The Coffin Texts

Sacred Spells of the Afterlife's Journey

Volume I

M L Ruscsak

Trient Press
3375 S Rainbow Blvd
#81710, SMB 13135
Las Vegas,NV 89180

Ordering Information:
Quantity sales. Special discounts are available on quantity purchases by corporations, associations, and others. For details, contact the publisher at the address above.
Orders by U.S. trade bookstores and wholesalers. Please contact Trient Press: Tel: (775) 996-3844; or visit www.trientpress.com.

Printed in the United States of America

Publisher's Cataloging-in-Publication data
Ruscsak, M.L.
A title of a book : The Coffin Texts: Sacred Spells of the Afterlife's Journey .
    ISBN

Hard Cover   979-8-88990-035-1

Paper Back   979-8-88990-037-5

Ebook   979-8-88990-036-8

The Coffin Texts

Chapter 1: Introduction to Coffin Texts

Definition and Purpose

The Coffin Texts refer to a collection of ancient Egyptian funerary spells and rituals inscribed on coffins and burial equipment during the Middle Kingdom period, which spans approximately 2055-1650 BCE. These texts hold immense importance as they provide insights into the religious and spiritual beliefs of ancient Egyptians, specifically concerning the afterlife and the journey of the deceased. The Coffin Texts serve as a bridge between the earlier Pyramid Texts and the later Book of the Dead, showcasing the evolution of Egyptian mortuary literature.

Explanation of their Purpose and Significance in Ancient Egyptian Funerary Practices

The Coffin Texts played a vital role in ancient Egyptian funerary practices, serving as a guidebook to assist the deceased in navigating the treacherous journey through the afterlife and ultimately achieving a favorable outcome in the judgment of their soul. These texts were primarily inscribed on the coffins, burial chambers, and other burial equipment of the deceased, ensuring that they had access to the spells and rituals necessary for a successful transition into the afterlife.

The purpose of the Coffin Texts was multi-faceted. Firstly, they aimed to protect the deceased from various dangers and malevolent forces encountered in the afterlife. These dangers included hostile deities, chaotic forces, and malevolent spirits that could potentially obstruct the deceased's journey towards a positive and eternal existence.

Secondly, the Coffin Texts provided guidance on how to navigate the complex cosmological landscape of the afterlife. They contained spells and rituals that enabled the deceased to align themselves with the gods, traverse different realms, and acquire knowledge and powers necessary for their journey. These texts were believed to provide the deceased with the necessary wisdom and magical formulas to overcome obstacles and successfully navigate the challenges encountered in the afterlife.

Furthermore, the Coffin Texts emphasized the preservation of the deceased's essential elements, such as the ba (soul) and the ka (life force). The spells and rituals described in the texts aimed to ensure the unity and preservation of these crucial components, preventing their dissolution or destruction, and enabling the deceased to retain their identity and continuity in the afterlife.

Lastly, the Coffin Texts were closely associated with the concept of ma'at, the fundamental principle of balance and harmony in Egyptian cosmology. They emphasized the deceased's adherence to moral and ethical conduct, while also providing opportunities for redemption and purification. By following the instructions and reciting the appropriate spells, the deceased sought to align themselves with the principles of ma'at, thereby ensuring a positive judgment and the eternal rewards associated with it.

The significance of the Coffin Texts extends beyond their role in ancient Egyptian funerary practices. They offer invaluable insights into the religious, cosmological, and socio-cultural beliefs of ancient Egyptians. The texts shed light on the complex interplay between the divine, the natural world, and human beings, revealing the Egyptians' profound understanding of the metaphysical and spiritual realms. Furthermore, the Coffin Texts serve as a testament to the continuity and resilience of ancient Egyptian religious traditions, as many of the concepts and rituals found within them continued to influence later funerary practices and texts, such as the Book of the Dead.

In conclusion, the Coffin Texts occupy a significant place in ancient Egyptian religious and funerary practices. These texts provided guidance, protection, and spiritual empowerment to the deceased, ensuring a successful journey through the afterlife. Moreover, they offer valuable insights into the religious beliefs and worldview of ancient Egyptians, highlighting their rich understanding of the afterlife, cosmology, and the intricate relationship between gods and humans. The Coffin Texts are a testament to the profound spiritual legacy of ancient Egypt and continue to captivate scholars and enthusiasts alike with their complex rituals, symbolic imagery, and profound wisdom.

Origins and Development

The origins of the Coffin Texts can be traced back to earlier funerary texts known as the Pyramid Texts. The Pyramid Texts were inscribed on the walls of pyramids during the Old Kingdom period (c. 2686-2181 BCE) and were intended exclusively for the pharaohs. These texts contained spells and rituals aimed at ensuring the pharaoh's successful journey to the afterlife and their eventual assimilation with the gods.

The Coffin Texts, although distinct from the Pyramid Texts, were influenced by them and incorporated many of their themes and concepts. The earlier Pyramid Texts served as a foundation upon which the Coffin Texts were built, sharing similarities in terms of cosmological beliefs, rituals, and the focus on the afterlife journey. The Coffin Texts expanded upon and adapted the Pyramid Texts to cater to a broader range of individuals beyond the pharaohs, including the elite and members of the royal court.

Evolution and Development of the Coffin Texts during the Middle Kingdom Period

The Middle Kingdom period (c. 2055-1650 BCE) marked a significant phase in the development of Egyptian religious and funerary practices, including the evolution of the Coffin Texts. During this time, the Coffin Texts experienced a transformation in both content and scope.

Initially, the Coffin Texts were primarily inscribed on the inner sides of coffins, coffinettes, and other burial equipment. However, as the Middle Kingdom progressed, the texts expanded to include other surfaces such as burial chambers, sarcophagi, and papyri. This expansion allowed for a more comprehensive representation of the spells and rituals required for the afterlife journey.

In terms of content, the Coffin Texts expanded beyond the pharaoh-centric focus of the Pyramid Texts. They incorporated a wider range of individuals, including members of the elite and those closely associated with the royal court. The texts became more accessible and allowed individuals of high social standing to aspire to an afterlife similar to that of the pharaohs. The Coffin Texts also reflected a more personalized approach, incorporating the names and titles of the deceased within the spells and rituals.

Additionally, the Coffin Texts incorporated new spells and rituals, reflecting the changing religious and cosmological beliefs of the Middle Kingdom period. Concepts such as divine judgment, the role of the gods in the afterlife, and the importance of moral conduct became more prominent. The texts provided instructions on how to navigate the complexities of the afterlife and emphasized the need for the deceased to align themselves with the principles of ma'at (balance and justice).

Relationship with Earlier Pyramid Texts

The Coffin Texts maintained a strong relationship with the earlier Pyramid Texts. While the Coffin Texts expanded upon and adapted the Pyramid Texts, they also preserved many of the core beliefs and rituals found in their predecessors.

Many spells and rituals found in the Pyramid Texts were incorporated into the Coffin Texts, demonstrating a continuity of religious ideas and practices. The core themes of protection, guidance, and empowerment of the deceased in the afterlife were preserved in the Coffin Texts, albeit with new additions and adaptations.

However, the Coffin Texts also represented an evolution and broadening of the funerary texts. They moved away from the exclusive focus on pharaohs found in the Pyramid Texts and embraced a more inclusive approach, making the afterlife journey accessible to a broader range of individuals. The Coffin Texts reflected the changing social dynamics and aspirations of the Middle Kingdom society, allowing individuals of high status to seek a more elaborate and enriched afterlife experience.

In conclusion, the Coffin Texts emerged as a development and expansion of the earlier Pyramid Texts during the Middle Kingdom period. They drew influence from the Pyramid Texts while adapting to the changing religious and social landscape of ancient Egypt. The Coffin Texts evolved to include a wider range of individuals and incorporated new spells and rituals that reflected the beliefs and aspirations of the Middle Kingdom society. Nonetheless, the Coffin Texts maintained a strong connection with the Pyramid Texts, preserving their core themes and providing a bridge between the Old Kingdom and the subsequent funerary texts, such as the Book of the Dead.

Discovery and Study

The discovery of Coffin Texts spans several archaeological expeditions and excavations throughout Egypt. These texts were found in various burial sites, including tombs, mastabas, and burial chambers, providing valuable insights into ancient Egyptian funerary practices.

The first significant discovery of Coffin Texts occurred in the late 19th century. Notable examples were found in the tombs of pharaoh Mentuhotep II and the nobleman Ankhtifi at Deir el-Bersha. These early findings piqued the interest of scholars, leading to subsequent excavations in different regions of Egypt.

Excavations at sites like Asyut, El-Bersheh, Saqqara, and Deir el-Medina revealed a wealth of Coffin Texts inscriptions on coffins, sarcophagi, and other burial equipment. The texts were meticulously inscribed on the inner sides of coffins, providing a comprehensive corpus of spells and rituals.

Pioneering Scholars and Their Contributions to the Study of Coffin Texts

Several pioneering scholars made significant contributions to the study of Coffin Texts, advancing our understanding of these ancient funerary texts. Their meticulous work laid the foundation for subsequent research and interpretation.

One such scholar was Sir Alan Gardiner, a British Egyptologist who played a crucial role in deciphering and categorizing the Coffin Texts. Gardiner meticulously studied the texts and classified them into numbered spells, providing a standardized framework for future analysis.

Another influential figure in the study of Coffin Texts was Raymond O. Faulkner, an Egyptologist known for his translations and commentaries on ancient Egyptian texts. Faulkner's expertise in Egyptian language and grammar enabled him to produce authoritative translations of the Coffin Texts, making them accessible to a wider audience.

Further contributions were made by scholars such as R. O. F. Gurney, Adolf Erman, and Wolfram Grajetzki, who provided valuable insights into the religious, mythological, and linguistic aspects of the Coffin Texts.

Challenges and Methods of Deciphering and Interpreting the Texts

Deciphering and interpreting the Coffin Texts posed several challenges to scholars. The texts were often inscribed in a complex and condensed manner, with hieroglyphic signs closely arranged and sometimes lacking clear divisions between words or phrases. This required a deep understanding of the Egyptian language, grammar, and religious symbolism.

To decipher the texts, scholars relied on a combination of linguistic analysis, comparison with other known texts, and contextual understanding of ancient Egyptian culture and beliefs. The study of grammar, vocabulary, and syntax allowed scholars to unlock the meaning of individual words and phrases within the texts.

Comparative analysis with other funerary texts, such as the Pyramid Texts and the Book of the Dead, provided important contextual clues and helped establish connections and developments in religious concepts and rituals.

Symbolic imagery and religious iconography depicted in the Coffin Texts were also crucial for interpretation. Understanding the underlying religious beliefs and cosmology of ancient Egyptians aided scholars in deciphering the symbolic language employed in the texts.

Additionally, the collaboration between scholars from various fields, such as Egyptology, linguistics, religious studies, and anthropology, played a vital role in unraveling the complexities of the Coffin Texts. Their interdisciplinary approach allowed for a more comprehensive understanding of the texts and the ancient Egyptian funerary practices they represented.

In conclusion, the discovery and study of Coffin Texts have been instrumental in deepening our understanding of ancient Egyptian funerary practices. Pioneering scholars, through their meticulous work, deciphered and interpreted these texts, shedding light on the religious beliefs, rituals, and cosmology of ancient Egyptians. Although challenges existed, scholars employed linguistic analysis, comparative studies, and contextual understanding to unlock the meanings of the texts. The collaborative efforts of experts from various fields further enhanced our knowledge of the Coffin Texts and their significance in ancient Egyptian culture.

Structure and Classification

The Coffin Texts exhibit a structured organization, with spells and rituals arranged in a specific order to guide the deceased through their journey in the afterlife. The texts were inscribed on the inner sides of coffins, coffinettes, burial chambers, and other burial equipment, creating a comprehensive guidebook for the deceased.

The organization of the Coffin Texts can be divided into different sections or chapters, each addressing specific aspects of the afterlife journey. These sections cover a wide range of topics, including protection from malevolent forces, offerings to the gods, spells for transformation, and knowledge acquisition. The texts progress systematically, ensuring that the deceased is equipped with the necessary spells and rituals to navigate the afterlife successfully.

Explanation of How the Texts Were Classified and Numbered

The classification and numbering of the Coffin Texts were primarily established by the Egyptologist Sir Alan Gardiner in the early 20th century. Gardiner carefully examined and cataloged the texts, assigning them numbers based on their content and context.

The Coffin Texts consist of individual spells, each designated with a unique number. Gardiner assigned the numbers consecutively, resulting in a system where each spell has its own specific identifier. This classification system allowed scholars to refer to specific spells with ease and facilitated comparative studies across different collections.

The numbering system starts from spell 1 and progresses sequentially, although some gaps exist due to missing or damaged texts. Each spell is identified by its corresponding number, and subsequent editions and translations of the Coffin Texts often refer to these assigned numbers to maintain consistency and facilitate cross-referencing.

Variations and Discrepancies in Different Collections of Coffin Texts

It is important to note that variations and discrepancies exist among different collections of Coffin Texts. These variations can arise due to a range of factors, including the specific burial context, regional differences, and the time span over which the texts were produced.

Different burial sites and regions within Egypt yielded varying collections of Coffin Texts. These regional differences can manifest in the inclusion or exclusion of specific spells, variations in wording, or alternative versions of certain spells. The diversity in Coffin Texts collections provides valuable insights into the localized beliefs and practices within ancient Egyptian society.

Additionally, the Coffin Texts were produced over a significant time span, spanning several centuries of the Middle Kingdom period. As a result, changes in religious beliefs, rituals, and linguistic conventions can be observed. These changes contribute to discrepancies and variations in different collections of Coffin Texts.

Furthermore, the preservation of the texts themselves can vary across different burial sites and tombs. Some texts may be damaged, fragmentary, or partially erased, leading to gaps and uncertainties in the interpretation and understanding of specific spells.

Scholars acknowledge these variations and discrepancies, and their studies aim to analyze and compare different collections to gain a more comprehensive understanding of the Coffin Texts as a whole.

In conclusion, the Coffin Texts exhibit a structured organization with spells and rituals arranged in a specific order. The texts were classified and numbered by Sir Alan Gardiner, providing a systematic reference system. However, variations and discrepancies exist among different collections of Coffin Texts, reflecting regional differences, the passage of time, and the preservation conditions of the texts. Scholars continue to explore and analyze these variations to gain a deeper understanding of the Coffin Texts and their cultural significance.

Themes and Content

The Coffin Texts are replete with recurring themes and motifs that reflect the religious and cosmological beliefs of ancient Egyptians. These themes and motifs serve to guide the deceased on their journey through the afterlife and ensure their successful assimilation into the realm of the gods. Some of the prominent themes and motifs include:

Protection and Safeguarding: The Coffin Texts contain numerous spells and rituals aimed at protecting the deceased from malevolent forces and dangers they may encounter in the afterlife. This includes protection from demons, snakes, and other supernatural entities. The texts emphasize the need for the deceased to be shielded and fortified on their journey.

Transformation and Metamorphosis: The Coffin Texts present the concept of transformation as a crucial aspect of the afterlife journey. Spells and rituals in the texts seek to facilitate the transformation of the deceased into a divine being, allowing them to navigate the complex realms of the afterlife and become united with the gods.

Knowledge Acquisition: The acquisition of knowledge and wisdom is a recurring theme in the Coffin Texts. The texts emphasize the importance of the deceased gaining knowledge of magical spells, rituals, and secret names of gods, which empower them to navigate the afterlife successfully.

Offerings and Sustenance: The Coffin Texts emphasize the necessity of providing offerings and sustenance to the gods in the afterlife. Rituals and spells detail the offerings to be made and the methods for ensuring the continuous provision of food, drink, and other necessities for the deceased.

Divine Judgment and Ma'at: The concept of divine judgment and the adherence to ma'at (balance, justice, and truth) are central to the Coffin Texts. The texts highlight the necessity for the deceased to demonstrate moral conduct, honesty, and righteousness during their earthly life to pass the judgment of the gods and secure a favorable afterlife outcome.

Overview of the Spells and Rituals Contained in the Texts

The Coffin Texts comprise a vast array of spells and rituals designed to aid the deceased in their afterlife journey. These spells cover a wide range of aspects, including protection, transformation, knowledge acquisition, and interaction with the divine realm. Some of the notable spells and rituals contained in the texts include:

Rituals for Opening the Mouth: These rituals involve the symbolic opening of the deceased's mouth, enabling them to speak and eat in the afterlife. The spells associated with these rituals ensure the restoration of vital functions necessary for sustenance and communication.

Spells for Navigation and Travel: The Coffin Texts include spells that provide guidance and protection for the deceased during their journey through the various realms of the afterlife. These spells often invoke the assistance of deities and depict the deceased traversing mythical landscapes and encountering supernatural obstacles.

Spells for Transformation and Metamorphosis: The texts contain spells and rituals aimed at facilitating the transformation of the deceased into a divine being or a specific deity. These transformative rituals enable the deceased to assume different forms and gain the powers associated with those forms.

Rituals for Protection and Defense: A significant portion of the Coffin Texts is dedicated to spells and rituals intended to safeguard the deceased from harm. These rituals invoke deities, magical symbols, and protective spells to ward off evil spirits, demons, and other malevolent forces.

Spells for Knowledge and Wisdom: The acquisition of knowledge and wisdom is emphasized in the Coffin Texts. Spells provide instructions for gaining access to secret knowledge, such as the names of gods, the rituals to be performed, and the understanding of magical formulas.

Discussion of the Religious and Cosmological Beliefs Reflected in the Texts

The Coffin Texts provide valuable insights into the religious and cosmological beliefs of ancient Egyptians during the Middle Kingdom period. The texts reflect the overarching belief in the existence of an afterlife and the necessity for the deceased to navigate and assimilate into the divine realm. Some key religious and cosmological beliefs reflected in the Coffin Texts include:

Concept of the Afterlife: The texts present a comprehensive understanding of the afterlife as a complex realm where the deceased continue their existence. The afterlife is depicted as a multifaceted landscape with various realms, each requiring specific rituals, spells, and knowledge to successfully traverse.

Divine Hierarchy: The Coffin Texts portray a well-defined hierarchy of gods and goddesses, each with their own specific roles and attributes. The texts often invoke these deities for protection, guidance, and intercession on behalf of the deceased.

Belief in Divine Judgment: The texts reflect the belief in a judgment process in the afterlife, where the deceased's actions and moral conduct during their earthly life are evaluated. The judgment is based on the concept of ma'at, ensuring that the deceased's heart is weighed against the feather of truth.

Connection with the Natural World: The Coffin Texts demonstrate the interconnectedness between the deceased and the natural world. The texts incorporate spells and rituals related to the elements of nature, such as the sun, stars, water, and the Nile, symbolizing the vital forces that sustain life and enable the afterlife journey.

Importance of Ritual and Magic: The Coffin Texts underscore the significance of ritual and magic in the religious and cosmological beliefs of ancient Egyptians. The texts provide detailed instructions for performing specific rituals, invoking deities, and utilizing magical spells and formulas to achieve desired outcomes in the afterlife.

In conclusion, the Coffin Texts exhibit recurring themes and motifs that reflect the religious and cosmological beliefs of ancient Egyptians. The spells and rituals contained in the texts cover a wide range of aspects, including protection, transformation, knowledge acquisition, and divine interaction. The texts reveal the belief in a structured afterlife journey, divine judgment, and the importance of maintaining ma'at. The Coffin Texts provide valuable insights into the religious and cosmological worldview of ancient Egyptians during the Middle Kingdom period.

Relationship with the Book of the Dead

The transition from the Coffin Texts to the Book of the Dead marks a significant evolution in ancient Egyptian funerary practices and beliefs. While the Coffin Texts were primarily used during the Middle Kingdom period (approximately 2055-1650 BCE), the Book of the Dead gained prominence during the New Kingdom period (approximately 1550-1070 BCE).

The transition can be attributed to several factors, including changes in religious and cultural practices, shifts in political power, and the desire for more personalized funerary texts. The Book of the Dead gradually replaced the Coffin Texts as the preferred funerary text, offering a more standardized and comprehensive compilation of spells and rituals.

Influence and Incorporation of Coffin Texts into the Book of the Dead

The Book of the Dead incorporates and expands upon many of the concepts, spells, and rituals found in the Coffin Texts. It can be seen as an elaboration and refinement of the Coffin Texts, with additional spells and illustrations.

Many spells and sections from the Coffin Texts were directly incorporated into the Book of the Dead. For example, spells for protection, transformation, and judgment from the Coffin Texts found their place in the Book of the Dead, often with slight modifications and additions. The inclusion of these Coffin Texts spells ensured the continuity of important funerary rituals and beliefs.

Contrasts and Similarities between the Two Funerary Texts

While the Book of the Dead builds upon the foundation of the Coffin Texts, there are notable contrasts and similarities between the two texts.

Organization and Structure: The Coffin Texts exhibit a more varied and flexible structure compared to the Book of the Dead. The Coffin Texts were inscribed directly on coffins and burial equipment, allowing for a more personalized arrangement of spells. In contrast, the Book of the Dead follows a standardized format, with chapters and spells organized in a consistent manner.

Length and Elaboration: The Coffin Texts are generally longer and more elaborate than the Book of the Dead. The Coffin Texts include extensive instructions, descriptions, and detailed rituals. The Book of the Dead, while still containing a significant amount of text, tends to be more concise and streamlined.

Focus on the Afterlife Journey: Both the Coffin Texts and the Book of the Dead center around the journey of the deceased in the afterlife. However, the Coffin Texts place greater emphasis on the physical aspects of the journey, with detailed instructions for traversing specific realms and encountering supernatural entities. The Book of the Dead, on the other hand, incorporates a more spiritual and introspective approach, focusing on the transformation of the deceased's soul and their ultimate union with the divine.

Illustrations and Visual Elements: The Book of the Dead is renowned for its richly illustrated vignettes, depicting scenes from the afterlife and the rituals described in the text. While some Coffin Texts also include illustrations, they are generally less elaborate and fewer in number compared to the Book of the Dead.

Despite these contrasts, the Coffin Texts and the Book of the Dead share many similarities. Both texts address the concerns of the deceased in the afterlife, provide guidance for navigating the realms of the gods, and emphasize the importance of rituals, spells, and judgment. Both texts reflect the core religious and cosmological beliefs of ancient Egyptians, albeit with variations in emphasis and presentation.

In conclusion, the transition from the Coffin Texts to the Book of the Dead marks a significant development in ancient Egyptian funerary practices. While the Coffin Texts served as the primary funerary texts during the Middle Kingdom, the Book of the Dead emerged as a more standardized and comprehensive compilation of spells and rituals during the New Kingdom. The Book of the Dead incorporated and expanded upon the Coffin Texts, preserving and refining important elements of ancient Egyptian funerary beliefs and practices. Despite their differences in structure, length, and emphasis, both texts share a common focus on the afterlife journey and reflect the core religious and cosmological beliefs of ancient Egyptians.

Legacy and Significance

The Coffin Texts exerted a profound influence on later Egyptian religious and funerary practices, particularly during the New Kingdom and subsequent periods. The transition from the Coffin Texts to the Book of the Dead marked a shift towards more standardized and widely-used funerary texts. The spells, rituals, and concepts introduced in the Coffin Texts continued to shape the religious and cosmological beliefs of ancient Egyptians for centuries.

Many of the themes and motifs found in the Coffin Texts, such as the importance of protection, transformation, divine judgment, and the acquisition of knowledge, were perpetuated in later funerary texts. The Book of the Dead, which incorporated and expanded upon the Coffin Texts, became the preeminent funerary text of ancient Egypt, influencing subsequent religious and funerary practices well into the Greco-Roman period.

Legacy and Impact of the Coffin Texts on the Understanding of Ancient Egyptian Culture

The Coffin Texts have played a pivotal role in the understanding of ancient Egyptian culture, religion, and beliefs. These texts provide valuable insights into the complex cosmology, religious rituals, and concepts of the afterlife held by ancient Egyptians during the Middle Kingdom.

The Coffin Texts shed light on the Egyptians' deep reverence for the gods, their belief in an intricate afterlife journey, and their understanding of the importance of moral conduct and ma'at. The texts reveal a sophisticated understanding of the interconnectedness between the natural and supernatural realms, as well as the role of magic and ritual in maintaining cosmic balance.

Furthermore, the Coffin Texts offer glimpses into the social, cultural, and artistic aspects of ancient Egyptian society. The illustrations and scenes depicted in the texts provide valuable evidence of religious iconography, burial practices, and the material culture of the Middle Kingdom period.

Importance of the Coffin Texts in the Study of Egyptology and Ancient Civilizations

The Coffin Texts hold immense importance in the field of Egyptology and the study of ancient civilizations. These texts serve as a crucial source of primary evidence for researchers, allowing them to reconstruct and interpret the religious and funerary practices of ancient Egyptians.

Through the study of the Coffin Texts, scholars have gained insights into the development and evolution of religious beliefs, ritual practices, and cosmological concepts over time. The texts provide a window into the cultural and intellectual world of ancient Egyptians, revealing their concerns, aspirations, and worldview.

Moreover, the Coffin Texts contribute to the broader understanding of the ancient civilizations of the Near East and their belief systems. By comparing the Coffin Texts with other funerary texts, such as the Pyramid Texts and the Book of the Dead, researchers can discern similarities, differences, and cross-cultural influences, shedding light on the interconnectedness of ancient societies and their religious beliefs.

In conclusion, the Coffin Texts have left a lasting legacy and exerted a significant impact on later Egyptian religious and funerary practices. They have deepened our understanding of ancient Egyptian culture, provided insights into their religious beliefs and cosmology, and served as important sources for the study of Egyptology and ancient civilizations. The Coffin Texts continue to be a testament to the profound spiritual and intellectual traditions of the ancient Egyptians.

Conclusion

In this chapter, we have explored the fascinating world of the Coffin Texts, a collection of ancient Egyptian funerary spells and rituals inscribed on coffins and burial equipment during the Middle Kingdom period. We have delved into their definition, purpose, and significance in ancient Egyptian funerary practices.

The Coffin Texts, traditionally identified as 1,185 spells, are not fixed in number, as different scholars may include additional or exclude certain texts based on their interpretations and criteria. These texts vary in length and complexity, ranging from single lines to elaborate compositions. They provide instructions and formulas for the deceased to navigate the afterlife journey, gain protection, acquire wisdom, and face divine judgment.

We have discussed the origins and development of the Coffin Texts, highlighting their precursors and influences, as well as their relationship with the earlier Pyramid Texts. The Coffin Texts emerged during the Middle Kingdom and played a significant role in shaping the religious and funerary practices of ancient Egyptians during that period.

The discovery and study of the Coffin Texts have presented their own set of challenges. We have explored the overview of their discovery in various burial sites and the contributions of pioneering scholars in deciphering and interpreting these ancient texts. The methods employed in deciphering the Coffin Texts have involved a combination of linguistic analysis, contextual understanding, and comparisons with other related texts.

The structure and classification of the Coffin Texts have been discussed, highlighting their organization and the criteria used for their classification and numbering. We have also addressed the variations and discrepancies that exist among different collections of Coffin Texts, emphasizing the flexibility and evolving nature of their compilation.

Furthermore, we have examined the recurring themes and motifs present in the Coffin Texts, providing an overview of the spells and rituals contained within them. We have also discussed the religious and cosmological beliefs reflected in the texts, including the concept of the afterlife, the divine hierarchy, the belief in divine judgment, the connection with the natural world, and the importance of ritual and magic.

The transition from the Coffin Texts to the Book of the Dead marks a significant development in ancient Egyptian funerary practices. We have explored the influence of the Coffin Texts on later Egyptian religious and funerary practices, as well as their legacy and impact on the understanding of ancient Egyptian culture. Additionally, we have highlighted the importance of the Coffin Texts in the study of Egyptology and ancient civilizations, showcasing their significance as primary sources for unraveling the mysteries of the ancient world.

Having covered these key points, we have set the stage for the subsequent chapters dedicated to specific Coffin Texts. In the following chapters, we will delve into the spells, rituals, and themes of the first 200 Coffin Texts, exploring their nuances, interpretations, and cultural context. Through this comprehensive study, we will gain a deeper appreciation and understanding of the rich tapestry of ancient Egyptian funerary beliefs and practices encapsulated within the Coffin Texts.

Note: The Coffin Texts do not have an exact numbering system, and different sources may have variations in the numbering.

CT 1: Spell for Protection: Protecting the deceased in the afterlife and ensuring their well-being.

Utterance:
"Oh, gods of the Netherworld, hear my plea,
Grant protection to this noble soul that rests before thee.
Shield them from all evil, both seen and unseen,
Let no harm befall them, in the realms serene.

May the four winds carry my words to the divine,
Calling upon the powers that eternally shine.
Wrap this blessed soul in your embrace so tight,
Protect them from darkness, and guide them to the light.

Let no malevolent spirit or demon draw near,
For this soul is pure, deserving of love and cheer.
Stand guard, O gods, with your powerful might,
Banish all foes, and ensure a safe flight.

By the divine words inscribed upon this tomb,
May protection surround this soul, banishing gloom.
Grant them peace, joy, and eternal repose,
As their spirit soars where the sacred river flows.

Oh, gods of the afterlife, I humbly implore,
Extend your divine shield, forevermore.
With your watchful gaze, may this soul thrive,
In the eternal realms where gods and spirits connive.

So be it, this spell of protection I cast,
Ensuring the safety of the deceased, steadfast.
Let no harm befall them in this ethereal plane,
May they find solace and harmony, free from all pain."

This spell for protection illustrates the ancient Egyptian belief in the power of divine intervention and the importance of safeguarding the deceased in their journey through the afterlife. By invoking the gods and requesting their protection, the spell aims to create a shield around the deceased, warding off any malevolent forces or harm. The repetition of divine names and the emphasis on the purity and worthiness of the soul emphasize the plea for benevolent intervention.

CT 2: Spell for Lighting the Darkness: Providing light and illumination for the deceased.

Utterance:
"O, radiant sun, whose rays pierce the night,
I beseech thee to bestow thy sacred light.
Illuminate the path of this noble soul,
In the depths of darkness, make them whole.

With the flicker of a flame, banish the gloom,
Let the brilliance of your presence consume.
Guide this departed spirit through shadowed lands,
With your divine radiance, held in their hands.

As Ra ascends in the morning sky,
May his light in the afterlife never die.
Let it shine brightly, a beacon of hope,
Leading the way where gods and souls elope.

I summon the power of the sacred fire,
To ignite the darkness, higher and higher.
May its glow dispel all fear and despair,
Granting solace to this soul, fair and square.

With each flickering flame and every gleam,
Let the brightness grow, like a precious dream.
Illumine the path, reveal what's unseen,
Envelop this spirit, as if in a gleaming sheen.

Oh, guardians of light, I call upon thee,
To grant this gift of luminosity.
Bring forth the torches, torches of divine,
Bathing this soul in your radiant shrine.

May the darkness retreat, as light takes its place,
Guiding this spirit with grace and embrace.
Illuminate the way, through eternity's veil,
Where divine realms and spirits prevail.

So it is spoken, so it shall be done,
Light the darkness, until the journey is won.

Let the brilliance shine, with celestial might,
For this departed soul, in eternal flight."

This spell for lighting the darkness demonstrates the ancient Egyptian belief in the power of light and its ability to dispel darkness and bring clarity and guidance to the deceased. By invoking the sun and the sacred fire, the spell seeks to illuminate the path of the departed, ensuring that they are not lost in the shadows of the afterlife. The imagery of flickering flames and the emphasis on divine radiance symbolize the hope, enlightenment, and protection sought for the soul's journey.

CT 3: Spell for Transformation into a Falcon of Gold: Granting the deceased the ability to transform into a divine bird for mobility and protection.

Utterance:
"O, winged falcon of the heavens high,
I beseech thee, hear my fervent cry.
Grant this noble soul the power to soar,
Transform them into a falcon, forevermore.

With feathers of gold, radiant and bright,
Let them take flight, in the day and night.
Grant them swiftness and agility untold,
A divine bird, resplendent and bold.

Let their wings span wide, like the sun's embrace,
As they traverse the realms with celestial grace.
Grant them the eyes of the falcon, keen and sharp,
To perceive all dangers, both near and far.

In the form of a falcon, they shall ascend,
Navigating the realms, without apprehend.
Grant them freedom of movement, unbounded and free,
To explore the sacred realms, in harmony.

May their golden plumage reflect divine light,
Shining with brilliance, powerful and bright.
Let them be protected, as they soar on high,
Shielded from all harm, as the falcon flies.

O, guardians of transformation, hear my plea,
Bestow this gift upon the departed, with glee.
Let their mortal form be shed, like a cocoon,
As they embody the falcon, under the moon.

By the power of ancient rites and sacred words,
Let this transformation unfold, like soaring birds.
Grant them the blessings of flight and might,
As a falcon of gold, they take their flight.

So it is spoken, so it shall be done,

Grant this transformation, until their journey is won.
Let them be reborn as a falcon divine,
Guided and protected, in the celestial line."

This spell for transformation into a falcon of gold illustrates the ancient Egyptian belief in the ability of the deceased to take on the form of a sacred bird for enhanced mobility and protection in the afterlife. By invoking the falcon and its attributes, the spell seeks to grant the departed soul the ability to soar through the realms with swiftness, agility, and heightened senses.

The imagery of golden feathers symbolizes the divine nature of the transformation, while the emphasis on flight and freedom highlights the soul's liberation from the limitations of the mortal realm. The spell calls upon the guardians of transformation to bestow this gift upon the departed, ensuring their safe passage and empowerment as they navigate the spiritual realms.

CT 4: Spell for Encountering the Great Ennead: Allowing the deceased to interact with the nine major deities of the Egyptian pantheon.

Utterance:
"O, mighty deities of the Great Ennead,
I call upon your divine presence, indeed.
Grant this noble soul the privilege to meet,
The nine major gods, in a sacred retreat.

Open the gates to the celestial realm,
Where gods reside, at the helm.
Grant them an audience with the divine,
So that their presence may intertwine.

Let the deceased stand in awe and wonder,
As they encounter gods in their divine splendor.
May Ra, the Sun God, shine his light,
Illuminating their path, ever so bright.

Osiris, the Lord of the Underworld and rebirth,
Extend your hand, offering guidance on this unearth.
Isis, the nurturing goddess, bring your grace,
Surround them with love, in this sacred space.

Horus, the falcon-headed god, protector and heir,
Bestow your blessings, shielding them with care.
Let Thoth, the wise scribe, impart his knowledge,
Granting wisdom and insight, from his celestial college.

May Hathor, the goddess of joy and dance,
Fill their hearts with mirth, in a divine trance.
Let Sekhmet, the lioness, fierce and bold,
Lend her strength, as their journey unfolds.

Set, the god of chaos, bring balance and strife,
Teaching lessons and tests, in this afterlife.
And lastly, Nephthys, the guardian and guide,
Lead them through the realms, side by side.

O, gods of the Great Ennead, hear my plea,
Grant this soul the privilege to interact with thee.

Let them feel your divine presence and grace,
In this encounter, within the sacred space.

So it is spoken, so it shall be done,
Allow this connection, until their journey is won.
May the deceased commune with the gods, so grand,
As they traverse the celestial land."

This spell for encountering the Great Ennead showcases the ancient Egyptian belief in the ability of the deceased to interact with the major deities of the Egyptian pantheon. By invoking the gods of the Great Ennead, the spell seeks to grant the departed soul the privilege of meeting and communing with these powerful divine beings.

Each deity mentioned in the spell holds a distinct role and significance within the Egyptian pantheon. They represent various aspects of life, creation, protection, wisdom, and balance. The spell calls upon these gods, such as Ra, Osiris, Isis, Horus, Thoth, Hathor, Sekhmet, Set, and Nephthys, to bestow their presence, guidance, and blessings upon the deceased as they navigate the afterlife.

The encounter with the Great Ennead offers the deceased an opportunity for divine communion, receiving knowledge, protection, and support from the gods. It highlights the belief in the interconnectedness between the mortal and divine realms, emphasizing the role of the deities in guiding and assisting the departed on their spiritual journey.

CT 5: Spell for Breathing Air: Ensuring that the deceased can breathe in the afterlife.

Utterance:
"O, ancient winds that carry life's breath,
I beseech thee to grant this soul no death.
In the realm beyond, where spirits reside,
Grant them the gift of breath, so vital and wide.

Let the air fill their lungs, with each inhale,
As they journey through realms, without fail.
Breathe life into their essence, once more,
As they traverse the afterlife's sacred shore.

May their breath be sustained, forevermore,
In the eternal realm, where they now soar.
Let no suffocation or deprivation befall,
Grant them the breath, the essence of all.

By the power of the elements, wind and air,
Bestow upon this soul, a breath beyond compare.
Let them inhale the sacred essence divine,
Filling their being, with the breath of time.

Like a gentle breeze that rustles the trees,
Let the breath of life put their spirit at ease.
Inhaling the freshness of the divine air,
Revitalizing their soul, with tender care.

So it is spoken, so it shall be done,
Grant this gift of breath, until their journey is won.
May the deceased breathe freely, without strife,
In the afterlife's realm, the breath of eternal life."

This spell for breathing air reflects the ancient Egyptian belief in the importance of breath for sustaining life, even in the afterlife. By invoking the ancient winds and the essence of air, the spell seeks to ensure that the deceased can continue to breathe and receive the life-giving force in the spiritual realms.

The spell emphasizes the eternal nature of breath, symbolizing the continuity of existence and the connection between the mortal and the divine. It calls upon the powers of the elements, specifically wind and air, to bestow the gift of breath upon the departed soul. The breath serves as a vital source of life force, providing sustenance and vitality in the afterlife journey.

In the ancient Egyptian worldview, the ability to breathe in the afterlife was considered essential for the well-being and existence of the deceased. This spell highlights the belief in the continuity of life, where the departed soul is granted the opportunity to breathe and partake in the spiritual realm's energies.

CT 6: Spell for Not Dying a Second Time: Protecting the deceased from further death or destruction.

Utterance:
"O, ancient guardians of eternal life,
I beseech thee, ward off death's strife.
Protect this noble soul from further demise,
Preserve their essence, as the sun shall rise.

Let not the jaws of death claim them again,
Shield them from destruction, sorrow, and pain.
Bind their spirit to the eternal realm's embrace,
Ensuring their existence, in sacred grace.

With powerful words and spells of might,
Banish death's grip, vanquishing its blight.
Guard them from the realm of shadows and decay,
Grant them eternal preservation, come what may.

May their spirit be fortified, undying and strong,
Immune to death's call, where darkness belongs.
Protect their essence, the spark of divine light,
Shield them from mortality's eternal night.

By the power of the gods, ancient and revered,
Let this soul be saved, its destiny cleared.
Forbid the reaper's touch, the cold hand of demise,
Preserving their essence, where immortality lies.

So it is spoken, so it shall be done,
Protect this soul, from death's grasp overrun.
Grant them eternal life, free from mortal strife,
Not dying a second time, in the afterlife."

This spell for not dying a second time reflects the ancient Egyptian belief in the preservation and protection of the deceased from further death or destruction in the afterlife. By invoking the ancient guardians and employing powerful words and spells, the spell seeks to safeguard the departed soul from the perils of mortality's grasp.

The spell emphasizes the desire to shield the deceased from the realm of shadows and decay, ensuring their existence in the eternal realm of the afterlife. It calls upon the gods and divine forces to fortify the spirit, making it impervious to death's call and preserving the essence of the departed in everlasting life.

The notion of not dying a second time highlights the belief in the continuity of existence and the rejection of further mortality in the afterlife. It symbolizes the ultimate goal of achieving immortality and eternal preservation for the deceased.

CT 7: Spell for Reassembling the Body: Assisting in the restoration and reconstitution of the deceased's body.

Utterance:
"O, divine forces of creation and renewal,
I beseech thee to restore, to reassemble.
Gather the scattered fragments, piece by piece,
Reconstitute this body, bring it release.

From the sands of time, from dust and clay,
Let the limbs and organs find their way.
Mend the broken pieces, mend the divide,
Let the body be whole, unified.

By the power of Isis, the great goddess of life,
Let her magic touch, alleviate the strife.
She who gathers, she who mends,
Assist in reassembling, making amends.

Osiris, the lord of rebirth and restoration,
Bless this body with divine manifestation.
Let the ba and the ka be joined as one,
Reunite the body, until life's journey is done.

May Anubis, the guardian of the necropolis,
Lend his guidance, his healing solace.
Guide the fragments, guide the bones,
Reconstruct this vessel, with sacred tones.

With each utterance, with each spell,
Restore this body, make it well.
Piece by piece, let it be formed anew,
Revive the deceased, their essence imbue.

So it is spoken, so it shall be done,
Reassemble this body, with each rising sun.
May the deceased find wholeness, restored and complete,
In the afterlife's realm, their form is replete."

This spell for reassembling the body reflects the ancient Egyptian belief in the restoration and reconstitution of the deceased's physical form in the afterlife. By invoking the powers of creation and renewal, as well as the deities associated with resurrection and healing, the spell seeks to gather the scattered fragments of the body and reconstruct it, ensuring its wholeness and unity.

The spell highlights the belief in the sacredness of the body and its integral role in the afterlife journey. It calls upon the divine forces, including Isis, Osiris, and Anubis, to assist in the process of reassembly. These deities are associated with life, rebirth, and restoration, making them ideal figures to invoke for the task at hand.

The reassembling of the body symbolizes the reunification of the ba (the soul) and the ka (the life force) with their physical vessel. It signifies the completeness and rejuvenation of the deceased, preparing them for their eternal existence in the afterlife.

CT 8: Spell for Protection against Animals: Safeguarding the deceased from harmful or hostile animals in the afterlife.

Utterance:
"O, ancient protectors of the realms untamed,
I call upon thee, to safeguard unblamed.
Grant protection to this soul, from creatures fierce,
Shield them from harm, let no danger pierce.

Let the lions of the desert bow in reverence,
The serpents of venomous fangs show deference.
Keep at bay the crocodiles, fierce and wild,
Ensure the deceased's safety, undefiled.

By the power of Horus, the mighty falcon,
Let his wings spread wide, as a shield unbroken.
With eyes keen, he watches from above,
Guarding against creatures that harm and shove.

Let the jackals, guardians of the sacred night,
Refrain from causing fright, hold their bite.
May the scorpions and vipers crawl away,
Leaving the deceased unharmed, I pray.

Invoke the spirits of the benevolent gods,
To banish aggression, where harmony nods.
May Anubis, the protector of the dead,
Guide them safely, where danger won't tread.

Envelop this soul in a shield of divine light,
Repelling animals' aggression, out of sight.
Grant them passage through realms serene,
Free from harm, untouched, and clean.

So it is spoken, so it shall be done,
Protect this soul from creatures that would stun.
May the deceased find refuge, untroubled and secure,
In the afterlife's realm, where peace is pure."

This spell for protection against animals reflects the ancient Egyptian belief in safeguarding the deceased from harmful or hostile creatures in the afterlife. By invoking the ancient protectors and benevolent gods associated with animal symbolism, the spell seeks to create a shield of divine light and guidance, ensuring the safety of the departed soul.

The spell emphasizes the need for protection against predatory and dangerous animals that could pose a threat to the deceased's well-being in the afterlife. It calls upon revered deities such as Horus, Anubis, and others to watch over and repel any aggression or harm from animals that may cross the path of the deceased.

The invocation of these deities symbolizes their role as guardians and protectors, capable of exerting their divine power to create a barrier between the deceased and potentially hostile animals. Their presence brings assurance and peace of mind, allowing the soul to navigate the afterlife without fear or danger.

CT 9: Spell for Repelling Snakes: Warding off snakes or serpent-like creatures in the afterlife.

Utterance:
"O, guardians of ancient wisdom and might,
I call upon thee to repel the serpents' bite.
Shield this noble soul from the venomous fangs,
Protect them from harm with divine yangs.

Let the hissing snakes be driven away,
Their slithering forms banished, I say.
By the power of Ra, the sun god of light,
Make them retreat, vanish from sight.

Invoke the magic of Wadjet, the protective cobra,
With her fiery gaze, repel the reptiles' aura.
Let the uraeus on her brow strike fear,
Keeping the deceased safe, forever clear.

May the scales of Apep, the serpent of chaos,
Shrink away, repelled by divine ethos.
Banish their presence, their venomous sting,
Preserve the deceased from their poisonous wring.

With the spell's utterance, let them flee,
The snakes and serpents, away from thee.
Create a barrier, a forcefield secure,
Keeping the deceased untainted and pure.

By the power of sacred incantations,
Shield this soul from serpentine temptations.
May they traverse the afterlife, unharmed and free,
Protected from snakes, their guardians shall be.

So it is spoken, so it shall be done,
Repel the snakes, safeguard this one.
May the deceased find solace, far from harm,
In the afterlife's realm, serene and warm."

This spell for repelling snakes reflects the ancient Egyptian belief in protecting the deceased from the presence and harm of snakes or serpent-like creatures in the afterlife. By invoking the guardians associated with serpents and employing divine powers, the spell seeks to create a barrier of protection, ensuring the safety and well-being of the departed soul.

The spell emphasizes the need to repel and banish the threat posed by venomous snakes or serpent-like creatures in the afterlife. It calls upon revered deities such as Ra, the sun god, and Wadjet, the protective cobra, to exert their power and drive away these dangerous reptiles. Their presence symbolizes divine protection and the ability to repel harm.

The invocation of these deities and the mention of Apep, the serpent of chaos, illustrate the ancient Egyptians' belief in the power of divine magic and sacred incantations to ward off evil forces. The aim is to create a sense of security and ensure the unimpeded journey of the deceased in the afterlife.

CT 10: Spell for Becoming the Phoenix: Allowing the deceased to transform into a mythical phoenix and experience rebirth.

Utterance:
"O, ancient spirits of divine transformation,
Grant this soul the power of resurrection.
Let the deceased soar with wings unfurled,
As a phoenix rising, in a new world.

By the fires of immortality, burn bright,
Ignite the spirit, in celestial flight.
Let the body be consumed, purified by flame,
From ashes to glory, a rebirth to acclaim.

Invoke the essence of the phoenix's grace,
Its radiant plumage, a celestial embrace.
Grant the deceased the ability to ascend,
In vibrant colors, their existence transcend.

By the power of Atum, the creator god,
Let the deceased be reborn, shed the mortal facade.
Like the phoenix, let them rise from the pyre,
Renewed and radiant, their essence inspire.

May the wings of Isis, goddess of magic and rebirth,
Wrap around the deceased, their spirit's worth.
Guide them through the cycles of transformation,
Grant them eternal life, a divine proclamation.

Let the flames of rejuvenation embrace,
Purify the soul, in eternal grace.
As the phoenix soars high in the skies,
May the deceased experience rebirth, arise.

So it is spoken, so it shall be done,
Grant this soul the transformation begun.
May they become the phoenix, in glorious flight,
Experiencing rebirth, forever alight."

This spell for becoming the phoenix reflects the ancient Egyptian belief in the transformative power of the mythical bird and its association with rebirth and immortality. By invoking the spirits of transformation and drawing upon the divine energy of Atum and Isis, the spell seeks to grant the deceased the ability to transcend mortality and experience a new life as the phoenix.

The spell highlights the symbolism of the phoenix, representing the cycles of life, death, and rebirth. It calls upon the fires of immortality to consume and purify the deceased's body, allowing them to rise anew from the ashes. The mention of Atum, the creator god, and Isis, the goddess of magic and rebirth, signifies their roles in the process of transformation and renewal.

The invocation of these deities and the imagery of the phoenix's wings and vibrant plumage evoke a sense of transcendence and spiritual elevation. The aim is for the deceased to soar with the phoenix's grace, shedding their mortal form and embracing an existence beyond earthly limitations.

CT 11: Spell for Passing by the Guards: Ensuring safe passage through the gates and guardians of the afterlife.

Utterance:
"O, gatekeepers and guardians of the realms beyond,
I invoke your mercy, with reverence, I respond.
Grant this noble soul safe passage, I implore,
Through gates and barriers, to the other shore.

Let the guardians of the afterlife stand aside,
Open the path, where the blessed souls reside.
By the power of Ma'at, the goddess of balance,
Guide the deceased through each challenge, each expanse.

May the scales of judgment tip in their favor,
Their heart as light as a feather's savor.
Let the guardians recognize their purity and worth,
Granting passage, unimpeded, to the afterlife's berth.

Invoke the protection of Anubis, the jackal-headed god,
As the deceased approaches, along the sacred road.
May his keen senses discern their righteous intent,
Ensuring safe passage, without impediment.

By the power of Thoth, the god of wisdom and scribes,
Let the gates open wide, as the soul subscribes.
May the deceased recite the sacred words with grace,
Gaining entrance to the realms, their destined place.

Let the deities of the celestial realms intervene,
Bestow favor upon this soul, unseen.
Guide them past the obstacles, the guardians' watch,
Grant them passage, without a deterring notch.

So it is spoken, so it shall be done,
Safe passage granted, the journey begun.
May the deceased traverse the afterlife's domain,
With the blessings of guardians, their presence sustain."

This spell for passing by the guards reflects the ancient Egyptian belief in the need for safe passage through the gates and guardians of the afterlife. By invoking the gatekeepers, the power of Ma'at, and the protection of Anubis and Thoth, the spell seeks to ensure that the deceased can navigate the challenges and obstacles in the realms beyond.

The spell emphasizes the importance of balance and righteousness in the judgment of the deceased. It calls upon Ma'at, the goddess of balance, to tip the scales in their favor, affirming their purity of heart and worthiness for passage. The mention of Anubis, the jackal-headed god, and Thoth, the god of wisdom and scribes, signifies their roles as protectors and guides, assisting the deceased in their journey.

The invocation of these deities and the concept of reciting sacred words underscore the belief in the power of ritual and divine intervention to secure safe passage. The aim is for the guardians of the afterlife to recognize the deceased's righteous intent and allow them to pass through the gates, unhindered.

CT 12: Spell for Rejoining the Bones: Assisting in the reassembling and reuniting of the deceased's skeletal remains.

Utterance:
"O, ancient spirits of restoration and might,
Hear my plea, grant this soul's bones their rightful right.
Reassemble the fragmented pieces, I pray,
Let the deceased's skeletal form hold sway.

By the power of Osiris, the lord of the dead,
Let the scattered bones be carefully led.
Guide each fragment to its rightful place,
Reuniting the deceased, with divine grace.

Invoke the essence of Ptah, the craftsman god,
With skilled hands, let the bones be awed.
May he mold and reshape, with expert precision,
Each piece fitting perfectly, a divine decision.

By the divine breath of Ankh, the symbol of life,
Revitalize the bones, dispelling strife.
Let the deceased's skeletal framework revive,
Reinstate their form, so they may thrive.

May the guardians of Duat, the realm of the dead,
Assist in the rejoining, with favor widespread.
Hold the bones together, in sacred embrace,
Preserving the deceased's essence, in eternal grace.

By the sacred rites, let the reassembly commence,
The deceased's skeletal unity, recompense.
Each bone finding its rightful position,
Restoring the deceased's skeletal composition.

So it is spoken, so it shall be done,
Rejoin the bones, as a unified one.
May the deceased's skeletal form be complete,
In the afterlife's realm, eternal and sweet."

This spell for rejoining the bones reflects the ancient Egyptian belief in the importance of restoring the deceased's skeletal remains for their continued existence and preservation in the afterlife. By invoking the spirits associated with restoration, such as Osiris and Ptah, and the symbolism of divine breath, the spell seeks to assist in the reassembling and reuniting of the scattered bones.

The spell emphasizes the role of divine entities in the meticulous process of rejoining the fragmented pieces of the deceased's skeletal structure. It calls upon Osiris, the lord of the dead, to guide and oversee the reassembly, ensuring that each bone finds its rightful place. The invocation of Ptah, the craftsman god, highlights the skillful craftsmanship required to mold and reshape the bones with precision.

The mention of Ankh, the symbol of life, signifies the restoration of vitality to the bones, revitalizing them and dispelling any previous damage or fragmentation. The involvement of the guardians of Duat, the realm of the dead, underscores their assistance in holding the reassembled bones together, preserving the deceased's essence and ensuring their eternal unity.

CT 13: Spell for Being Reborn in Memphis: Granting the deceased the opportunity for rebirth in the city of Memphis, a significant religious center.

Utterance:
"O, ancient spirits of Memphis, hear my plea,
Grant this soul the chance for rebirth, I decree.
Let the deceased find solace in your sacred land,
A new life in Memphis, divinely planned.

By the power of Ptah, the creator god,
Let the deceased's rebirth be divinely awed.
In the heart of Memphis, a center of worship,
Grant them a fresh start, their spirit to equip.

Invoke the blessings of Hathor, the goddess of love,
May she nurture the deceased, like a gentle dove.
In Memphis, let them find compassion and care,
A rebirth with joy and love, beyond compare.

By the sacred Nile, let the waters cleanse,
Washing away the past, redeeming any offense.
May the ancient spirits guide the deceased's way,
To a new beginning, in Memphis they shall stay.

Grant them the wisdom of Thoth, the god of knowledge,
In Memphis, let them find enlightenment at the college.
May they learn and grow, their spirit refined,
In the city of Memphis, their destiny aligned.

By the power of the sacred temples that stand,
May the deceased be reborn, in the divine land.
Let them embrace the rituals and traditions,
A new life in Memphis, free from afflictions.

So it is spoken, so it shall be done,
Grant this soul a rebirth, a new life begun.
In Memphis, let them find solace and grace,
A divine opportunity, in this sacred place."

This spell for being reborn in Memphis reflects the ancient Egyptian belief in the significance of the city as a religious center and its association with rebirth and spiritual renewal. By invoking the spirits of Memphis, such as Ptah, Hathor, and Thoth, the spell seeks to grant the deceased the opportunity for a fresh start and a new life in this sacred and revered city.

The spell highlights the power and influence of Ptah, the creator god, in orchestrating the deceased's rebirth in Memphis. It calls upon the blessings of Hathor, the goddess of love, to provide nurturing and care in their new existence. The mention of Thoth, the god of knowledge, signifies the importance of wisdom and enlightenment in the rebirth process.

The invocation of the sacred Nile and the reference to the ancient spirits of Memphis symbolize the cleansing and guidance necessary for the deceased's transition into their new life. The spell emphasizes the embracing of rituals and traditions in Memphis, as the city holds the key to the deceased's destiny and spiritual growth.

CT 14: Spell for Sailing with Ra: Enabling the deceased to join the solar deity Ra in his celestial boat.

Utterance:
"O, radiant Ra, the great solar god,
I beseech thee, guide this soul with your nod.
Grant the deceased the privilege to sail,
In your celestial boat, beyond the earthly veil.

As you journey through the heavens high,
May the deceased be by your side, drawing nigh.
Let them bask in your divine light and glow,
Sailing with you, wherever you may go.

By the power of the sun's rays, so bright,
Illuminate the path, casting away the night.
May the deceased embark on this sacred quest,
Joined with Ra, their souls divinely blessed.

Invoke the winds of Ma'at, the goddess of truth,
That they may carry the deceased, in eternal youth.
Guide them through the celestial realms with grace,
In your celestial boat, a sacred space.

By the sacred rudder, steer the vessel true,
Through the cosmic waters, ever blue.
Grant the deceased the company of your divine entourage,
Navigating the celestial realms, a joyous voyage.

May the gods and goddesses of the heavens unite,
Welcoming the deceased with joy and delight.
In the company of Ra, let their spirits ascend,
As they sail together, their earthly ties transcend.

By the sacred rituals of the sun's embrace,
Let the deceased join Ra in celestial grace.
A celestial boat, a sacred vessel to sail,
Joined with Ra, their destinies prevail.

So it is spoken, so it shall be done,
The deceased sailing with Ra, their souls as one.

In the celestial boat, a divine union unfurled,
Embracing the journey through the celestial world."

This spell for sailing with Ra reflects the ancient Egyptian belief in the opportunity for the deceased to accompany the solar deity Ra on his celestial boat, traversing the celestial realms and experiencing a divine union. By invoking Ra's guidance, the power of the sun's rays, and the assistance of Ma'at, the goddess of truth, the spell seeks to enable the deceased to sail alongside Ra in his celestial vessel.

The spell emphasizes the privilege of joining Ra on his celestial boat, as he represents the ultimate manifestation of solar power and divine radiance. It calls upon Ra to illuminate the path and cast away the darkness, ensuring that the deceased can embark on this sacred journey in his divine light.

The invocation of the winds of Ma'at symbolizes the need for balance and truth in the celestial voyage. It highlights the role of Ma'at in facilitating the passage of the deceased through the celestial realms, guided by the gentle and guiding winds of righteousness.

The spell envisions the deceased in the company of Ra's divine entourage, sailing through the cosmic waters and being welcomed by the gods and goddesses of the heavens. It depicts the celestial boat as a sacred vessel, uniting the deceased's spirit with the radiant presence of Ra, transcending earthly ties and embracing the boundless possibilities of the celestial world.

CT 15: Spell for Traveling in the Netherworld: Facilitating the journey of the deceased through the underworld.

Utterance:
"O, guardians of the Netherworld, hear my plea,
Guide the deceased through the realms they must see.
Grant them safe passage on this sacred path,
Navigating the underworld, free from wrath.

By the power of Anubis, the jackal-headed god,
May the deceased find guidance, where e'er they trod.
Let them traverse the Duat, the realm of the dead,
With Anubis as their protector, their fears be shed.

Invoke the presence of Osiris, the lord of the underworld,
May he receive the deceased with kindness, unfurled.
In his domain, let them find solace and rest,
Embracing the journey, divinely blessed.

By the sacred rituals and spells inscribed,
May the deceased overcome the challenges prescribed.
Grant them the knowledge of the hidden realms,
As they travel through the netherworld's helm.

Invoke the aid of Isis, the divine mother,
May she nurture and comfort the deceased like no other.
In her embrace, let them find strength and peace,
As they navigate the realms, their anxieties cease.

By the scales of Ma'at, the goddess of truth,
Let the deceased's heart be weighed, resolute.
May they find balance and righteousness within,
Passing the judgment, absolved of all sin.

By the light of Ra, the sun god so bright,
Illuminate their path, dispelling the night.
Guide them through the underworld's winding way,
As they journey to eternal life's bay.

So it is spoken, so it shall be done,
The deceased traveling in the netherworld, their journey begun.

Protected by Anubis, guided by Osiris and Isis so fair,
Through the underworld they travel, divinely aware.

May the guardians of the Netherworld pave their way,
As the deceased embarks on this sacred relay.
Grant them safe passage, free from despair,
As they navigate the realms with utmost care."

This spell for traveling in the Netherworld reflects the ancient Egyptian belief in the journey of the deceased through the underworld, guided by various deities and protected by powerful entities. By invoking the guardians of the Netherworld, such as Anubis, Osiris, Isis, and Ma'at, the spell seeks to facilitate the safe passage of the deceased through the realms of the dead.

The spell highlights the role of Anubis, the jackal-headed god, as the protector and guide of the deceased on their journey through the Netherworld. It calls upon Anubis to provide guidance and safeguard the deceased from any harm or malevolent forces they may encounter.

The invocation of Osiris, the lord of the underworld, and Isis, the divine mother, signifies the importance of their nurturing presence and benevolent guidance. It portrays Osiris as the welcoming and compassionate figure who receives the deceased in his domain, providing them with solace and rest.

The spell emphasizes the significance of the rituals and spells inscribed in the Coffin Texts, which provide the deceased with the knowledge and tools necessary to overcome the challenges of the Netherworld. It highlights the role of Ma'at, the goddess of truth, in ensuring that the deceased's heart is weighed with righteousness and finds balance in the judgment.

By invoking the light of Ra, the spell seeks to dispel the darkness and illuminate the path of the deceased as they journey through the underworld. It symbolizes the divine guidance and protection provided by the sun god on their quest for eternal life.

CT 16: Spell for Acquiring the Soul: Ensuring that the deceased's soul is properly integrated into their new existence in the afterlife.

Utterance:
"O, ancient spirits and divine beings,
Hear my words and heed my pleadings.
Grant the deceased their rightful soul,
Complete their being, make them whole.

By the power of Osiris, lord of the dead,
May the deceased's soul be duly wed.
Integrate it into their new existence,
With divine essence, fill their essence.

Invoke the presence of the ba and ka,
Assemble them in harmonious array.
Let the ba, the soul's earthly part,
Merge with the ka, the vital spark of the heart.

By the rites and rituals prescribed,
May the deceased's soul be unified.
Bind it to their eternal essence,
Secure its place with divine presence.

O, Anubis, the embalmer divine,
Guide the soul to its rightful shrine.
Lead it through the realms, serene,
Where eternal peace and solace convene.

By the sacred spells and incantations,
Secure the soul's everlasting station.
Ensure its integration into the divine tapestry,
A seamless part of the afterlife's tapestry.

O, Hathor, goddess of joy and love,
Bless the soul with blessings from above.
Let it experience eternal bliss,
In the realm of everlasting happiness.

By the scales of Ma'at, the goddess of truth,

Let the soul's worth be weighed, uncouth.
May it be deemed righteous and pure,
Ascending to realms of eternal allure.

So it is spoken, so it shall be done,
The deceased's soul acquired, integration begun.
By the powers of the divine and sacred art,
Secure their place in the afterlife's chart.

May the ba and ka unite in divine embrace,
As the deceased finds their eternal place.
With Osiris as their guide and protector,
May their soul find eternal joy and splendor."

This spell for acquiring the soul reflects the ancient Egyptian belief in the integration of the deceased's soul into their new existence in the afterlife. By invoking various deities, such as Osiris, Anubis, Hathor, and Ma'at, the spell seeks to ensure the proper integration and unity of the soul within the divine realms.

The spell highlights the role of Osiris, the lord of the dead, as the central figure in overseeing the acquisition of the deceased's soul. It calls upon Osiris to integrate the soul into its new existence, filling the deceased with divine essence and completeness.

The invocation of the ba and ka represents the two essential components of the soul in Egyptian belief. The ba represents the individual's unique personality and earthly existence, while the ka represents the vital life force and spiritual essence. The spell seeks to merge these two aspects harmoniously, ensuring the complete integration of the deceased's soul.

Anubis, the embalmer divine, is invoked as the guide who leads the soul through the realms of the afterlife, ensuring its safe passage and arrival at its rightful destination. Hathor, the goddess of joy and love, blesses the soul with eternal happiness and bliss in the realms of everlasting joy.

The spell emphasizes the importance of the sacred spells, rites, and rituals prescribed in the Coffin Texts for securing the soul's integration into the divine tapestry of the afterlife. It emphasizes the significance of Ma'at, the goddess of truth, in weighing the soul's worth and ensuring its righteousness and purity for ascending to the realms of eternal allure.

By uniting the ba and ka in divine embrace and with the guidance and protection of Osiris, the spell seeks to secure the deceased's place in the afterlife's chart, where their soul can experience everlasting joy and splendor.

CT 17: Spell for Providing the Ka with Food: Supplying the deceased's spiritual double, the Ka, with sustenance.

Utterance:
"O, divine providers of sustenance and nourishment,
Hear my words and grant your blessed endorsement.
Bestow upon the deceased's Ka its rightful share,
Satisfy its hunger, fulfill its spiritual fare.

By the offerings presented on sacred altars,
Let the Ka partake in these divine favors.
Fill its essence with the essence of life,
Nourish its spirit, relieve its strife.

Invoke the presence of the gods and goddesses,
Who govern the bountiful earthly processes.
Osiris, the god of agriculture and fertility,
Grant the Ka abundance, infinite serendipity.

O, fertile fields and flourishing crops,
Let your abundance extend beyond mortal stops.
Provide sustenance to the Ka's ethereal form,
Grant it vitality, protect it from harm.

By the sacred rituals and offerings made,
Ensure the Ka's satisfaction does not fade.
Let the fragrance of incense fill the air,
As the Ka partakes in this sacred affair.

O, Sekhmet, lioness goddess of nourishment,
Bless the Ka with your divine encouragement.
Provide it with the life-sustaining essence,
Preserve its vitality, guard its presence.

By the bread, fruits, and libations offered,
May the Ka's hunger and thirst be properly buffered.
Sustain its existence in the realm of the dead,
With divine nourishment, ensure it is fed.

By the powers of Ma'at, the goddess of balance,
Let the Ka's sustenance find divine resonance.

Maintain harmony in the afterlife's domain,
As the Ka thrives, free from hunger and pain.

So it is spoken, so it shall be done,
The deceased's Ka fed, its hunger won.
By the grace of the gods and goddesses divine,
Provide nourishment to the Ka's ethereal shrine.

May the offerings and rituals duly performed,
Sustain the Ka, its hunger transformed.
With the divine provisions bestowed with care,
Let the Ka flourish in the afterlife's rare."

This spell for providing the Ka with food reflects the ancient Egyptian belief in supplying the deceased's spiritual double with sustenance in the afterlife. By invoking the divine providers of nourishment, such as Osiris and Sekhmet, the spell seeks to ensure that the Ka is properly fed and its hunger relieved.

The spell emphasizes the importance of offerings presented on sacred altars as a means to provide nourishment to the Ka. It calls upon the gods and goddesses who govern earthly processes, particularly Osiris, the god of agriculture and fertility, to bestow abundance and serendipity upon the Ka.

The invocation of Sekhmet, the lioness goddess of nourishment, highlights her role in blessing the Ka and preserving its vitality. The spell seeks her divine encouragement and protection to provide the Ka with the life-sustaining essence it requires.

The rituals and offerings made, including bread, fruits, and libations, are emphasized as a means to ensure the Ka's satisfaction and vitality. The fragrance of incense symbolizes the sacredness of the offering and the Ka's participation in the ritual.

The spell acknowledges the powers of Ma'at, the goddess of balance, in maintaining harmony in the afterlife's domain. By invoking her, the spell seeks to align the provision of nourishment to the Ka with the divine order and balance of the universe.

Through the proper performance of offerings and rituals, the spell aims to sustain the Ka's existence in the realm of the dead, ensuring it is free from hunger and pain. It emphasizes the role of divine provisions in allowing the Ka to flourish and thrive in the afterlife.

CT 18: Spell for Creating an Abode in the Duat: Assisting in the construction of a dwelling place for the deceased in the underworld.

Utterance:
"O, divine architects and builders of the Duat,
Hear my plea and fulfill this sacred task.
Assist in the creation of a dwelling place,
A sanctuary for the deceased's eternal embrace.

By the power of Ptah, the master craftsman,
Let the abode in the Duat take form and begin.
Weave the essence of the deceased's desire,
Construct a sanctuary that will never tire.

Invoke the presence of Hathor, the goddess of beauty,
Bless the abode with splendor and serenity.
Adorn its walls with celestial hues,
Creating a dwelling fit for eternal views.

O, Anubis, guardian of the Netherworld,
Guide the construction, may it unfurl.
Ensure the stability and strength of the abode,
A sanctuary that will forever withhold.

By the sacred rituals and incantations,
May the abode defy time's limitations.
Let its walls withstand the test of eternity,
A haven for the deceased's tranquility.

O, Isis, divine mother and protector,
Wrap the abode with love, make it a reflector.
Shield it from malevolent forces and harm,
Preserve its sanctity, a place of charm.

By the wisdom of Thoth, the god of knowledge,
Let the abode be filled with divine homage.
Inscribe the walls with sacred spells,
Empowering the dwelling, where darkness dwells.

So it is spoken, so it shall be done,

The abode in the Duat, its construction begun.
By the hands of divine architects and builders,
Create a sanctuary, free from earthly filters.

May the abode provide solace and rest,
A dwelling place where the deceased is blessed.
In the realm of the Duat, let it stand,
A haven crafted by divine hand."

This spell for creating an abode in the Duat reflects the ancient Egyptian belief in the construction of a dwelling place for the deceased in the underworld. By invoking the divine architects, such as Ptah and Hathor, and seeking the guidance and protection of Anubis, Isis, and Thoth, the spell aims to assist in the creation of a sanctuary that will provide eternal solace and tranquility for the deceased.

Ptah, known as the master craftsman, is invoked to bring the abode in the Duat to life. It calls upon Ptah to weave the essence of the deceased's desires and construct a dwelling that will never tire, providing a fitting sanctuary in the afterlife.

Hathor, the goddess of beauty, is called upon to bless the abode with splendor and serenity. The spell requests her presence to adorn the walls of the dwelling with celestial hues, creating an aesthetically pleasing and harmonious environment for the deceased.

Anubis, as the guardian of the Netherworld, is asked to guide the construction of the abode, ensuring its stability and strength. It is his role to safeguard the dwelling and make it a secure sanctuary that will endure throughout eternity.

The rituals and incantations performed during the construction of the abode are emphasized as integral to its endurance. The spell invokes the wisdom of Thoth, the god of knowledge, to inscribe the walls with sacred spells, empowering the dwelling and protecting it from malevolent forces.

Isis, the divine mother and protector, is invoked to wrap the abode with love and shield it from harm. Her presence ensures the preservation of its sanctity, making it a place of charm and safety for the deceased.

The spell concludes with the affirmation that the construction of the abode has begun under the guidance of the divine architects and builders. It seeks a dwelling that provides solace and rest, a haven where the deceased can find blessings and eternal peace in the realm of the Duat.

CT 19: Spell for Receiving Offerings: Enabling the deceased to receive offerings and provisions from their loved ones.

Utterance:
"O, spirits of the departed and ancestral kin,
Hear my call and let the offering begin.
Open the channels between realms unseen,
So the deceased may receive provisions serene.

By the power of Anubis, the guardian of the tomb,
Let the connection between worlds fully bloom.
Guide the offerings from the earthly plane,
To the awaiting hands of the deceased's domain.

O, Nephthys, goddess of mourning and lament,
Carry the prayers and offerings, let them be sent.
Wrap them in your gentle embrace,
As you journey to the deceased's resting place.

By the sacred rituals and heartfelt devotion,
Let the offerings reach their intended destination.
May the fragrance of incense fill the air,
As loved ones show their deep love and care.

O, Osiris, lord of the afterlife and renewal,
Bless the offerings with your divine approval.
Grant the deceased the sustenance they require,
Nourish their spirit, fulfill their desire.

By the sacred rites and spoken words,
Let the offerings become a divine accord.
As they pass from the living to the dead,
May the bond between realms be firmly spread.

O, Hathor, goddess of joy and abundance,
Shower the offerings with your gracious radiance.
Fill them with your blessings and divine grace,
As they reach the deceased in their resting place.

By the love and memories that bind,
Let the offerings bring solace to the deceased's mind.

May they feel the presence of their loved ones near,
As provisions and offerings of love appear.

So it is spoken, so it shall be done,
The deceased receives offerings, their connection won.
By the power of the spirits and deities divine,
Let the provisions reach the deceased's shrine.

May the offerings bring comfort and peace,
As the deceased's journey in the afterlife finds release.
Through the bond between realms, strong and true,
Loved ones' offerings ensure their presence anew."

This spell for receiving offerings reflects the ancient Egyptian belief in the importance of providing provisions to the deceased in the afterlife. By invoking the spirits of the departed and ancestral kin, as well as the guidance of Anubis, Nephthys, Osiris, and Hathor, the spell seeks to enable the deceased to receive offerings and provisions from their loved ones.

Anubis, the guardian of the tomb, is called upon to open the channels between the earthly plane and the realm of the deceased. It is through his guidance that the offerings are guided to their intended destination, reaching the deceased's domain.

Nephthys, the goddess of mourning and lament, is asked to carry the prayers and offerings to the deceased's resting place. Her gentle embrace ensures the safe passage of the offerings as she journeys between the realms.

The sacred rituals and heartfelt devotion of the living are emphasized as essential in ensuring that the offerings reach the deceased. The fragrance of incense symbolizes the spiritual connection and serves as a means for loved ones to demonstrate their love and care.

Osiris, the lord of the afterlife and renewal, is invoked to bless the offerings with his divine approval. His presence ensures that the deceased receives the sustenance they require, nourishing their spirit and fulfilling their desires in the afterlife.

Hathor, the goddess of joy and abundance, is called upon to shower the offerings with her gracious radiance. Her blessings and divine grace infuse the offerings, bringing comfort and solace to the deceased as they sense the presence of their loved ones.

The spell concludes with the affirmation that the deceased receives the offerings, establishing a strong and true connection between the realms. The provisions symbolize the love, memories, and continued presence of the living in the afterlife, bringing comfort and peace to the deceased.

CT 20: Spell for Ascending to the Sky: Facilitating the ascent of the deceased's spirit to the celestial realms.

Utterance:
"O, divine celestial beings, guardians of the sky,
Hear my plea as I call upon your power high.
Guide the spirit of the deceased on its ascent,
To the realms above, where celestial wonders are meant.

By the authority of Ra, the sun god supreme,
Let the spirit soar in the celestial dream.
Lend your wings, mighty falcons of the sky,
Carry the spirit upwards, let it fly.

O, Nut, goddess of the sky's expanse,
Open your starry vault, give the spirit a chance.
Create a path of shimmering stars and light,
Leading the spirit to realms beyond sight.

By the sacred utterances and divine incantations,
Let the spirit transcend earthly limitations.
Break free from the bonds of mortality's hold,
Ascend to the heavens, to the realm of gold.

O, Horus, falcon-headed god of divine ascent,
Guide the spirit with your celestial intent.
Soar with the spirit upon your wings,
To the realms where eternal joy sings.

By the wisdom of Thoth, the god of knowledge,
Let the spirit transcend earthly bondage.
Grant it passage through the celestial gate,
To join the company of the blessed, its fate.

O, Ma'at, goddess of truth and cosmic balance,
Align the spirit with the celestial dance.
Weigh its heart against the feather of truth,
Ensure its ascent, its eternal youth.

By the sacred rites and spoken words,
Let the spirit rise, like soaring birds.

May it reach the celestial abode on high,
Where eternal bliss and radiance lie.

So it is spoken, so it shall be done,
The spirit ascends to realms beyond the sun.
By the power of the celestial beings divine,
Guide the spirit on its ascent, let it shine.

May the spirit soar to celestial heights,
Where it finds eternal peace and delights.
In the embrace of the celestial realms above,
May the spirit bask in eternal love."

This spell for ascending to the sky reflects the ancient Egyptian belief in the journey of the deceased's spirit to the celestial realms. By invoking the divine celestial beings, such as Ra, Nut, Horus, Thoth, and Ma'at, the spell seeks to facilitate the ascent of the deceased's spirit to the heavenly realms.

Ra, the sun god, is called upon to lend his power and grant the spirit the ability to soar in the celestial dream. The spell invokes Ra's authority to allow the spirit to break free from earthly limitations and ascend to the realms where celestial wonders reside.

Nut, the goddess of the sky, is asked to open her starry vault and create a path of shimmering stars and light. Her role is to guide the spirit and provide a celestial pathway leading to realms beyond earthly sight.

Horus, the falcon-headed god, is invoked to guide the spirit with his divine intent and carry it upon his wings. It is through Horus' assistance that the spirit is able to ascend and join the company of the blessed in the realms where eternal joy awaits.

Thoth, the god of knowledge, is called upon to bestow wisdom upon the spirit, allowing it to transcend earthly bondage. His guidance ensures the spirit's safe passage through the celestial gate, leading to its ultimate destination.

Ma'at, the goddess of truth and cosmic balance, is invoked to align the spirit with the celestial dance. She weighs the heart of the deceased against the feather of truth, ensuring its ascent and eternal youth in the celestial abode.

The spell concludes with the affirmation that the spirit ascends to realms beyond the sun. Through the power of the divine celestial beings, the spirit is guided on its ascent, where it finds eternal peace, love, and bliss.

CT 21: Spell for Not Being Repulsed by the Gatekeeper: Ensuring a favorable reception and acceptance by the gatekeeper of the afterlife.

Utterance:
"O gatekeeper of the afterlife, guardian of the celestial gate,
Look upon the deceased with kindness, do not seal their fate.
Grant them passage through your hallowed threshold,
Let their spirit unfold in the realm untold.

By the power of the sacred words I speak,
May the gatekeeper's heart not repel or critique.
Open the gate wide, let the deceased pass,
To the realm of eternity, where serenity does amass.

O gatekeeper, witness the deeds of the deceased,
See their worthiness and grant them release.
May their heart be light as the feather of Ma'at,
In balance with truth, their virtues intact.

By the sacred symbols and the divine names,
Let the gatekeeper relinquish his judgments and claims.
See the deceased's journey, their trials and strife,
And welcome them into eternal life.

O Anubis, guide of the souls in transition,
Intercede on behalf of the deceased's admission.
Present their case with wisdom and care,
And ensure they are received in the afterlife fair.

By the scales of justice and divine decree,
May the gatekeeper find the deceased worthy.
Let them pass through the gate with ease,
To partake in the eternal cosmic mysteries.

O gatekeeper, do not repulse or deny,
The deserving soul that seeks to comply.
Look upon them with favor and grace,
And grant them a rightful place in the sacred space.

By the power vested in the divine order,

Let the gatekeeper welcome the deceased as a border.
Release them from earthly bonds and strife,
And embrace them in the realm of eternal life.

So it is spoken, so it shall be done,
The gatekeeper's acceptance, a battle won.
May the deceased pass through the celestial gate,
And find eternal bliss in their destined fate."

This spell for not being repulsed by the gatekeeper reflects the ancient Egyptian belief in the presence of a guardian at the entrance of the afterlife, who assesses the worthiness of the deceased for admission. By invoking the gatekeeper and the assistance of Anubis, the spell seeks to ensure a favorable reception and acceptance of the deceased into the afterlife.

The gatekeeper of the afterlife is called upon to look upon the deceased with kindness and to grant them passage through the celestial gate. The spell emphasizes the hope that the gatekeeper's heart will not repel or judge the deceased, but instead open the gate wide, allowing the spirit to enter the realm of eternity.

Anubis, the god of embalming and guide of the souls in transition, is invoked to intercede on behalf of the deceased's admission. His wisdom and care are sought to present the case of the deceased and advocate for their acceptance into the afterlife. The spell emphasizes that Anubis should present the deeds and virtues of the deceased, highlighting their worthiness and eligibility for eternal life.

The spell also references the importance of the deceased's heart being light as the feather of Ma'at, symbolizing their alignment with truth and cosmic balance. By aligning their virtues with the scales of justice, the spell implores the gatekeeper to recognize the righteousness of the deceased and welcome them into the afterlife.

The conclusion of the spell emphasizes the desire for the gatekeeper to relinquish any judgments or claims and to see the journey and trials of the deceased. It implores the gatekeeper to open their heart and embrace the deserving soul, granting them a rightful place in the sacred space of the afterlife.

CT 22: Spell for Sailing through the Sky: Assisting the deceased in navigating the celestial realms.

Utterance:
"Oh, celestial expanse, vast and divine,
Guide the spirit of the deceased as it takes flight.
Grant it passage through your radiant gates,
To traverse the heavens and transcend mortal states.

With sails unfurled and winds as allies,
Let the deceased embark on this celestial voyage.
May the boat of the sun be their vessel,
As they navigate the skies, resolute and fearless.

Oh, Ra, the great solar deity,
Bestow upon the deceased your divine energy.
Let your boat carry them on its golden wings,
As they soar through the heavens, a wondrous offering.

Oh, Nut, celestial goddess of the sky,
Extend your protective mantle from on high.
Wrap the deceased in your starry embrace,
Guiding their path with celestial grace.

With each passing hour, with each celestial sphere,
May the deceased advance without fear.
Navigating the constellations and celestial maps,
They journey through realms, transcending earthly traps.

Oh, wise Thoth, master of knowledge and time,
Illuminate the path with your celestial rhyme.
Guide the deceased through astral dimensions,
With wisdom and insight, dispelling all confusions.

As the boat of the sun sails through the skies,
May the deceased witness celestial wonders with their eyes.
The realms of gods and stars, a spectacle to behold,
Their spirit emboldened, their destiny enfolded.

By the power of ancient cosmic laws,
Let the deceased traverse celestial shores.

Grant them safe passage, free from harm,
As they embark on this celestial charm.

Soaring through the sky, their spirit unbound,
Connected to the universe, forever profound.
Oh, celestial expanse, embrace their flight,
And lead them to realms of eternal light.

With gratitude and reverence, this spell is cast,
To aid the deceased on their celestial sojourn, unsurpassed.
May they sail through the sky with ease and grace,
Guided by celestial forces, to their destined place."

This spell for sailing through the sky reflects the ancient Egyptian belief in the celestial realms and the journey of the deceased's spirit through the heavens. It seeks to assist the deceased in navigating the celestial expanse, ensuring a safe and purposeful journey.

The spell calls upon the celestial expanse, the vast and divine sky, to guide the spirit of the deceased as it takes flight. It implores the celestial gates to open, granting passage to the deceased as they traverse the heavens and transcend mortal states.

Ra, the great solar deity, is invoked as the one who carries the deceased on the boat of the sun. The spell asks for Ra's divine energy to empower the deceased's journey, as they soar through the skies on the golden wings of the sun boat.

Nut, the celestial goddess of the sky, is called upon to extend her protective mantle and guide the path of the deceased. With her starry embrace, she provides celestial grace, ensuring the safe navigation of the deceased through the astral realms.

Thoth, the wise master of knowledge and time, is invoked for his guidance and wisdom. The spell seeks Thoth's assistance in illuminating the path of the deceased through the celestial dimensions, dispelling any confusions and ensuring a clear course.

The boat of the sun sailing through the skies symbolizes the journey of the deceased's spirit as they witness celestial wonders and traverse through realms beyond earthly confines. The spell emphasizes the awe-inspiring nature of the celestial realms and the profound connection between the deceased and the universe.

The conclusion of the spell expresses gratitude and reverence for the assistance provided, as it seeks to aid the deceased on their celestial sojourn. It implores the celestial expanse to embrace their flight and lead them to realms of eternal light, where their spirit can find its destined place.

CT 23: Spell for Protection against Crocodiles: Safeguarding the deceased from crocodile-related dangers in the afterlife.

Utterance:
"Oh, mighty guardians of the Nile's depths,
Fierce crocodiles that lurk in murky waters.
I beseech your attention and heed my call,
Protect the deceased from your jaws' mighty slaughter.

Let not their sharp teeth tear the spirit's form,
Nor their powerful jaws crush the essence within.
By the power of ancient words and sacred spells,
Create a shield, a barrier against crocodile's sin.

Oh, Sobek, powerful god of crocodiles,
Hear this plea and lend your divine protection.
Wrap the deceased in your formidable might,
Shield them from harm with your fierce affection.

May your scales be their armor, impenetrable and strong,
Guarding their spirit from crocodile's grip.
Let your eyes see all dangers that may arise,
Alerting the deceased to dangers that might slip.

Oh, Netjeru, gods and goddesses divine,
Unite your forces in this protective design.
By your combined strength and watchful eye,
Keep the deceased safe as they journey by.

With the power of Ra, the sun's radiant light,
Banish the darkness that hides crocodile's might.
Illuminate the path, reveal their lurking presence,
So the deceased may evade their deadly essence.

Oh, magicians and sorcerers of ancient lore,
Unleash your spells to safeguard forevermore.
Enchant the deceased with crocodile-repelling might,
Making them invisible in their perilous flight.

By the power of this sacred incantation,
I invoke the protection of all creation.

May the crocodiles bow to your divine decree,
And spare the deceased from their jaws' decree.

This spell for protection against crocodiles reflects the ancient Egyptian belief in the dangers posed by these fierce creatures in the afterlife. Crocodiles were seen as symbols of chaos and were associated with the threat of destruction. Therefore, this spell seeks to safeguard the deceased from the perils and harm that crocodiles represent.

The spell begins by addressing the mighty guardians of the Nile's depths, the fierce crocodiles that lurk in the waters. It implores their attention and asks for their protection, urging them to refrain from tearing the spirit's form or crushing its essence within their jaws.

Sobek, the powerful god of crocodiles, is invoked as the primary protector. The spell calls upon Sobek to lend his divine might and create an impenetrable shield for the deceased. Sobek's scales become the armor that guards the spirit from the grip of crocodiles, while his vigilant eyes detect any lurking dangers and alert the deceased to potential threats.

The Netjeru, the collective term for the gods and goddesses of ancient Egypt, are invoked to unite their forces in protecting the deceased. Their combined strength and watchful eye ensure the safety of the deceased as they journey through the afterlife.

Ra, the sun god, is called upon for his illuminating power. His radiant light banishes the darkness that conceals the presence of crocodiles, allowing the deceased to see and evade their deadly essence.

The spell also acknowledges the wisdom of the ancient magicians and sorcerers, who are invoked to unleash their protective spells. These spells enchant the deceased with the ability to repel crocodiles, making them invisible to the creatures and ensuring their safe passage.

The conclusion of the spell affirms the power of the sacred incantation and invokes the protection of all creation. It calls upon the crocodiles to bow to the divine decree, sparing the deceased from their jaws' decree.

CT 24: Spell for Greeting Osiris: Allowing the deceased to approach and pay homage to the god Osiris, ruler of the underworld.

Utterance:
"Oh, Osiris, great lord of the Duat,
King of the underworld, judge of the deceased.
With reverence and devotion, I come before thee,
To offer my homage and seek thy blessed peace.

Grant me passage to your divine presence,
That I may stand in your hallowed court.
Guide me through the realms of the afterlife,
As I journey towards the eternal resort.

Oh, Osiris, mighty judge and ruler supreme,
With your wisdom and grace, make my presence known.
Open the gates of your glorious abode,
So I may approach your sacred throne.

May my heart be pure, my intentions sincere,
As I kneel before you, O Osiris, divine.
With words of adoration, I greet your name,
And seek your favor in this sacred shrine.

Grant me audience, O merciful Osiris,
As I offer my praises and reverence to thee.
Accept my offerings and pleas for protection,
And bestow your blessings upon me.

May my voice reach your ears, O Lord of the Dead,
As I declare my loyalty and devotion.
Let my words resonate within your realm,
And bring me closer to eternal salvation.

Oh, Osiris, compassionate ruler of souls,
Receive me as a faithful servant of the divine.
Guide me through the trials of the afterlife,
And lead me to the eternal life that shall be mine.

With every step I take in your presence,

I honor your name and acknowledge your might.
Oh, Osiris, the great god of resurrection,
I bow before you, consumed by your eternal light.

In this spell for greeting Osiris, the deceased seeks permission and guidance to approach the god Osiris, who is revered as the ruler of the underworld and the judge of the deceased. The spell begins by addressing Osiris as the great lord of the Duat, the Egyptian underworld, and acknowledges his role as the king and judge of the deceased.

The deceased expresses their reverence and devotion to Osiris, approaching him with humility and a sincere desire to pay homage. They request passage to his divine presence and guidance through the realms of the afterlife, seeking his assistance and protection on their journey.

The spell invokes Osiris as the mighty judge and ruler, asking him to make the presence of the deceased known and to open the gates of his abode. The goal is to gain access to Osiris' sacred court and to approach his sacred throne with respect and awe.

The deceased emphasizes the purity of their heart and the sincerity of their intentions as they kneel before Osiris. They greet his name with words of adoration, acknowledging his divine status and seeking his favor in the sacred shrine.

The spell implores Osiris to grant the deceased an audience and to accept their offerings and pleas for protection. The deceased seeks to establish a connection with Osiris, asking for his blessings and favor in their journey through the afterlife.

The deceased expresses their devotion and loyalty to Osiris, declaring themselves as a faithful servant of the divine. They ask for his guidance through the trials of the afterlife and seek his leadership in attaining eternal life.

The spell concludes with the deceased bowing before Osiris, acknowledging his power as the great god of resurrection. They submit themselves to Osiris' eternal light and honor his name with every step they take in his presence.

Through this spell, the deceased seeks the approval and favor of Osiris, the ruler of the underworld, to ensure a smooth and successful journey through the afterlife and to ultimately attain eternal life in Osiris' divine presence.

CT 25: Spell for Receiving the Necessities of Life: Ensuring that the deceased is provided with essential sustenance and supplies for their existence in the afterlife.

Utterance:
"O provider of life, bestow your blessings upon me,
In this realm of the eternal afterlife.
Grant me the necessities I require to sustain my existence,
As I journey through the realms beyond mortal strife.

O generous spirits, hear my plea,
Bring forth the abundance of sustenance and supplies.
Let the offerings of food and drink be plentiful,
To nourish my spirit as it forever flies.

May the fertile fields yield bountiful harvests,
With grains and fruits in abundance overflowing.
Let the rivers flow with sweet and refreshing waters,
Satisfying my thirst, their life-giving essence bestowing.

Grant me the bread that sustains,
The meat that nourishes, and the milk that comforts.
Fill my storerooms with provisions aplenty,
That I may partake of them in endless assortments.

O guardian spirits, bring forth the offerings,
The delicacies and libations of rich and savory taste.
Let them be presented to me with reverence and honor,
In this realm where my eternal existence is embraced.

May the scent of incense fill the air,
A fragrance of devotion and sacredness divine.
Let it rise as an offering to the heavens,
In reverence to the gods, in their presence we align.

As I traverse the afterlife's realms,
May the necessities of life never be in shortage.
Provide me with all that I need to thrive,
To sustain my spirit in this eternal pilgrimage.

With gratitude, I receive these offerings,

Knowing they are essential for my eternal bliss.
May they replenish and satisfy my every need,
As I dwell in the afterlife's eternal abyss.

In this spell for receiving the necessities of life, the deceased appeals to the provider of life and the generous spirits of the afterlife to ensure their provision in the eternal realm. The utterance begins by invoking the provider of life and seeking their blessings in the afterlife, emphasizing the importance of receiving the necessities required for sustenance.

The deceased addresses the generous spirits, requesting their assistance in bringing forth abundance in the form of food and drink. They seek the plentiful offerings of nourishment, including grains, fruits, and other essential sustenance, to sustain their spirit as they journey through the realms beyond mortal existence.

The spell entreats the spirits to ensure the fertility of fields, yielding bountiful harvests and abundant crops. It calls for the rivers to flow with sweet and refreshing waters, quenching the thirst of the deceased and providing the life-giving essence they require.

The deceased asks for a variety of provisions, including bread, meat, milk, and other nourishing substances, to be stored in their afterlife abode. They express the desire for a plentiful and diverse supply of food, symbolizing the satisfaction of their physical and spiritual needs.

The spell appeals to the guardian spirits, requesting that they bring forth offerings of delicacies and libations with reverence and honor. The aroma of incense is invoked as a sacred offering, rising to the heavens and aligning the deceased's presence with the gods.

The deceased expresses gratitude for the offerings, acknowledging their essential role in ensuring eternal bliss. They trust that these provisions will replenish and satisfy their every need as they dwell in the eternal abyss of the afterlife.

Through this spell, the deceased seeks the assurance that they will receive the necessary sustenance and supplies to thrive in the afterlife. It reflects the belief in the continuation of life beyond death and the importance of spiritual nourishment for eternal existence.

CT 26: Spell for Becoming a Star: Allowing the deceased to transform into a celestial star and join the heavenly realm.

Utterance:
"O radiant one, grant me transformation divine,
To transcend the earthly bounds, to brightly shine.
In this afterlife journey, I seek a celestial fate,
To become a radiant star, my eternal state.

Like the luminous sun in the vast expanse above,
Let me ascend to the heavens, a beacon of love.
Grant me the wings of a celestial being,
To soar through the cosmos, ever free and gleaming.

In the celestial realm, let my essence reside,
As a star among stars, my spirit glorified.
Illuminate the night sky with my eternal light,
Guiding the way for souls, in the darkness of night.

Grant me the brilliance to rival the moon's glow,
A radiant presence in the celestial show.
May my light twinkle with the spirits of the blessed,
In the tapestry of stars, eternally impressed.

I shed the mortal coil, my earthly form released,
Embracing the celestial realm, my soul finds peace.
Through the realms of eternity, I now traverse,
As a star among stars, my destiny rehearsed.

O celestial powers, hear my fervent plea,
Grant me this transformation, so mote it be.
Let my essence blend with the celestial spheres,
As a star, shining bright throughout the years.

As I ascend to the heavens, I leave behind,
The confines of the earthly realm, no longer confined.
I become a beacon of light, a celestial fire,
A radiant star, fulfilling my soul's deepest desire.

In this spell for becoming a star, the deceased beseeches a higher power to grant
them the divine transformation into a celestial being. They yearn to transcend the

earthly boundaries and shine brightly in the celestial realm, akin to the luminous sun and the radiant stars above.

The utterance expresses the desire to ascend to the heavens, to become a guiding light and a source of love and inspiration. The deceased seeks wings that will allow them to soar through the cosmos, free and radiant, experiencing the vastness of the celestial realm.

The spell invokes the imagery of the celestial realm, where the essence of the deceased will reside as a star among stars, their spirit glorified. They aspire to illuminate the night sky, guiding lost souls and offering comfort in the darkness.

The deceased implores the higher powers to grant them the brilliance that rivals the moon's glow, to become a radiant presence in the celestial tapestry. They envision their light twinkling alongside other blessed spirits, eternally imprinted in the celestial realms.

Through the transformation into a star, the deceased sheds their earthly form and embraces the celestial realm, finding peace and transcendence. They embark on a journey through the realms of eternity, fulfilling their destiny as a star among stars.

The spell concludes with a plea to the celestial powers, affirming the earnestness of the request. The deceased seeks to blend their essence with the celestial spheres, becoming a shining star that will endure throughout the ages.

This spell reflects the belief in the potential for the deceased to transcend earthly limitations and join the celestial realm. It embodies the desire for eternal luminosity, guiding and inspiring others as a radiant star in the cosmic expanse.

CT 27: Spell for Receiving Offerings in the Afterlife: Ensuring that the deceased continues to receive offerings and provisions from the living.

Utterance:
"O benefactors of the living, hear my plea,
In this eternal realm where my spirit now be.
Grant me the continuation of offerings divine,
That I may thrive in the afterlife's sacred shrine.

O loved ones and kin, remember me with care,
In this realm where I dwell, beyond mortal affair.
Bring forth the offerings of food and libations,
Sustaining my spirit with your sacred dedications.

Let the incense rise, carrying your prayers and love,
To reach my abode in the realms above.
With reverence and devotion, present the offerings rare,
In this eternal bond, our connection we share.

May the bread of life be laid before my shrine,
Symbolizing nourishment, a sustaining sign.
Let the fruits of the earth, ripe and succulent,
Satisfy my hunger, their essence abundant.

Pour the libations, the sacred liquid of life,
Quenching my thirst, dispelling all strife.
Let the aroma of incense fill the air,
As an offering of devotion, rising with care.

O generous souls, shower me with your grace,
As you offer provisions in this sacred space.
For it is through your offerings, love, and devotion,
That I receive sustenance in this eternal ocean.

As you honor me with your prayers and gifts,
I am embraced by the love that uplifts.
In this afterlife journey, your offerings bestow,
Abundance and sustenance, a perpetual flow.

May your remembrance of me never cease,

As you provide offerings, my soul finds peace.
Together we forge a bond that transcends time,
In this eternal realm, where love's light will shine.

In this spell for receiving offerings in the afterlife, the deceased calls upon the benefactors of the living to ensure the continuation of offerings and provisions in the eternal realm. The utterance begins with an appeal to loved ones and kin, urging them to remember the deceased with care and dedication.

The deceased implores their loved ones to bring forth offerings of food, libations, and incense, symbolizing nourishment, sustenance, and devotion. They emphasize the importance of these offerings in sustaining their spirit and maintaining a sacred bond between the realms of the living and the afterlife.

The spell emphasizes the significance of bread, representing the bread of life, and the fruits of the earth as sources of nourishment for the deceased. It highlights the pouring of libations, the sacred liquid of life, to quench the thirst of the deceased and provide spiritual refreshment.

The aroma of incense is invoked as an offering of devotion, rising to the heavens and serving as a connection between the living and the deceased. The deceased acknowledges the generosity of souls who shower them with grace through prayers and offerings, recognizing the love and upliftment that such gestures provide.

The spell concludes with a plea for the remembrance of the deceased and a perpetual flow of offerings and sustenance. It emphasizes the enduring bond between the living and the deceased, forged through offerings and the eternal light of love.

This spell reflects the belief in the continued connection between the realms of the living and the afterlife. It underscores the importance of offerings in providing sustenance and maintaining a spiritual bond between the deceased and their loved ones.

CT 28: Spell for Defeating Enemies: Providing protection and assistance to the deceased in overcoming adversaries or hostile forces.

Utterance:
"O mighty protectors, lend me your strength,
In this realm where adversaries seek to impede.
Grant me the power to vanquish all foes,
And safeguard my spirit, in the afterlife's creed.

O guardians of the divine, hear my plea,
As I face the challenges that lie ahead.
Bolster my spirit with courage and might,
To confront my enemies with a heart unwavering and steadfast.

Let my enemies be as dust beneath my feet,
Their plots and schemes crumbling into naught.
May their malicious intent be turned aside,
By the divine forces that protect me, I am taught.

With the strength of the gods, I shall prevail,
Against those who seek to harm and assail.
Grant me the weapons to strike down my foes,
With each blow, their resistance shall fail.

May my spirit be shielded from their dark designs,
As I navigate the realms of the afterlife divine.
Protect me from their snares and illusions,
With wisdom and discernment, let victory be mine.

O spirits of justice, guide my hand,
As I confront my adversaries, take a stand.
Fill my heart with resolve and righteous fury,
To overcome the obstacles, in this sacred land.

By the power of the divine, I am shielded,
From the machinations of those who would harm.
Their malevolent intentions shall be dispersed,
As I invoke the protective forces with this charm.

With this spell for defeating enemies, I proclaim,

My spirit is fortified, and my enemies I shall tame.
In the afterlife's realm, I stand resolute,
Protected and victorious, in the divine's holy name.

In this spell for defeating enemies, the deceased invokes the aid of mighty protectors and guardians of the divine to provide strength and assistance in overcoming adversaries. The utterance begins with a plea for the protectors to lend their power and shield the deceased from the adversities they may face in the afterlife.

The spell beseeches the divine forces to bolster the spirit of the deceased with courage and might, enabling them to confront their enemies with unwavering determination. The aim is to render the adversaries powerless, turning their plots and schemes into dust and thwarting their malicious intent.

The deceased invokes the strength of the gods, seeking their assistance in striking down their foes and ensuring the failure of their resistance. They call upon divine protection to shield their spirit from the dark designs of their enemies, relying on wisdom and discernment to achieve victory.

The spell acknowledges the presence of spirits of justice, who guide the hand of the deceased as they confront their adversaries. The aim is to navigate the realms of the afterlife with resolve and righteousness, overcoming obstacles and dispelling the snares and illusions set by their enemies.

By invoking the power of the divine, the deceased proclaims their shielded status, protected from the harm and machinations of their enemies. The spell concludes with a declaration of victory and fortification, as the deceased stands resolute and victorious in the sacred realm of the afterlife.

This spell reflects the belief in the existence of adversaries or hostile forces in the afterlife and seeks divine assistance in overcoming them. It underscores the importance of protection and resilience in facing challenges and highlights the power of the divine forces in defeating enemies.

CT 29: Spell for Becoming a Divine Falcon: Granting the deceased the ability to transform into a divine falcon and navigate the spiritual realms.

Utterance:
"O divine falcon, with wings spread wide,
Grant me the power to join your celestial flight.
Transform my being into your majestic form,
As I navigate the realms of spiritual light.

May my mortal limitations be cast aside,
As I embody your grace and celestial might.
Grant me the sight to see beyond the mundane,
And soar through the realms of eternal sight.

With each beat of my wings, I ascend higher,
Beyond the boundaries of earthly constraints.
Grant me the swiftness to traverse the heavens,
As I explore the realms where divine presence remains.

Grant me the keen eyesight of the falcon,
To perceive the hidden truths and mysteries untold.
Let me pierce the veil that separates the worlds,
And witness the wonders that the divine enfold.

In the form of a divine falcon, I am free,
To travel between realms and transcend mortality.
Guide me, O sacred bird, in my spiritual quest,
As I embrace the transformation and rise in totality.

With the wings of a falcon, I transcend time,
Navigating the spiritual realms with ease.
Grant me the wisdom to discern the sacred,
And connect with the divine essence that frees.

As a divine falcon, I embody power and grace,
Resplendent in flight, soaring through sacred space.
Through this spell, I embrace my avian form,
As I embark on a journey of spiritual embrace.

In this spell for becoming a divine falcon, the deceased beseeches the assistance of the falcon, a symbol of divine power and grace, to grant them the ability to transform into this majestic bird and navigate the spiritual realms. The utterance begins by invoking the divine falcon and requesting its power to join its celestial flight, shedding the limitations of mortal existence.

The spell asks for a transformation of the deceased's being into the form of a divine falcon, enabling them to traverse the realms of spiritual light. The aim is to transcend the constraints of earthly existence and perceive beyond the mundane, exploring the realms where divine presence resides.

The deceased seeks the attributes of the falcon, including keen eyesight to perceive hidden truths and mysteries, and the swiftness to traverse the heavens. The spell emphasizes the falcon's ability to pierce the veil that separates worlds and witness the wonders that the divine encompasses.

In the form of a divine falcon, the deceased experiences freedom and the ability to travel between realms, transcending the limitations of time and mortality. They request the guidance of the sacred bird in their spiritual quest, embracing the transformation and rising in totality.

The spell highlights the transformative power of assuming the form of a divine falcon, allowing the deceased to navigate the spiritual realms with ease and connect with the sacred essence. It emphasizes the embodiment of power, grace, and wisdom in the avian form, as the deceased embarks on a profound journey of spiritual embrace.

This spell reflects the belief in the transformative abilities of the deceased in the afterlife and their aspiration to connect with the divine in a profound and transcendent way. It symbolizes the liberation of the spirit and the quest for spiritual enlightenment and understanding.

CT 30: Spell for Opening the Earth: Assisting the deceased in traversing the earth and accessing hidden or secret knowledge.

Utterance:
"O Earth, ancient and wise,
I beseech you to open wide.
Unveil the secrets buried deep,
Allow me passage, let me peep.

Grant me access to hidden realms,
Where ancient knowledge overwhelms.
Open the doors to hidden lore,
That lies concealed forevermore.

With reverence, I approach your core,
Seeking wisdom, forevermore.
Guide my steps through your sacred soil,
As I unravel mysteries and ancient toil.

Let your depths yield their hidden truth,
As I journey through your sacred route.
Reveal the secrets of forgotten time,
And let their wisdom merge with mine.

By your power, O Earth, I am led,
To places where the living tread.
Through caverns and tunnels, I roam,
Exploring mysteries, making them known.

Grant me the strength to tread with care,
As I traverse your depths, unaware.
Protect me from harm, O Earth divine,
And guide me as I seek what's mine.

In this spell for opening the Earth, the deceased calls upon the ancient wisdom and power of the Earth itself to assist them in traversing its depths and accessing hidden or secret knowledge. The utterance begins by addressing the Earth, acknowledging its ancient and wise nature, and requesting it to open wide to reveal the secrets buried deep within its core.

The spell seeks the Earth's assistance in granting access to hidden realms where ancient knowledge resides. It implores the Earth to open the doors to hidden lore, allowing the deceased to peep into the depths of wisdom that lie concealed and forgotten.

The deceased approaches the Earth with reverence and seeks guidance as they journey through its sacred soil. They desire to unravel mysteries and ancient toil, accessing the hidden truths that lie within the Earth's depths.

The spell acknowledges the Earth's power and asks for its cooperation in revealing the secrets of forgotten time. It emphasizes the merging of the deceased's own wisdom with the ancient knowledge that is unveiled through their exploration.

The deceased acknowledges the responsibility and care required as they tread through the Earth's depths. They seek protection from harm and guidance as they navigate the unknown paths, ensuring their safety in their quest for knowledge.

This spell reflects the belief in the Earth as a repository of ancient wisdom and hidden knowledge. It symbolizes the deceased's aspiration to uncover the mysteries of the past and acquire the wisdom that lies within the Earth's depths. It is an invocation for guidance, protection, and illumination as the deceased embarks on a journey of exploration and discovery.

CT 31: Spell for Receiving the Breath of Life: Ensuring that the deceased is imbued with the breath of life, symbolizing vitality and renewal.

Utterance:
"O Breath of Life, come forth and bless,
Bestow upon me vitality, I profess.
In the realm of the afterlife, I dwell,
Grant me the essence that makes me swell.

Breathe into me the spark divine,
Revive my spirit, let it shine.
Infuse me with energy and zest,
That I may thrive, I manifest.

From the heavens, let the breath descend,
Like a gentle breeze, my soul to mend.
Fill my being with life's sweet breath,
Renew my essence, conquer death.

With each inhale, my spirit's renewed,
Exhaling darkness, embracing the light so true.
Let the breath of life flow through my veins,
Revitalizing my existence, breaking chains.

Breathe into me the joy and mirth,
Rekindle the flame, the spark of birth.
Awaken my senses, my consciousness awake,
In this eternal journey, my spirit will partake.

Grant me the strength to rise anew,
To face the challenges, to embrace what's true.
With the breath of life, I am imbued,
Vitality and renewal, forever pursued.

In this spell for receiving the breath of life, the deceased invokes the essence of vitality and renewal. The utterance calls upon the Breath of Life to come forth and bless the deceased, infusing them with the life force that symbolizes vitality and renewal.

The spell acknowledges the realm of the afterlife in which the deceased dwells and seeks the essence that will make their spirit swell with renewed energy and vitality. It emphasizes the desire to be revived and to have their spirit shine brightly.

The Breath of Life is invoked as a divine spark that revives the spirit and infuses the individual with energy and zest. The spell calls for the breath to descend from the heavens like a gentle breeze, mending the soul and filling the being with the life force that conquers death.

The spell emphasizes the transformative power of the breath, renewing the essence of the deceased and dispelling darkness. Each inhale brings renewal and exhales the darkness, embracing the light and the joy of existence.

The Breath of Life is invoked to flow through the veins of the deceased, revitalizing their entire being and breaking the chains of mortality. It is seen as a source of joy, awakening the senses and consciousness to fully partake in the eternal journey of the afterlife.

The deceased seeks the strength to rise anew, to face challenges and embrace the truth, knowing that with the breath of life, they are imbued with vitality and renewal. The spell embodies the belief in the transformative power of life's breath and the continuous pursuit of vitality and renewal in the eternal existence of the afterlife.

CT 32: Spell for Transformation into a Lotus: Allowing the deceased to transform into a sacred lotus, symbolizing purity and rebirth.

Utterance:
"O Lotus, flower of divine grace,
Grant me the power to transform my space.
In the realm of the afterlife, I seek,
To become a lotus, pure and meek.

Let my form blossom, petals unfold,
A symbol of purity, a sight to behold.
From the murky depths, I shall arise,
A radiant lotus, a heavenly prize.

Transform me, O sacred flower,
Into a vessel of rebirth and power.
In your petals, let my spirit reside,
A symbol of purity, where I'll abide.

Like a lotus floating on tranquil waters,
I'll embrace serenity, leaving behind earth's tethers.
My essence purified, my soul reborn,
In this transformation, my destiny's sworn.

Grant me the purity of your delicate bloom,
The rebirth of my spirit, a divine heirloom.
As a lotus, I shall rise above,
Transcending mortality, embracing eternal love.

In this spell for transformation into a lotus, the deceased seeks the power to assume the form of a sacred lotus, symbolizing purity and rebirth. The utterance calls upon the lotus, a flower associated with divine grace and spiritual transformation.

The spell expresses the desire to transform one's space in the realm of the afterlife and become a lotus, a symbol of purity and humility. The lotus is seen as an embodiment of divine beauty and represents the journey of the soul from the depths of darkness to spiritual enlightenment.

The deceased calls upon the lotus to let their form blossom, with petals unfolding to reveal their transformed self. They envision themselves emerging from the murky depths, rising as a radiant lotus, a symbol of purity and a heavenly sight to behold.

The spell entreats the lotus to transform the individual, allowing their spirit to reside within its petals. By becoming a lotus, the deceased seeks to embody purity and find a tranquil abode where they can reside in the afterlife.

The lotus is compared to floating on tranquil waters, representing serenity and detachment from earthly attachments. The transformation into a lotus is believed to purify the essence of the deceased and facilitate their rebirth, freeing them from the limitations of mortality.

The spell invokes the lotus to grant the purity of its delicate bloom, symbolizing the purification of the deceased's essence and the rebirth of their spirit. As a lotus, the deceased aspires to rise above earthly concerns and transcend the mortal realm, embracing the eternal love and divine destiny that awaits.

Through this spell, the deceased seeks the transformative power of the lotus, desiring to embody purity and experience the spiritual rebirth that comes with it. The lotus serves as a symbol of the transformative journey of the soul in the afterlife, where the pursuit of purity and eternal love is embraced.

CT 33: Spell for Reuniting with Loved Ones: Facilitating the reunion of the deceased with their deceased loved ones in the afterlife.

Utterance:
"O spirits of the departed, hear my plea,
Grant me the reunion I long to see.
In the realm of the afterlife, let us gather,
With loved ones, together, forever and further.

Open the gates that separate our souls,
Unite us in the embrace that consoles.
Through the veil of eternity, let us pass,
Reunited, bonded in love that shall surpass.

Bring forth the spirits of those I hold dear,
Let our paths converge, drawing near.
Guide us to each other in the afterlife's expanse,
Grant us the joy of an eternal dance.

May the ties of affection never fade,
In the afterlife's realm where we're remade.
Let our spirits intertwine, interlace,
Forever bound in love's sacred space.

O spirits of the departed, bridge the divide,
Reveal the path where our destinies coincide.
With each passing day, let our reunion grow,
United in love, with hearts all aglow.

Grant us the solace of shared presence,
In the realm of the afterlife's essence.
May our bond transcend the earthly strife,
And bring eternal joy, the elixir of life.

In this spell for reuniting with loved ones, the deceased appeals to the spirits of the departed, seeking a joyous reunion in the afterlife. The utterance acknowledges the separation that exists between the realms of the living and the deceased.

The spell implores the spirits to open the gates that separate the souls, allowing for the gathering and reunion of the deceased with their loved ones. It seeks to transcend the boundaries of time and space, drawing the spirits together in a shared embrace of comfort and solace.

The deceased calls upon the spirits to guide them and their loved ones to each other in the vast expanse of the afterlife. They yearn for the joy of an eternal dance, where paths converge and the bonds of affection are forever cherished.

The spell expresses the desire for an unbreakable connection with loved ones, emphasizing that the ties of affection should never fade in the afterlife's realm. The spirits are implored to bring forth the spirits of those held dear, allowing their paths to intersect and their spirits to intertwine.

The deceased entrusts the spirits to bridge the divide between the realms, revealing the path where destinies coincide. They seek a growing and enduring reunion with their loved ones, united in love and with hearts aglow.

The spell beseeches the spirits to grant the solace of shared presence in the afterlife's realm, where earthly strife is left behind. It acknowledges that the bond between the deceased and their loved ones transcends mortal limitations, bringing forth eternal joy and the elixir of life.

Through this spell, the deceased longs for the reunion and eternal connection with their loved ones in the afterlife. It reflects the belief in the continuation of relationships beyond death and the yearning for the enduring bonds of love to persist in the realm of the departed.

CT 34: Spell for Speaking the Words of Power: Granting the deceased the ability to invoke powerful divine words and command spiritual forces.

Utterance:
"O ancient gods, bestow upon me,
The gift of words that set me free.
Grant me the power to command and decree,
In the realm of spirits, let my voice be.

With sacred incantations, my tongue shall weave,
Words of power that make spirits believe.
Open the doors to hidden realms and gates,
As I invoke the authority that creation awaits.

Let my voice resound with divine might,
As I utter the words that ignite the light.
Grant me the knowledge of ancient lore,
The wisdom to invoke, the force to explore.

By the gods' decree, I speak with authority,
Words that bend the spirits to my reality.
The language of the divine, I now possess,
To summon forces, and chaos suppress.

With each syllable, I call upon the divine,
Commanding spirits, and their will align.
Grant me the ability to navigate the unseen,
To unravel mysteries, and truths intervene.

Through sacred words, I bind and release,
Channeling the power that grants me peace.
May my voice resonate with the heavens above,
Invoking the ancient, invoking the love.

O gods, in your grace, empower my speech,
To transcend boundaries, and secrets breach.
Grant me the wisdom to wield this gift,
With reverence, in your divine uplift.

In this spell for speaking the words of power, the deceased invokes the ancient gods, seeking the gift of commanding and decreeing in the realm of spirits. The utterance acknowledges the significance of sacred incantations and the power they hold.

The spell implores the gods to grant the ability to open doors to hidden realms and gates through the spoken words. The deceased seeks the authority that creation awaits, the power to invoke and command the spiritual forces.

The utterance emphasizes the importance of speaking with divine might, unleashing words that ignite the light and hold the knowledge of ancient lore. The deceased seeks the wisdom to invoke and explore, to navigate the unseen and unravel mysteries.

The spell acknowledges that by the gods' decree, the deceased speaks with authority, bending the spirits to their reality. The language of the divine is possessed, enabling the summoning of forces and the suppression of chaos.

Through the sacred words spoken, the deceased calls upon the divine, commanding the spirits and aligning their will. The spell seeks the ability to navigate the unseen, to access hidden truths and intervene in the course of events.

The utterance invokes the binding and releasing of energies through sacred words, channeling the power that brings peace. The deceased desires for their voice to resonate with the heavens, invoking the ancient and invoking love.

Finally, the spell humbly requests the gods' grace to empower the speech of the deceased, transcending boundaries and unveiling secrets. The wisdom to wield this gift is sought with reverence, acknowledging the divine uplift provided by the gods.

Through this spell, the deceased seeks the ability to speak the words of power, commanding and invoking the spiritual forces. It reflects the belief in the potency of sacred incantations and the role of language in harnessing and directing supernatural energies.

CT 35: Spell for Entering the Underworld: Assisting the deceased in gaining access to the realm of the dead and navigating its challenges.

Utterance:
"O gates of the underworld, open wide,
As I embark on this transformative stride.
Grant me passage to the realm of the dead,
To tread the path that countless souls have tread.

With reverence, I approach your mighty gates,
Seeking entrance to the realm that awaits.
May the guardians of the afterlife stand aside,
As I journey through the darkness with unyielding stride.

Guide my steps, O ancient spirits of the tomb,
Illuminate the path through shadow and gloom.
Grant me the wisdom to navigate the abyss,
To overcome challenges, my spirit shall persist.

Let the doors of the underworld reveal their way,
As I travel through realms where spirits sway.
Protect me from the perils that lie in wait,
As I venture into the realm of eternal fate.

O gods of the netherworld, hear my plea,
Assist me in this sacred journey to be.
Grant me passage through each perilous trial,
As I seek reunion beyond the earthly mile.

May my heart remain steadfast and true,
As I face the tests that I must go through.
Grant me the strength to overcome each test,
To emerge victorious, among the blessed.

By the power of divine names I invoke,
Let the gates of the underworld unlock.
Grant me passage to the realm beyond,
Where departed souls and deities respond.

In this spell for entering the underworld, the deceased calls upon the gates of the underworld to open wide, allowing them access to the realm of the dead. The utterance acknowledges the transformative nature of this journey and the countless souls who have traveled this path before.

The spell seeks the guidance of the ancient spirits of the tomb, requesting their illumination and wisdom to navigate the darkness and challenges of the underworld. The deceased expresses their determination to stride forward with unwavering resolve.

The utterance implores the guardians of the afterlife to stand aside, granting passage to the deceased as they journey through the realms of the dead. Protection from the perils that lie in wait is sought, acknowledging the inherent dangers of this sacred pilgrimage.

The spell invokes the gods of the netherworld, requesting their assistance in this journey. The deceased seeks their guidance and support as they face and overcome the trials that await, with the ultimate goal of reuniting with their departed loved ones.

The utterance emphasizes the need for a steadfast and true heart as the deceased encounters various tests in the underworld. They seek the strength to overcome each trial and emerge victorious among the blessed.

By invoking the power of divine names, the spell implores the unlocking of the gates of the underworld, granting the deceased passage to the realm beyond. The spell acknowledges the presence of departed souls and deities who await their arrival.

Through this spell, the deceased seeks assistance in entering the underworld, navigating its challenges, and ultimately reaching the realm of the dead. It reflects the belief in the importance of guidance, protection, and strength to overcome the tests encountered on the journey to the afterlife.

CT 36: Spell for Becoming an Imperishable Star: Granting the deceased eternal existence and transcendence as an imperishable star.

Utterance:
"O celestial realm, where stars reside,
Grant me the transformation, let me abide.
I yearn for eternal existence, beyond earthly decay,
To shine as an imperishable star, in the cosmic array.

Grant me transcendence, O divine celestial host,
As I leave behind the mortal coil, the earthly post.
Release me from the bounds of time and space,
And elevate my spirit to an eternal embrace.

Let my essence ascend to the heavens above,
Where the imperishable stars shine with eternal love.
Cloak me in radiance, in celestial splendor,
As I transcend the mortal realm, ever tender.

Grant me the immortality of the cosmic domain,
Where time stands still, free from mortal bane.
Let my light guide the way for those who seek,
A path to transcendence, where souls are meek.

As an imperishable star, I shall never fade,
A luminous beacon, undimmed by shade.
Let my spirit soar amidst the cosmic expanse,
In timeless existence, where eternity enchants.

I beseech the gods, the guardians of the night,
To bless me with this transcendental flight.
Grant me eternal existence, beyond earthly strife,
As I become an imperishable star, for eternal life.

By the power of celestial realms, I implore,
Transform me, O universe, forevermore.
Grant me the transcendence, the eternal embrace,
As I become an imperishable star, in infinite grace."

In this spell for becoming an imperishable star, the deceased invokes the celestial realm and seeks transformation into an eternal, transcendent existence beyond the limitations of earthly decay. They yearn to shine as an imperishable star among the cosmic array, symbolizing eternal radiance and transcendence.

The spell implores the divine celestial host to grant transcendence, allowing the spirit to leave behind the constraints of time and space, and ascend to the celestial heavens. The aim is to be cloaked in radiance, embraced by the cosmic splendor, and freed from the limitations of the mortal realm.

The deceased seeks to join the ranks of the imperishable stars, those celestial bodies that shine eternally and are unaffected by the passage of time. They aspire to guide others on the path to transcendence, illuminating the way for souls who seek eternal transformation.

The utterance calls upon the gods, the guardians of the night, to bless the deceased with the desired transcendental flight. The aim is to attain eternal existence, beyond earthly strife, and become an imperishable star in the cosmic expanse.

The spell acknowledges the power and enchantment of the celestial realms, seeking transformation and eternal embrace. The deceased desires to become an imperishable star, forever radiant and undimmed, experiencing timeless existence and the blessings of infinite grace.

Through this spell, the deceased yearns for transcendence, eternal existence, and the radiance of an imperishable star. It reflects the belief in the possibility of transcending the mortal realm and joining the cosmic order of the heavens, where the spirit shines eternally in timeless grace.

CT 37: Spell for Protection against Adversaries in the Afterlife: Safeguarding the deceased from malevolent spirits or entities in the afterlife.

Utterance:
"O spirits of protection, heed my plea,
In this realm beyond mortal decree.
Grant me strength and shield my soul,
From adversaries who seek to take their toll.

May the power of the gods surround me,
Their divine essence my sanctuary.
Keep at bay the malevolent spirits,
And safeguard me from their nefarious merits.

By the light of Ra, the sun's golden ray,
I am shielded from harm throughout the day.
Let his radiance envelop my being,
A barrier against all malicious scheming.

Through the invocation of sacred words,
I repel the forces that seek to disturb.
I am fortified with divine might,
Against all adversaries, day and night.

With the guidance of Ma'at, goddess of truth,
I am protected from deceit and uncouth.
May her scales balance justice in my favor,
Shielding me from harm with her unwavering savor.

O Anubis, guardian of the afterlife's gate,
Grant me safe passage, and ward off any trait.
Protect me from the spirits of chaos and strife,
Preserving my soul in eternal life.

By the power of Isis, the divine mother,
I am shielded from malevolence like no other.
Her wings wrap me in a protective embrace,
Keeping me safe in the afterlife's sacred space.

Let the spells of protection encircle me,

Forming an impenetrable barrier for all to see.
Banish the adversaries, repel their might,
And ensure my soul's serenity throughout the night.

By the ancient knowledge and wisdom I possess,
I ward off any harm that seeks to oppress.
I am fortified by the forces of light,
Shielded from adversaries with all my might.

With this spell, I declare my protection,
Against malevolent spirits' cruel intention.
I am safeguarded in the afterlife's domain,
Shielded from adversaries, free from any stain.

So mote it be, let this protection endure,
In the afterlife's realm, sacred and pure.
I am shielded from harm, eternally secure,
Against adversaries' forces, I am ensured."

In this spell for protection against adversaries in the afterlife, the deceased calls upon the spirits of protection and divine forces to safeguard their soul from malevolent entities. They seek strength and divine shielding to repel those who would cause harm in the afterlife.

The spell invokes the power of the gods and goddesses to surround the deceased and create a sanctuary of divine essence. The light of Ra, the sun god, is invoked to envelop the individual, serving as a barrier against malevolent forces throughout the day.

The utterance emphasizes the repelling of adversarial spirits through the invocation of sacred words and the fortification of the deceased with divine might. The forces that seek to disturb are kept at bay, ensuring the individual's safety and security in the afterlife.

Specific deities are invoked for protection. Anubis, the guardian of the afterlife's gate, is called upon to grant safe passage and ward off any traitorous spirits. The goddess Ma'at, associated with truth and justice, is invoked to maintain balance and shield the deceased from deceit and harm.

Isis, the divine mother figure, is called upon for her protective wings to wrap around the individual, offering a nurturing embrace and safeguarding them from malevolence. The power of ancient knowledge and wisdom possessed by the deceased is also emphasized as a source of protection.

The spell affirms the creation of an impenetrable barrier of protection through the recitation of sacred words. Adversaries are banished, their might repelled, ensuring the soul's serenity and security throughout the night in the afterlife.

The individual declares their protection and fortification, relying on the forces of light to shield them from harm. They assert their resilience and unwavering resolve to ward off any harm or oppression that seeks to threaten their eternal peace.

Through this spell, the deceased seeks to ensure their safety and protection from malevolent spirits or entities in the afterlife. It reflects the belief in the existence of opposing forces in the spiritual realm and the need for spiritual fortification to maintain a state of serenity and security.

CT 38: Spell for Uniting with Osiris: Facilitating the merging and unity of the deceased's essence with the god Osiris.

Utterance:
"O Osiris, great ruler of the afterlife,
I beseech thee to hear my plea.
Grant me the honor of uniting with thee,
In sacred union, my spirit shall be free.

As I journey through the realms of the dead,
I seek to merge with thy divine essence.
Let my soul intertwine with thine,
In eternal union, bound by love's presence.

Thou art the embodiment of resurrection,
The symbol of renewal and eternal life.
By merging with thee, I transcend mortality,
And embrace the divine, free from strife.

O Osiris, open thy divine embrace,
And welcome me into thy eternal realm.
Let my essence unite with thine,
In a bond that transcends the earthly realm.

Grant me the wisdom and knowledge,
That flows through thy divine being.
May thy strength and power be infused,
Within my spirit, evermore foreseeing.

As I merge with thee, O Osiris,
Let me partake in thy divine destiny.
Guide me through the realms of the afterlife,
In unity, our spirits shall forever be.

In this sacred union, I am transformed,
My mortal limitations left behind.
I become one with the eternal essence,
Unified with Osiris, divine and sublime.

Through this spell, I declare my desire,
To merge with Osiris, ruler of the dead.

In unity, I find eternal liberation,
As my essence is forever wed.

So mote it be, let this union be sealed,
As my spirit merges with Osiris divine.
In this eternal bond, I find solace and peace,
Forever united, our essences entwine."

In this spell for uniting with Osiris, the deceased entreats the great ruler of the afterlife to hear their plea and grant them the honor of merging with his divine essence. They seek to become one with Osiris, symbolizing a profound union and liberation of their spirit.

The spell acknowledges Osiris as the embodiment of resurrection, renewal, and eternal life. The deceased yearns to intertwine their soul with Osiris, transcending the limitations of mortality and embracing the divine essence that he represents.

The individual implores Osiris to open his divine embrace and welcome them into his eternal realm. They seek a deep bond and unity that transcends the earthly realm, allowing their essence to merge with Osiris' essence in a profound and transformative way.

The deceased seeks to partake in Osiris' wisdom, knowledge, strength, and power, desiring their spirit to be infused with his divine attributes. Through this merging, they aim to be guided through the realms of the afterlife, forever connected to Osiris in unity and shared destiny.

The spell emphasizes the transformation that occurs as the deceased merges with Osiris. They leave behind their mortal limitations and become one with the eternal essence, unified with the divine and transcending the boundaries of earthly existence.

Through this spell, the individual declares their desire for a sacred and eternal union with Osiris, finding solace, peace, and liberation in the merging of their essences. It reflects the belief in the possibility of a profound connection with the divine and the transformative power of such a union in the afterlife.

CT 39: Spell for Warding off Snakes and Serpents: Providing protection from venomous creatures and serpentine dangers in the afterlife.

Utterance:
"O guardians of the afterlife, hear my plea,
Grant me protection from serpentine harms.
Keep me safe from venomous creatures,
As I journey through the realm of eternal charms.

By the power of divine authority I invoke,
I ward off snakes and serpents with this spell.
Their venomous fangs shall not touch me,
Nor their coils bind me in their treacherous hell.

I call upon the ancient forces of protection,
To create a shield around me, strong and true.
Let it repel all serpentine dangers,
As I traverse the realms beyond mortal view.

May my presence be repulsive to serpents,
Causing them to slither away in fear.
Let them be unable to approach or harm me,
As I navigate this afterlife journey, crystal clear.

O spirits of the afterlife, aid me in my quest,
To be free from the perils that snakes bring.
Keep me safe and shielded from their venom,
So I may continue my ascent and sing.

With this spell, I command the serpents to retreat,
To keep their distance and never come near.
Let them be banished from my path,
Leaving me untouched by their venomous spear.

As I journey through the afterlife's expanse,
I am shielded and protected from serpentine strife.
No snake or serpent shall harm me,
For I am guarded by the power of eternal life.

By the authority of the gods and the ancient lore,

I ward off snakes and serpents, great and small.
With their venomous threats repelled,
I am safeguarded, standing tall.

So mote it be, let this protection be sealed,
As I journey through the afterlife's vast domain.
With this spell, I am shielded from serpentine harms,
Forever protected, free from venomous pain."

In this spell for warding off snakes and serpents, the deceased calls upon the guardians of the afterlife to provide protection from serpentine dangers. They seek to be kept safe from venomous creatures as they embark on their journey through the realm of eternal charms.

The individual invokes the power of divine authority to ward off snakes and serpents with the strength of their spell. They declare that the venomous fangs of these creatures shall not touch them, and their coils shall not bind them in treacherous entanglements.

The spell entreats the ancient forces of protection to create a shield around the individual, repelling all serpentine dangers that may cross their path. They ask for the power to repulse snakes, causing them to slither away in fear, unable to approach or harm the one reciting the spell.

The deceased calls upon the spirits of the afterlife to aid them in their quest to be free from the perils that snakes bring. They seek safety and shielding from the venomous threats that may be encountered during their journey beyond mortal existence.

The spell commands the serpents to retreat, ensuring they keep their distance and never come near the individual. The goal is to banish them from the individual's path, leaving them untouched by the venomous harm that serpents can inflict.

The spell emphasizes the desire to be shielded and protected from serpentine strife as the individual traverses the vast expanse of the afterlife. They declare that no snake or serpent shall harm them, as they are guarded by the power of eternal life and the protective forces invoked through this spell.

By the authority of the gods and the ancient lore, the individual proclaims their ability to ward off snakes and serpents, big or small. They express their gratitude for the seal of protection, ensuring their safety and freedom from venomous pain as they journey through the afterlife's domain.

Through this spell, the deceased seeks protection from serpentine dangers in the afterlife, acknowledging the symbolic and mythical significance of snakes and serpents as potential threats. It reflects the belief in the ability to repel and ward off these perils through the power of invocation and divine protection.

CT 40: Spell for Ascending to the Sky with Ra: Assisting the deceased in ascending to the heavens alongside the solar deity Ra.

Utterance:
"O radiant Ra, shining in the sky,
Guide me on my ascent as I fly.
Grant me wings to soar in your divine light,
And join you on your celestial flight.

I invoke your name, O mighty Ra,
The sun god who illuminates the way.
As you journey through the heavens high,
Let me ascend with you, drawing nigh.

With wings of falcon, swift and strong,
I soar through the heavens all day long.
Grant me the power to traverse the sky,
As we embark on this celestial journey up high.

I rise above the earthly realm below,
As your divine presence in my heart does glow.
Together we traverse the heavenly expanse,
In harmony, our spirits dance.

I ascend to the realms of eternal bliss,
Where celestial beings find their solace.
With every beat of my wings, I draw near,
To the realms of gods, forever clear.

O Ra, the giver of light and life,
Lead me through the celestial strife.
Grant me passage to the heavens above,
Where eternal joy and peace abound, my love.

On this journey, I leave behind the earthly ties,
As I ascend, reaching the celestial skies.
My spirit merges with the radiant sun,
In unity with Ra, our destinies are spun.

As we journey through the celestial sphere,

I am filled with awe and boundless cheer.
Grant me the vision to behold the divine,
As we soar together, forever entwined.

O Ra, my guide and celestial friend,
To your divine light, my spirit does ascend.
In your presence, I find eternal peace,
As we embark on this celestial release.

So mote it be, let this ascension be sealed,
As I join Ra on his celestial field.
Together we soar, forever connected,
In the realms above, my soul protected."

In this spell for ascending to the sky with Ra, the deceased invokes the solar deity Ra, seeking guidance and assistance in ascending to the heavens. They yearn to join Ra on his celestial journey, basking in his divine light and experiencing the wonders of the celestial realm.

The individual addresses Ra as the radiant sun god who illuminates the path. They implore Ra to grant them wings to soar in his divine light, allowing them to join him on his celestial flight. They express the desire for a celestial union and a shared journey through the heavens.

The spell emphasizes the invocation of Ra's name, recognizing his power and presence as they embark on this celestial ascent. The individual envisions themselves with the wings of a falcon, swift and strong, enabling them to traverse the sky and follow Ra's path.

As they ascend, the individual leaves behind earthly ties and rises above the mundane realm. They express their connection to Ra, feeling his divine presence within their heart, and experiencing the harmony of their spirits dancing together in the celestial expanse.

The individual longs to reach the realms of eternal bliss, where celestial beings find solace and divine joy. They trust in Ra's guidance and power to grant them passage to the heavens, where everlasting peace and serenity reside.

The spell invokes Ra as the giver of light and life, entrusting him to lead the individual through the celestial strife and grant them access to the celestial realms. The individual envisions their spirit merging with the radiant sun, achieving unity with Ra and aligning their destinies.

The celestial journey is described as a release from earthly ties, with the individual ascending to the celestial skies and leaving behind the limitations of the mortal realm. They express gratitude for the opportunity to behold the divine and experience the awe-inspiring wonders of the celestial sphere.

The spell concludes by sealing the ascension and the union with Ra, affirming the eternal connection between the deceased and the solar deity. They find solace and eternal peace in Ra's presence as they embark on their celestial journey together.

Through this spell, the deceased seeks the assistance of Ra in ascending to the heavens, symbolizing their transcendence beyond earthly limitations and their union with divine forces. It reflects the belief in the power of divine intervention and the yearning for spiritual elevation and eternal connection with the gods.

CT 41 : Spell for Receiving Nourishment from the Gods: Ensuring that the deceased is provided with divine sustenance and nourishment.

Utterance:
"O benevolent gods, hear my plea,
Bestow upon me your divine decree.
Grant me nourishment from your sacred feast,
That my spirit may be sustained, never to cease.

From your celestial realm, bestow upon me,
The food that nourishes, the essence that sets me free.
Let the ambrosia of your divine table be mine,
Filling my spirit with energy divine.

O gods of abundance, bless me with your grace,
Provide me with sustenance in this sacred space.
May your sacred offerings, like heavenly dew,
Satisfy my hunger, my spirit renew.

I invoke your names, O mighty deities,
In reverence, I offer my prayers and pleas.
From the realms beyond, bring forth the feast,
That I may partake and be forever released.

Let the bread of life be my daily sustenance,
Filling my spirit with your divine radiance.
May the nectar of the gods flow through my veins,
Reviving my essence, removing all strains.

In your divine presence, I find solace and peace,
As I partake in the blessings that never cease.
Your nourishment transcends the physical need,
Feeding my soul, fulfilling every creed.

With gratitude, I accept your divine gift,
In this eternal realm, my spirits uplift.
May your sustenance be a constant flow,
Nourishing my being, wherever I may go.

O gods of plenty, I offer my praise,

For the sustenance that blesses my days.
In unity with you, my spirit thrives,
As I partake in the feast, my eternal lives.

So mote it be, let this nourishment unfold,
As the gods' blessings within me are enfolded.
Forever nourished, my spirit shall shine,
As I embrace the divine, in unity divine."

In this spell for receiving nourishment from the gods, the deceased appeals to the benevolent gods to provide them with divine sustenance. They acknowledge the celestial nature of the gods and their ability to bestow nourishment from their sacred feast, ensuring the eternal sustenance of the spirit.

The deceased addresses the gods of abundance, seeking their grace and blessings to receive sustenance in the afterlife. They express the desire for the food and essence that nourish the spirit, allowing it to be sustained and liberated from earthly limitations. The divine table and the ambrosia of the gods are invoked as symbols of spiritual nourishment and energy.

The individual invokes the names of the mighty deities, offering prayers and pleas in reverence. They request that the gods bring forth the sacred feast from the realms beyond, allowing them to partake and be forever released from spiritual hunger. The bread of life is sought as a daily sustenance, filling the spirit with the divine radiance of the gods.

The spell acknowledges the transcendent nature of the gods' nourishment, surpassing physical needs and feeding the soul. The nectar of the gods is called upon to flow through the veins of the deceased, reviving their essence and removing all strains. The presence of the gods is seen as a source of solace, peace, and fulfillment.

Gratitude is expressed for the divine gift of sustenance, recognizing the gods of plenty and offering praise for the blessings that bless the days of the deceased. The individual embraces unity with the gods, acknowledging that their nourishment allows their spirit to thrive and shine eternally. They accept the constant flow of divine sustenance, nourishing their being in all realms.

Through this spell, the deceased seeks to ensure that they are continuously provided with divine nourishment, transcending physical needs and feeding their spiritual essence. It reflects the belief in the benevolence of the gods and the importance of spiritual sustenance for eternal existence.

CT 42: Spell for Rejuvenation and Youthfulness: Granting the deceased rejuvenation, vitality, and a youthful appearance in the afterlife.

Utterance:
"O divine forces of rejuvenation and youth,
Grant me the gift of eternal vitality and truth.
In this realm of the afterlife, let me be renewed,
With youthfulness and vigor that shall never elude.

From the sacred fountains of eternal life,
Let the waters of rejuvenation be rife.
Bathe my spirit in their revitalizing embrace,
Granting me a youthful radiance, full of grace.

O gods of eternal youth, hear my plea,
Bestow upon me the beauty I seek to see.
Remove the traces of age and decay,
Restore my appearance in a pristine display.

Like the lotus blooming in its youthful prime,
Let my spirit blossom in this eternal clime.
May my body be vibrant, my senses keen,
Forever youthful, age shall remain unseen.

Grant me the strength and energy divine,
To explore the realms of the afterlife sublime.
Let my spirit soar with boundless zeal,
As I embrace the eternal, in youthful appeal.

Banish the wrinkles, the signs of time,
Let my appearance radiate in its prime.
Revive the glow of youth upon my face,
Eternally vibrant, in your divine embrace.

With each passing moment, I am reborn,
Renewed and refreshed, no longer forlorn.
Grant me the vitality of eternal youth,
In this afterlife realm, where beauty finds truth.

O gods of rejuvenation, I express my gratitude,

For the gift of eternal youthfulness and fortitude.
In your divine presence, I shall forever thrive,
Embracing the eternal, where age cannot survive.

So mote it be, let rejuvenation unfold,
As my spirit and appearance are forever enfolded.
In the afterlife's realm, I shall forever shine,
Rejuvenated, youthful, in eternal divine."

In this spell for rejuvenation and youthfulness, the deceased beseeches the divine forces of rejuvenation and youth to grant them eternal vitality and a youthful appearance in the afterlife. They seek to be renewed and revitalized, free from the signs of age and decay.

The individual calls upon the sacred fountains of eternal life, where the waters of rejuvenation flow abundantly. They ask for their spirit to be bathed in these revitalizing waters, allowing them to possess a radiant and graceful youthfulness that will never fade.

The gods of eternal youth are invoked, and the individual requests their intervention to bestow upon them the desired beauty and appearance. They seek the removal of any traces of age and decay, with a restoration of their physical form to its pristine state.

Drawing inspiration from the lotus, a symbol of rejuvenation, the individual wishes for their spirit to blossom in its youthful prime. They desire a vibrant body and keen senses that will forever defy the passage of time, allowing them to explore the realms of the afterlife with boundless zeal.

The spell implores the gods to banish wrinkles and signs of time, replacing them with a perpetual glow of youth upon the individual's face. The request is made for the strength and energy divine to embrace the eternal and experience life in its youthful appeal.

Gratitude is expressed to the gods of rejuvenation, acknowledging their role in bestowing the gift of eternal youthfulness and fortitude. The individual recognizes that in the divine presence, they shall thrive and shine forever, free from the constraints of age.

Through this spell, the deceased seeks to attain rejuvenation, vitality, and a youthful appearance in the afterlife. It reflects the belief in the transformative power of the divine and the desire for eternal youth and beauty.

CT 43: Spell for Merging with the Sun Disk: Facilitating the merging of the deceased's essence with the divine solar disc, symbolizing unity with Ra.

Utterance:
"O radiant Sun, source of life and light,
I beseech thee to grant me a wondrous sight.
In this afterlife realm, let our essences merge,
As I become one with thy radiant surge.

Mighty Ra, ruler of the celestial domain,
I offer my spirit, devoid of any disdain.
Let my essence blend with thy divine fire,
As we unite in a celestial embrace, higher and higher.

Like a golden phoenix soaring through the sky,
Let my spirit ascend and forever fly.
Merge my being with thy radiant Sun Disk,
As we unite, divine unity, let it brisk.

Grant me the wisdom and knowledge profound,
As our essences intertwine, forever bound.
In the light of thy presence, all truths unfold,
As my spirit and the Sun become one, bold.

Illuminate my path with thy divine glow,
As we merge, let thy radiance freely flow.
Through this merging, I attain transcendence,
United with the Sun, in sacred essence.

As the sunbeams caress my spirit's core,
I become the embodiment of divine lore.
Let thy fiery energy ignite my soul,
As we merge, in divine unity, I am made whole.

O radiant Sun, hear my fervent plea,
In thy embrace, let me forever be.
Merging our essences, let the barriers dissolve,
As I become one with thee, in everlasting resolve.

So mote it be, let our essences align,

As I merge with the Sun, divine and sublime.
In this afterlife realm, unity shall prevail,
As my spirit merges with the Sun's celestial trail."

In this spell for merging with the Sun Disk, the deceased addresses the radiant Sun, symbolizing the life-giving and illuminating force of Ra. They beseech the Sun to grant them a wondrous sight and allow their essences to merge, forging a divine unity in the afterlife.

The individual acknowledges Ra as the mighty ruler of the celestial domain and offers their spirit without any disdain. They desire to blend their essence with the divine fire of the Sun, ascending together in a celestial embrace, soaring like a golden phoenix through the sky.

The spell implores Ra to grant wisdom and profound knowledge as their essences intertwine, forever bound in unity. In the light of Ra's presence, all truths are revealed, and the individual's spirit and the Sun become one, embracing divine unity in a bold and transformative manner.

The individual seeks the illumination of their path with the divine glow of Ra, as their essences merge and the radiant energy of the Sun freely flows within them. Through this merging, they aspire to attain transcendence and become united with the Sun in sacred essence.

They invoke the sunbeams to caress their spirit's core, becoming the embodiment of divine knowledge and wisdom. They ask for Ra's fiery energy to ignite their soul as the merging takes place, experiencing unity and wholeness in their eternal existence.

The individual expresses their fervent plea for the radiant Sun to hear them and allow them to forever be in its embrace. They envision the barriers dissolving as they merge with the Sun, experiencing divine unity that transcends the limitations of the mortal world.

Through this spell, the deceased seeks to merge their essence with the divine solar disc, symbolizing the unity with Ra and the attainment of higher knowledge and spiritual transcendence. It represents the longing to become one with the cosmic forces and embody the divine in the afterlife realm.

CT 44: Spell for Protection against Demons and Spirits: Safeguarding the deceased from malevolent spirits and demonic entities in the afterlife.

Utterance:
"O mighty guardians of the afterlife's domain,
I beseech thee for protection, free from any stain.
Shield me, O divine spirits, from demons' cruel might,
Keep me safe from their malevolence day and night.

With sacred power and celestial might,
Surround me now, banish darkness from sight.
Form a barrier impenetrable and strong,
Guard me against spirits that do me wrong.

Invisible shields, cast around my form,
Repel demons and spirits, their presence transform.
May they find no access to my sacred abode,
As I walk the paths of the afterlife, forever bestowed.

Ward off their temptations, their whispers of deceit,
Keep them at bay, far from my spirit's retreat.
Let their malevolent forces be repelled,
By the power of your divine spells.

O guardians of the afterlife, stand tall and firm,
Shield me from spirits that seek to harm.
With your watchful eyes and vigilant might,
Protect me in the eternal realms, day and night.

Invisible armor, encompassing my being,
Bar the way for spirits with intentions unseeing.
Let them perceive my spirit as invincible and bright,
Unable to approach, unable to ignite.

By your divine presence and heavenly grace,
I am shielded from demons' dark embrace.
May your protection be my fortress strong,
Defending me against evil all along.

So mote it be, let the guardians unite,

In this spell of protection, shining bright.
With their celestial power, my spirit defend,
Against demons and spirits, until the end."

In this spell for protection against demons and spirits, the deceased calls upon the mighty guardians of the afterlife's domain for safeguarding. They implore the divine spirits to shield them from the cruel might of demons and protect them from the malevolent intentions of spirits in the afterlife.

The individual invokes the sacred power and celestial might of the guardians, asking them to surround them with an impenetrable and strong barrier. They seek the guardians' assistance in forming an invisible shield that repels demons and transforms their presence. Through this protective barrier, they aim to ensure that demons find no access to their sacred abode as they traverse the paths of the afterlife.

The spell requests the guardians to ward off the temptations and deceitful whispers of demons, keeping them at a distance from the individual's spirit. They rely on the power of the guardians' divine spells to repel the malevolent forces that may seek to harm them.

The individual entreats the guardians to stand tall and firm, guarding them against spirits that harbor ill intentions. They rely on the watchful eyes and vigilant might of the guardians to provide protection in the eternal realms of the afterlife, day and night.

They visualize the guardians enveloping their being with invisible armor, barring the way for spirits with malicious intent. The individual desires that spirits perceive their spirit as invincible and bright, rendering them unable to approach or ignite any harm.

In the final part of the spell, the individual expresses their trust in the guardians' divine presence and heavenly grace. They rely on the guardians' protection as a strong and impenetrable fortress, defending them against the influence of evil throughout their eternal journey.

Through this spell, the deceased seeks the assistance of the guardians to shield them from the malevolent forces of demons and spirits in the afterlife. It represents the individual's desire for spiritual protection and the belief in the guardians' power to repel evil and ensure their well-being in the realms beyond.

CT 45: Spell for Becoming a Spirit: Allowing the deceased to transform into a spirit capable of traversing the spiritual realms.

Utterance:
"O ancient spirits, hear my plea,
Grant me the power to transcend mortality.
From earthly form, I seek release,
To traverse the realms of spiritual peace.

With sacred words and potent spells,
I shed my mortal shell, my earthly dwells.
Grant me the essence of ethereal flight,
To soar through realms, bathed in divine light.

Let my spirit be unbound and free,
A vessel of energy, untethered, you see.
No longer confined to earthly bounds,
But roaming the spiritual realms, without any bounds.

As I shed my mortal form, I embrace,
The transformation into a spirit's grace.
No longer weighed down by earthly strife,
But infused with the essence of eternal life.

Grant me the wisdom of ages past,
To navigate the spiritual realms vast.
Let me traverse the planes unseen,
With clarity of purpose and vision keen.

As a spirit, I am unbound by time,
Existing beyond mortal realms, sublime.
With the power of the ancient spirits' decree,
I transcend mortality and embrace eternity.

O ancient ones, guide me on my way,
Protect and illuminate my spirit's stay.
Grant me the knowledge and strength to endure,
As I traverse the realms, forever pure.

May my spirit be a beacon of light,
Guiding others through the realms of night.

With this transformation, I am reborn,
A spirit, eternal and unadorned.

So mote it be, let the transformation begin,
As I shed my mortal form and transcend within.
Becoming a spirit, I embrace the unknown,
Roaming the spiritual realms, forever grown."

In this spell for becoming a spirit, the deceased addresses the ancient spirits and seeks their assistance in transcending mortality. They yearn to be released from their earthly form and to traverse the realms of spiritual peace.

The individual invokes the power of sacred words and potent spells to shed their mortal shell and embrace the essence of ethereal flight. They long to soar through the realms, bathed in divine light, free from the confines of earthly existence.

The spell implores the ancient spirits to grant the individual the freedom and liberation of a spirit. They aspire to become vessels of energy, untethered from the earthly bounds, roaming the spiritual realms without limitations.

The individual desires to acquire the wisdom of ages past, enabling them to navigate the vastness of the spiritual realms with clarity and purpose. They seek to transcend time and exist beyond mortal realms, infused with the essence of eternal life.

The spell calls upon the ancient ones to guide and protect the individual on their journey as a spirit. They beseech the spirits for knowledge and strength to endure as they traverse the realms, forever pure in their essence.

The individual envisions their spirit as a beacon of light, capable of guiding others through the realms of darkness. They embrace the transformation into a spirit, recognizing it as a rebirth into eternity, free from earthly attachments.

In conclusion, through this spell, the deceased implores the ancient spirits to facilitate their transformation into a spirit. They seek liberation from mortal limitations and the ability to navigate the spiritual realms with wisdom and purpose. The spell symbolizes the individual's yearning for transcendence and the belief in the existence of an eternal, spiritual essence beyond earthly life.

CT 46: Spell for Illumination and Enlightenment: Providing the deceased with divine knowledge, insight, and enlightenment in the afterlife.

Utterance:
"O ancient sources of divine light,
Bestow upon me knowledge shining bright.
In the realms of the afterlife, I seek,
Illumination and wisdom, the truth to speak.

Grant me the radiance of your divine flame,
That my spirit may be forever aflame.
Illuminate my path with your sacred glow,
So that in darkness, wisdom I may know.

Open the doors to the halls of wisdom,
Reveal the secrets of the celestial kingdom.
Enlighten my mind with your cosmic insight,
Unveil the mysteries, make them clear and bright.

May my spirit be a vessel of divine knowing,
Absorbing wisdom from the realms overflowing.
Grant me clarity of thought, perception keen,
So that in your presence, divine truths are seen.

Through the ages, the wisdom has passed,
Ancient knowledge, eternal and steadfast.
Let it flow into my being, through every pore,
Empowering my spirit, forevermore.

In the afterlife's realms, I seek to explore,
The depths of knowledge, the truths to adore.
Illuminate my consciousness, expand my mind,
So that divine wisdom I may forever find.

O ancient sources of divine light,
Guide my spirit through eternal night.
With your illumination, I shall ascend,
To the heights of enlightenment, worlds without end.

Grant me the insight to perceive,

The mysteries of existence, the web we weave.
May divine knowledge fill my spirit's core,
In the afterlife's realms, forevermore.

As I embrace your radiance, divine and bright,
Illumination and enlightenment are my birthright.
With gratitude, I receive the wisdom you impart,
Forever enlightened, forever connected at heart.

So mote it be, let illumination descend,
As I seek divine wisdom, my spirit to transcend.
In the afterlife's realms, forever I shall shine,
With your sacred light, divine and sublime."

In this spell for illumination and enlightenment, the deceased addresses the ancient sources of divine light and beseeches them to bestow knowledge shining bright. The individual seeks illumination and wisdom in the realms of the afterlife, yearning to speak the truth.

The spell implores the ancient sources to grant the radiance of their divine flame, that the spirit may forever be aflame with knowledge. The individual longs for the illumination of their path and clarity in darkness, that they may discern wisdom.

The doors to the halls of wisdom are called to be opened, and the secrets of the celestial kingdom are sought to be revealed. The individual desires their mind to be enlightened with cosmic insight, unveiling the mysteries and making them clear and bright.

The spell requests the individual's spirit to be a vessel of divine knowing, absorbing wisdom that overflows from the realms. They seek clarity of thought and keen perception, to recognize divine truths in the presence of the ancient sources.

The ancient knowledge passed through the ages is invoked, and the individual seeks its flow into their being, empowering their spirit forever. They aspire to explore the depths of knowledge in the afterlife's realms, to adore the truths they unveil.

The ancient sources of divine light are called upon to guide the spirit through eternal night, illuminating consciousness and expanding the mind. The individual yearns for divine wisdom to fill their spirit's core in the realms of the afterlife, forevermore.

In conclusion, this spell invokes the ancient sources of divine light to grant illumination and enlightenment to the deceased. It reflects the individual's desire for profound knowledge, insight, and clarity in the afterlife. The spell symbolizes the eternal pursuit of wisdom and the belief in the transformative power of divine illumination.

CT 47: Spell for Receiving Guidance from Ancestors: Enabling the deceased to seek guidance and wisdom from their ancestral spirits.

Utterance:
"O spirits of my ancestors, hear my call,
In the realms of the afterlife, I stand tall.
From generation to generation, our lineage flows,
Grant me your wisdom, that I may truly know.

Ancient spirits, guardians of our kin,
With reverence and respect, I now begin.
I seek your guidance in this eternal realm,
To navigate the paths, the secrets overwhelm.

Let your voices echo through time's embrace,
Whispering truths, revealing the sacred space.
Guide me with your ancestral light,
Illuminate my path, dispelling the night.

In your presence, I find strength and solace,
Your wisdom resonates, transcending any malice.
Share with me the stories of our bloodline,
Unveil the lessons, the wisdom divine.

From the depths of the afterlife, I call on you,
Ancestral spirits, wise and true.
Grant me your counsel, your ancestral sight,
Illuminate my spirit with your guiding light.

In dreams and visions, let our souls unite,
Convey your wisdom, clear and bright.
Through the veil that separates our worlds,
Speak to me, as the sacred scroll unfurls.

In your wisdom, I find solace and peace,
Your ancestral guidance brings me release.
With gratitude and reverence, I receive,
The lessons you offer, as I believe.

O spirits of my ancestors, I honor your name,

Your presence in the afterlife remains the same.
Guide me through the realms unknown,
With your wisdom, my spirit has grown.

So mote it be, let the connection be strong,
As I seek your guidance, to which I belong.
In the afterlife's embrace, forever we unite,
Ancestral spirits, shining in eternal light."

In this spell for receiving guidance from ancestors, the deceased calls upon the spirits of their ancestors in the afterlife. They acknowledge the intergenerational lineage and seek the wisdom and guidance of their ancestral spirits.

The spell begins by addressing the spirits of the ancestors and expressing the individual's standing in the afterlife. They request the spirits to bestow their wisdom, enabling the deceased to truly know and understand.

The deceased acknowledges the ancient spirits as guardians of their kin and approaches them with reverence and respect. They seek the guidance of the ancestors to navigate the overwhelming secrets and paths of the eternal realm.

The spell implores the ancestral spirits to let their voices echo through time, whispering truths and revealing the sacred space. The deceased yearns for their ancestral light to guide their path and dispel the darkness.

The individual finds strength and solace in the presence of the ancestors, recognizing the resonance of their wisdom that transcends any malice. They desire to hear the stories of their bloodline and uncover the divine wisdom and lessons embedded within.

The deceased calls upon the ancestral spirits to share their counsel and ancestral sight, illuminating their spirit with guiding light. They seek connection through dreams and visions, where the wisdom of the ancestors can be conveyed and the sacred scroll of knowledge unfurls.

With gratitude and reverence, the deceased receives the lessons offered by the ancestral spirits, understanding the solace and peace they bring. They honor the spirits of their ancestors and acknowledge the enduring presence and guidance in the afterlife.

In conclusion, this spell serves as a heartfelt plea for guidance and wisdom from the spirits of the deceased's ancestors. It reflects the deep respect and appreciation for ancestral heritage and the belief in the power of ancestral guidance in navigating the afterlife. The spell symbolizes the enduring connection between the living and the deceased and the profound wisdom that can be passed down through generations.

CT 48: Spell for Becoming a Sahu (Akhu): Granting the deceased the ability to transform into a divine Akhu, a glorified and radiant spirit.

Utterance:
"O divine spirits, hear my plea,
Grant me the transformation I seek to be.
From mortal form to radiant soul,
A glorified Akhu, forever whole.

Through the veil of the afterlife I pass,
Leaving behind my earthly mass.
Shedding the mortal coil of flesh,
Embracing the divine, the eternal mesh.

Grant me the wings of ethereal flight,
To soar in realms of everlasting light.
Clothe me in radiant attire sublime,
With the splendor of the divine, I will shine.

Let my essence glow with celestial fire,
A luminous being, divinely inspired.
Release me from the bounds of mortality,
To embody the transcendence of immortality.

Grant me the vision of all-seeing eyes,
To behold the mysteries that eternally rise.
Endow me with wisdom, knowledge divine,
A radiant Akhu, with brilliance that shines.

May my spirit ascend to realms above,
In the company of deities, united in love.
Bathed in the glory of celestial bliss,
A transformed Sahu, eternally amiss.

In the divine realm, let my presence be known,
As a radiant spirit, gloriously shown.
Unite me with the spirits of the ancient past,
In the eternal embrace, our spirits will last.

With gratitude and reverence, I accept,

The transformation, the eternal concept.
As a Sahu, radiant and sublime,
I transcend time, forever in divine rhyme.

So be it, let the transformation unfold,
As I embrace the divine, my spirit's stronghold.
In the afterlife's embrace, forever I'll be,
A glorified Akhu, radiant and free."

In this spell for becoming a Sahu (Akhu), the deceased appeals to the divine spirits, seeking a transformation into a glorified and radiant spirit. The utterance emphasizes the desire to transcend mortal form and embrace a higher, eternal existence.

The spell begins by addressing the divine spirits, calling upon them to hear the plea and grant the transformation being sought. The deceased seeks to shed their earthly form and become a luminous Akhu, a radiant and complete spirit.

The individual expresses the intention to pass through the veil of the afterlife, leaving behind their mortal body and embracing a higher spiritual state. They yearn to transcend the limitations of flesh and merge with the divine essence that permeates the eternal realms.

The spell implores the divine spirits to grant wings of ethereal flight, enabling the transformed spirit to soar in realms of everlasting light. The deceased seeks to be clothed in radiant attire, symbolizing the splendor and magnificence of the divine.

The individual requests their essence to glow with celestial fire, emanating a luminosity that reflects their divine inspiration. They yearn to be released from the bounds of mortality and embody the transcendence of immortality.

The spell seeks the bestowment of all-seeing eyes, granting the transformed spirit the vision to behold the eternal mysteries. The deceased desires to be endowed with wisdom and divine knowledge, embodying a radiant Akhu whose brilliance shines brightly.

The individual aspires for their spirit to ascend to realms above, joining the company of deities and uniting in divine love. They yearn to be bathed in the glory of celestial bliss, experiencing the transformation into a radiant Sahu, forever beyond mortal limitations.

The spell concludes with the acceptance of the transformation, expressing gratitude and reverence. The individual acknowledges the eternal concept of becoming a Sahu, a radiant and sublime spirit. They embrace the notion of transcending time and existing in divine harmony.

In summary, this spell represents a heartfelt plea for transformation into a Sahu (Akhu), a glorified and radiant spirit in the afterlife. It symbolizes the desire to shed mortal limitations and embrace a higher spiritual state of being. The spell reflects the belief in the eternal nature of the soul and the aspiration to join the company of divine beings in the realms beyond.

CT 49: Spell for Protection against Evil Forces: Safeguarding the deceased from malevolent forces, curses, and negative influences.

Utterance:
"By the power of divine light, I stand,
A shielded spirit in this sacred land.
I invoke the guardians of the afterlife,
To shield me from harm and banish strife.

Evil forces, I command you to depart,
From the sacred realm, you must not chart.
With the strength of the gods, I repel your might,
Banishing darkness, embracing divine light.

I call upon the ancient spirits of protection,
To surround me with their divine connection.
Let their power shield me from every harm,
Keeping me safe, secure, and warm.

May the amulets of sacred symbols I bear,
Repel curses, ward off evil, and beware.
With each breath I take, I am fortified,
Protected from harm, with spirits by my side.

Evil eye, black magic, and negativity,
I cast you away with divine positivity.
May your influence wane and diminish,
As divine protection ensures evil's extinguish.

I stand firm in the face of adversity,
With divine light as my guiding emissary.
No malevolent force shall break my defense,
For I am shielded by divine providence.

As I traverse the afterlife's domain,
Protection surrounds me like a steadfast chain.
Evil forces, be banished from my sight,
In this sacred realm, only goodness shall alight.

So mote it be, let the spell be cast,

By the powers of protection that will forever last.
In the divine embrace, I find sanctuary,
Shielded from evil, I am safe and free."

In this spell for protection against evil forces, the deceased invokes the power of divine light and calls upon the guardians of the afterlife to shield them from harm and banish negativity. The utterance emphasizes the command to evil forces to depart and the embrace of divine light and protection.

The spell asserts the strength of the gods and their ability to repel evil and banish darkness. The deceased calls upon the ancient spirits of protection to surround them and establish a divine connection. It is their power that shields from harm and ensures safety and security.

Amulets of sacred symbols are invoked as a means to repel curses, ward off evil, and be aware of potential dangers. The deceased recognizes the power of these symbols and their ability to fortify their spirit and protect from malevolent influences.

The spell acknowledges the existence of the evil eye, black magic, and negativity, but confidently casts them away with divine positivity. The influence of these malevolent forces is declared to wane and diminish as divine protection ensures their extinction.

The individual stands firm in the face of adversity, guided by divine light as their steadfast emissary. They assert that no malevolent force shall break their defense, as they are shielded by divine providence.

As the deceased traverses the afterlife's domain, they affirm that protection surrounds them like an unbreakable chain. Evil forces are commanded to be banished from their sight, allowing only goodness to prevail in the sacred realm.

The spell concludes with the affirmation of the cast spell, invoking the powers of protection that will endure eternally. The deceased finds sanctuary in the divine embrace, shielded from evil and embracing safety and freedom.

Overall, this spell represents a powerful invocation for protection against evil forces in the afterlife. It emphasizes the power of divine light, the guardians of the afterlife, and sacred symbols to repel malevolent energies and ensure the safety and well-being of the deceased.

CT 50: Spell for Uniting with the Sun God: Facilitating the union and fusion of the deceased's essence with the sun god, symbolizing divinity.

Utterance:
"O radiant Sun God, source of eternal light,
I beseech your presence in this sacred rite.
In the afterlife's realm, I seek to unite,
With your divine essence, shining ever bright.

I offer my devotion, my spirit, and my heart,
As I call upon your radiance to impart.
Merge with my being, O glorious one,
Grant me divinity, let our essence become one.

Like the sun's rays that spread across the land,
May your divine power touch me, expand.
Infuse me with your brilliance and might,
As we merge in harmony, shining through the night.

In this sacred union, I transcend mortal bounds,
Becoming divine, with immortal resounds.
May my spirit radiate with your divine fire,
As I ascend to heights that never tire.

Grant me the wisdom of your celestial gaze,
As we merge, enlightening my eternal days.
Let me bask in your warmth, your eternal embrace,
As I become a vessel of your divine grace.

In this sacred fusion, I am reborn,
A being of light, from darkness torn.
United with you, O Sun God so fair,
I shine with your brilliance, beyond compare.

Forever bound, our essences entwined,
In the realms of eternity, our union defined.
As I join the celestial chorus of your light,
I embody divinity, shining ever bright.

So mote it be, let the spell be cast,

In the union of our essence that will forever last.
I am one with the Sun God's divine flame,
A radiant being, forever to acclaim."

In this spell for uniting with the sun god, the deceased invokes the presence of the radiant Sun God and seeks to unite their essence with the divine deity. The utterance expresses the desire to merge with the sun god's essence, symbolizing the attainment of divinity.

The individual offers their devotion and calls upon the sun god's radiance to impart upon them. They seek to merge their being with the glorious sun god, granting them divinity and becoming one with their essence.

The spell compares the sun's rays that spread across the land to the divine power of the sun god, and the individual asks for their brilliance and might to infuse them. The goal is to be filled with the sun god's brilliance and shine through the night of the afterlife.

Through this sacred union, the individual aims to transcend mortal boundaries and become divine, resonating with immortal energy. They seek the wisdom of the sun god's celestial gaze and the enlightenment that comes with the merging of their essences.

The individual yearns to bask in the warmth and eternal embrace of the sun god, becoming a vessel of divine grace. They acknowledge that through this fusion, they are reborn and become a being of light, shining with the sun god's brilliance.

The spell affirms the eternal bond between the individual and the sun god, their essences forever entwined in the realms of eternity. The individual becomes part of the celestial chorus of the sun god's light, embodying divinity and shining brightly.

The utterance concludes by affirming the casting of the spell and the eternal nature of the union with the sun god. The individual proclaims their oneness with the divine flame of the sun god, forever to be acclaimed as a radiant being.

Overall, this spell represents a powerful invocation for the union with the sun god in the afterlife. It seeks to merge the essence of the deceased with the divine energy of the sun god, symbolizing the attainment of divinity and eternal radiance.

CT 51: Spell for preserving one's memory from fading in the afterlife

In the realm of the eternal, where memories reside,
I invoke the power to make them abide.
Through the shifting sands of time's embrace,
I seek to preserve my memories in this sacred space.

O spirits of remembrance, hear my plea,
Grant me the gift to retain my memory.
In the afterlife's vast and boundless domain,
Let not my recollections wane.

By the strength of my will and the force of my intent,
I safeguard my memories, as they were meant.
Like an ancient tome, treasured and sealed,
I preserve the essence of all I have revealed.

Let not the winds of oblivion blow,
Erasing the moments I long to know.
May the tapestry of my life, vibrant and true,
Unfurl in the afterlife, as I once knew.

With each breath I take and each word I speak,
I anchor my memories, strong and unique.
Etched in the fabric of my soul's embrace,
They withstand the test of time and space.

Through the ages, my memories endure,
A testament to the life I once knew for sure.
In the afterlife's embrace, they shall remain,
A guiding light amidst the ethereal plane.

By the power of my will and the strength of my soul,
I ensure my memories remain whole.
No fading, no drifting, no loss in the abyss,
For my memories persist in eternal bliss.

As I pass into the afterlife's gentle hold,
I carry my memories, steadfast and bold.
No matter the challenges that may arise,

My recollections stand, a cherished prize.

So mote it be, let it be done,
My memories preserved, one by one.
In the tapestry of eternity, they shall reside,
As a testament to the life I once lived wide.

By the spirits of remembrance, I am blessed,
With memories preserved, in the afterlife's quest.
With gratitude and reverence, I embrace this grace,
Preserving my memories in this sacred space.

CT 52: Spell for escaping the clutches of the god of sorrow

In the realm of sorrow, where shadows lay,
I seek release from its suffocating sway.
With heavy heart and burdened soul,
I call upon the magic to make me whole.

O god of sorrow, loosen your grip,
Release me now from this sorrowful trip.
I refuse to be held in your despairing embrace,
I claim my freedom in this sacred space.

With every breath I take, I exhale the pain,
Releasing the sorrow that once did reign.
I embrace the light that banishes the dark,
Igniting the flame within my heart.

I call upon the guardians of joy and delight,
To lift me high, like a soaring kite.
Fill my spirit with laughter and cheer,
And let sorrow's chains quickly disappear.

I invoke the power of hope and grace,
To lift me up and guide my pace.
No longer bound by sorrow's chains,
I break free from its consuming strains.

I dance with joy, I sing with glee,
In this moment, I choose to be free.
I release the tears that held me tight,
And embrace the dawn's awakening light.

With each step forward, I leave sorrow behind,
No longer a captive, no longer confined.
I reclaim my happiness, my heart restored,
As I walk this path with courage, I move toward.

By the strength within, I break the bonds,
Escaping sorrow's grasp, my spirit responds.
I am resilient, I am strong,
I rise above sorrow, where I belong.

With every beat of my heart, I find solace and peace,
As I let go of sorrow, my worries release.
I am free, I am whole, I am alive,
No longer captive to sorrow's strive.

So mote it be, let it be done,
I am liberated, my sorrow undone.
I embrace joy and the blessings it brings,
Escaping the clutches of sorrow's sting.

In this sacred space, I find my way,
Embracing life's beauty, day by day.
I am free from sorrow's hold,
With a heart that's light and a spirit bold.

By the power of my will and the strength of my soul,
I escape the clutches of sorrow's control.
I reclaim my joy, my spirit renewed,
For in this spell's casting, my freedom is pursued.

As I step into the light, I leave sorrow behind,
Embracing the happiness that I now find.
With gratitude and love, I embrace my tomorrow,
Released from the clutches of the god of sorrow.

CT 53: Spell for warding off the god of chaos and disorder

In the face of chaos, I stand strong and firm,
With this spell, I protect and affirm.
I call upon the powers of order and control,
To keep chaos at bay and maintain my soul.

Oh god of chaos, I ward you away,
Your destructive forces I will not sway.
With clarity and balance, I create my space,
In harmony and order, I find my place.

I invoke the guardians of stability and peace,
To guard my path and make chaos cease.
With their guidance and watchful eye,
I ward off chaos, no room for it to pry.

I weave a shield, a barrier of light,
To keep chaos at bay, out of sight.
With every breath, I breathe in calm,
And chaos's influence I disarm.

I cleanse my space of discord and strife,
Inviting peace and harmony into my life.
I banish chaos with each sacred word,
Restoring balance, like a graceful bird.

I call upon the forces of structure and law,
To keep chaos's chaos from my door.
I embrace discipline and clarity of mind,
Leaving chaos and disorder far behind.

I affirm my intentions, focused and clear,
To create a world free from chaos and fear.
I stand tall in the face of uncertainty,
For chaos has no power over me.

By the power within, I reclaim control,
Warding off chaos, making it unfold.
With every action, I bring order and peace,
Allowing chaos and disorder to cease.

As I walk my path with purpose and grace,
Chaos's influence I will deface.
I am the architect of my own destiny,
Creating a world of harmony and serenity.

By the strength of this spell and my will,
I ward off chaos, my spirit to fulfill.
I embrace order and structure's embrace,
Shielding myself from chaos's chase.

So mote it be, let it be done,
With this spell, chaos is shunned.
I am protected, my spirit is secure,
Warding off chaos, of this I am sure.

In this sacred space, I find my peace,
As chaos and disorder continue to decrease.
I am grounded, centered, and strong,
Warding off chaos, where I belong.

With gratitude and harmony in my heart,
I ward off chaos, I set myself apart.
I walk in balance, free from disorder's blight,
Protected and guided by the powers of light.

By the power of order and control, I am blessed,
Warding off chaos, I am truly impressed.
I stand in harmony, chaos at bay,
With this spell, I keep chaos away.

CT 54: Spell for attaining the protection of the guardian deities of the afterlife

In the realm of the afterlife, I seek protection,
From the guardian deities, a divine connection.
I call upon the powers that guard this sacred place,
To guide and shield me with their grace.

Oh guardian deities, I invoke your might,
Wrap me in your arms, protect me in your light.
With your wisdom and strength, I am secure,
As I journey through this realm pure.

I seek your presence, your watchful eyes,
To guide me through the afterlife's skies.
Keep me safe from harm, from negative sway,
As I navigate this mystical pathway.

Oh guardian deities, I offer my devotion,
To receive your blessings and eternal protection.
Surround me with your divine embrace,
Shielding me from any dark embrace.

I honor you with reverence and respect,
In your presence, I find solace and reflect.
Guide me with your wisdom and profound,
As I traverse the afterlife's sacred ground.

Grant me your guidance and steadfast care,
As I face the challenges that may ensnare.
Protect me from malevolent forces that roam,
Preserve my spirit, my eternal home.

By your divine presence, I am fortified,
Against any danger, I will not hide.
With you as my guardians, I am blessed,
Protected and guided through the afterlife's quest.

I offer my gratitude for your watchful gaze,
For keeping me safe in this mystical haze.
May your protection be with me every day,

As I walk the path in the afterlife's array.

Oh guardian deities, I thank you for your grace,
For surrounding me in this sacred space.
With your protection, I fear no plight,
Guided and guarded in the afterlife's light.

By the power of this spell, I call upon thee,
Guardian deities, protect and guide me.
In your embrace, I find eternal peace,
In the afterlife's realm, my spirit finds release.

CT 55: Spell for avoiding the judgment of the god of destiny

In the realm of fate and destiny's sway,
I seek to navigate my own chosen way.
I call upon the forces that govern all,
To protect me from the god of destiny's call.

Oh god of destiny, I humbly plea,
Grant me the freedom to shape my own decree.
Let not your judgment cloud my path,
But rather, let me forge my own aftermath.

I ask for the power to choose my own course,
To shape my destiny without remorse.
May your gaze upon me be one of leniency,
As I strive to live a life of authenticity.

I acknowledge the importance of destiny's hand,
But also the autonomy to make my stand.
Guide me, oh god of destiny, with gentle sway,
So I may walk a path that leads my own way.

Grant me the wisdom to make choices true,
To align my actions with what I value and pursue.
Let not your judgment be harsh or severe,
But rather, let me learn and grow without fear.

I embrace the responsibility that comes with free will,
To shape my own fate, my own journey fulfill.
Oh god of destiny, I seek your understanding,
To walk a path that is authentic and expanding.

By the power of this spell, I seek to be free,
From the judgment of destiny, let me flee.
Guide me on a path that resonates within,
Where my choices and actions align and begin.

CT 56: Spell for acquiring the power to manipulate the astral plane

In the realm of ethereal realms, I seek to dwell,
Where the astral plane weaves its mysterious spell.
I call upon the forces that govern the astral light,
Grant me the power to traverse this celestial flight.

Oh astral plane, I beseech thee now,
Bestow upon me the ability to freely bow,
To the currents and currents of cosmic energy,
And manipulate the astral realm with profound synergy.

Grant me the sight to perceive the astral thread,
To navigate its vastness with wisdom widespread.
May my astral form soar with grace and ease,
As I explore dimensions beyond earthly seas.

I call upon the celestial guardians of this plane,
To guide and protect me from harm or bane.
With their wisdom and guidance, let me be blessed,
As I traverse the astral realms with zest.

Grant me the power to shape and mold,
The energies of the astral plane untold.
Let me harness its mysteries, its divine flow,
To manifest my desires and intentions in this astral glow.

By the power of this spell, I command and decree,
The ability to manipulate the astral plane, set me free.
May my intentions align with cosmic will,
As I harness the power of the astral realm, skill by skill.

CT 57: Spell for escaping the torment of the god of regret

In the realm of eternal spirits, where regrets reside,
I seek liberation from the torment deep inside.
By the power of incantations and sacred plea,
I break free from regret's grip, and set my spirit free.

Oh, mighty forces of the afterlife's realm,
Release me from the shackles of remorse's helm.
Grant me strength to overcome regret's weight,
To rise above its grasp, and reclaim my fate.

With each word uttered, with each thought conceived,
I sever the ties that hold me, and believe.
I banish regret from my spirit and mind,
Leaving no trace of its torment behind.

Oh, god of regret, I bid you farewell,
I cast off your burden, no longer under your spell.
My spirit is free, released from your hold,
With newfound freedom, my destiny unfolds.

I embrace the present, and the future unknown,
No longer bound by the regrets I have sown.
I walk a path of healing, forgiveness, and grace,
Escaping the torment, finding solace in embrace.

CT 58: Spell for warding off malevolent spirits in the realm of lost souls

In the realm where lost souls wander astray,
I invoke the power to keep darkness at bay.
By sacred words and symbols of protection,
I shield myself from malevolent detection.

Spirits of light, guardians of the divine,
Wrap me in your love, let your presence shine.
With your guidance, I ward off the night's gloom,
Keeping malevolent spirits sealed in their tomb.

By the strength of the sacred amulet I wear,
I repel evil entities, banishing despair.
No lost soul's anguish shall attach to me,
For I am shielded, safe and spiritually free.

I call upon the ancient wisdom of the ages,
To guard my spirit throughout life's stages.
With every step I take, in every realm I roam,
I am protected, my soul a sacred home.

Evil spirits, I command you to depart,
In the light's presence, you cannot impart.
I am shielded from your ill-intentioned sway,
As I walk the path of truth and light each day.

CT 59: Spell for avoiding the judgment of the god of compassion

Oh merciful god, whose compassion knows no bound,
I call upon you, my voice in reverence resound.
Grant me your mercy, your understanding divine,
Let your judgment upon me, oh god, kindly shine.

In your presence, I seek solace and reprieve,
May your compassion and forgiveness relieve.
Guide me through the trials of the afterlife's gate,
Shield me from judgment, let mercy be my fate.

As you weigh my heart against the feather of truth,
May your compassion outweigh the deeds of my youth.
Look upon me with kindness, oh god of compassion,
And spare me from the harshness of divine retribution.

I beseech you, oh god, with a humble plea,
Grant me your mercy, for I seek your decree.
With contrite heart, I acknowledge my flaws,
In your compassion, I find the highest cause.

May your compassion shine upon me like a light,
Guiding me through the darkness, from day to night.
I pledge my devotion, my faith, and my trust,
In your mercy, oh god, I place my soul's thrust.

CT 60: Spell for Warding off Evil Spirits: Providing protection against evil spirits and malevolent supernatural entities in the afterlife.

Utterance:
"O spirits of darkness, I bid you away,
From the realms where I traverse, I command you to stay.
In the afterlife's expanse, I claim my space,
With this spell of protection, your influence I erase.

By the power of divine light, I am shielded,
No evil force can harm, for I am firmly yielded.
I call upon the guardians of the afterlife's gate,
To stand as sentinels, protecting my fate.

Let my presence be cloaked in sacred light,
A shield against malevolence, shining ever bright.
May the purity of divine energy surround,
Repelling evil spirits, leaving no ground.

I invoke the ancient words of protection,
Uttering them with conviction, with no hesitation.
Let their power resonate through the ether,
Creating a barrier that evil cannot wither.

By the authority of the gods, I proclaim,
This sacred space, evil cannot claim.
I am shielded from all wicked intent,
No malevolent spirit shall my path torment.

O benevolent ancestors, guide and guard,
Watch over me with vigilance, ever on guard.
Send forth your blessings, your wisdom and might,
Shield me from harm, in the afterlife's night.

Evil spirits, I banish you with this spell,
Into the depths of darkness, where you shall dwell.
You have no power here, no influence to wield,
For I am protected, my spirit sealed.

So mote it be, let the spell be cast,

May its power endure, forever to last.
I am safeguarded from malevolence's sway,
In the afterlife's realms, I find my way."

In this spell for warding off evil spirits, the deceased calls upon the power of divine light and protection to repel malevolent entities in the afterlife. The utterance emphasizes the claim of personal space and the banishment of evil influence.

The individual invokes the guardians of the afterlife's gate to stand as sentinels, safeguarding their path and ensuring their protection. They seek the cloak of sacred light, creating a shield against malevolence and darkness, allowing no ground for evil spirits to harm.

The spell relies on the power of ancient words of protection, uttered with conviction and confidence. It calls upon the resonance of these words through the ether, forming a strong barrier that evil cannot overcome.

The individual proclaims their authority and invokes the gods to secure their sacred space, ensuring that no wicked intent can penetrate their defenses. They rely on the benevolent ancestors to guide and guard, sending forth blessings, wisdom, and protection.

The spell explicitly addresses the evil spirits, commanding their banishment into the depths of darkness where they will dwell. It asserts the individual's authority and declares that the evil spirits have no power or influence within their presence.

The spell concludes by affirming the casting of the spell and the enduring power it possesses. The individual declares their protection from malevolence and their ability to find their way in the afterlife's realms.

Overall, this spell provides a potent invocation for protection against evil spirits and malevolent entities in the afterlife. It draws upon the power of divine light, the guardians of the afterlife, and ancestral guidance to create a shield that repels and banishes all forms of wickedness.

CT 61: Spell for preserving one's ba (soul) from dissolution

In the realm of eternal souls, I make my plea,
To protect my ba, my essence, so it may forever be.
By the power of ancient words and sacred rites,
I shield my ba from dissolution's blights.

Oh, great guardians of the afterlife's gate,
Hear my cry and come to my aid, I await.
Wrap your wings around me, offer your divine embrace,
Shield my ba from the forces that seek to erase.

By the strength of this spell, I invoke your might,
Preserve my ba from the realms of endless night.
Keep it whole, untarnished, and forever pure,
Shield it from dissolution, make its essence endure.

Let no chaos or decay touch my ba's essence,
Let no darkness or oblivion cloud its presence.
May it retain its identity, its eternal flame,
Forever preserved, its divine essence shall remain.

As the stars guide my path through the afterlife's domain,
May my ba shine brightly, its essence sustain.
With this spell, I bind my ba to eternal preservation,
Shielded from dissolution, it shall know no cessation.

CT 62: Spell for attaining the blessings of the wind god Shu

Oh mighty Shu, god of the winds and breath,
I beseech you for your blessings, I confess.
Grant me the power to soar on gentle air,
To feel your presence, your guidance, and care.

With each gust of wind that brushes my face,
Fill me with strength, with your divine grace.
Let your breath empower me in all I do,
In every endeavor, let me be renewed.

Oh Shu, who separates the sky from the earth,
Bestow upon me the gift of rebirth.
As you bring life to the lifeless, stale air,
Infuse my being with your vital flair.

Grant me the wisdom to navigate life's maze,
To find my way through its ever-changing phase.
With your guidance, I shall not go astray,
Carried by your winds, I'll find my own way.

Oh wind god Shu, I offer my gratitude,
For your blessings, your protection, and fortitude.
With your power, I shall face any storm,
For I am blessed, in your embrace, I am warm.

CT 63: Spell for acquiring the ability to perceive the hidden realms

By the power of the ancient ones and the mystic lore,
I seek to open the gates and unlock the hidden door.
Grant me, oh gods, the sight beyond mortal perception,
Reveal to me the realms hidden from ordinary conception.

With eyes wide open, I delve into the depths unknown,
Piercing the veil that separates the seen and the shown.
Let my senses transcend the boundaries of the mundane,
So I may witness the secrets that in shadows remain.

Grant me the keen perception of the seer and the sage,
To see the ethereal realms, beyond time and age.
With heightened senses, I perceive the unseen,
Unveiling mysteries and realms yet to be seen.

Let my mind be attuned to the subtle vibrations,
That resonate in dimensions beyond our known sensations.
Reveal to me the beings that dwell in hidden abodes,
The spirits, the fae, the guardians of secret codes.

With clarity of vision, I navigate the astral plane,
Discovering the wonders that therein lie arcane.
Grant me the ability to comprehend the esoteric signs,
And to decipher the hidden messages in ancient designs.

By the power vested in me, I open my inner sight,
To perceive the hidden realms with clarity and might.
I embrace the knowledge that lies beyond the mundane,
And with reverence, I explore the realms that remain.

CT 64: Spell for preserving one's spirit from annihilation in the realm of darkness

In the realm of darkness, where shadows hold sway,
I invoke the ancient powers to guide my way.
Protect me, oh guardians of eternal light,
Preserve my spirit from the depths of endless night.

By the sacred words, I ward off the abyss,
Shielding my essence from the void's deadly kiss.
Let not the darkness consume my inner flame,
For in this realm, I shall eternally claim.

I call upon the forces that banish despair,
To safeguard my spirit with utmost care.
May the light within me never fade away,
Even in the darkest of nights, I shall not sway.

With each step I take, let the path be lit,
Leading me away from the shadows that befit.
No darkness shall overcome the strength I possess,
For my spirit is resilient, it shall never regress.

I am the beacon amidst the darkness' embrace,
Shining bright with divine grace and embrace.
Guide me, oh deities, with your celestial might,
As I traverse the realm of eternal night.

By the power vested in me, I declare,
My spirit remains whole, unyielding to despair.
In the realm of darkness, my light shall persist,
Defying annihilation, forever I exist.

CT 65: Spell for escaping the grasp of the god of despair

Oh, god of despair, release your hold on me,
I break free from your clutches, I shall be free.
No longer shall I succumb to sorrow's plight,
For I shall rise above, embracing joy and light.

With every breath I take, I defy your chains,
I banish the darkness that within me remains.
No longer shall despair cloud my heart and mind,
In its place, hope and resilience I shall find.

I call upon the ancient powers of renewal,
To cleanse my spirit and make me whole.
Grant me strength and courage to face the night,
And emerge victorious in the battles I fight.

Oh, god of despair, your reign ends today,
I reclaim my life, I walk my own way.
With each step I take, your influence fades,
My spirit soars high, above the dark shades.

I am a beacon of hope, a warrior of light,
Guided by purpose, fueled by inner might.
No longer shall despair define who I am,
For I am stronger than you, oh god of dam.

Release me now, relinquish your grip,
In the realm of hope, I shall surely eclipse.
I am free from your clutches, forevermore,
Embracing a future filled with joy and more.

CT 66: Spell for warding off the god of lies and deceit

Oh, god of lies, your web of deceit unraveled shall be,
I invoke the powers of truth to set me free.
With every word spoken, I see through your guise,
Your illusions shattered, revealing the lies.

I call upon the guardians of honesty and light,
To shield me from deception, to keep my path bright.
May their presence surround me, a shield so strong,
Protecting me from falsehood, all my life long.

Oh, god of deceit, your influence shall wane,
As truth and integrity firmly take their reign.
My heart is a fortress, guarded and true,
No deception shall penetrate, no falsehoods accrue.

I walk a path of righteousness and authenticity,
Imbued with the strength of truth's purity.
No longer swayed by your manipulative ways,
I stand firm, immune to your wicked plays.

With every step I take, truth shall guide me,
A beacon of light, shining for all to see.
I reject your whispers, your misleading call,
For I am anchored in truth, standing tall.

Oh, god of lies, your power diminished,
By the light of truth, you are banished.
I embrace honesty, sincerity, and trust,
In their embrace, I find strength and robust.

By the power of truth, I ward off your deceit,
No longer a victim, but a victor I shall meet.
Your illusions shattered, your hold released,
I walk a path of truth, forever at peace.

CT 67: Spell for attaining the protection of the guardian spirits of the underworld

Oh, guardian spirits of the underworld, hear my plea,
Wrap me in your embrace, protect and guide me.
As I journey through the realms of the deceased,
I seek your shelter, your wisdom, your inner peace.

With each step I take in the realm of the dead,
May your presence surround me, like a cloak spread.
Shield me from malevolent forces that may arise,
With your strength and power, make them vaporize.

Guardian spirits, fierce and unwavering in your might,
Keep me safe from darkness, from eternal night.
Let not the perils of the underworld consume me,
But guide me through its depths, forever free.

Embrace me with your light, with your ethereal grace,
As I navigate the paths of this sacred place.
Bestow upon me your knowledge, your ancient lore,
That I may traverse the underworld, forevermore.

In the company of guardians, I find solace and trust,
For in their presence, I am shielded from all that's unjust.
With each passing moment, their protection I feel,
Their essence intertwining with mine, making me whole and real.

Oh, guardian spirits of the underworld, I invoke your might,
In your protection, I take refuge day and night.
Guide me on my journey, with your wisdom and care,
For in your presence, I find peace beyond compare.

CT 68: Spell for Avoiding the Judgment of the God of Mercy

Oh, god of mercy, with your discerning eyes,
I stand before you, humble and wise.
Grant me clemency, your benevolent grace,
As I face your judgment in this sacred space.

In life, I've stumbled and made mistakes,
But now in death, my soul awakes.
I seek your forgiveness, your divine reprieve,
From the burdens of transgressions, I wish to be relieved.

With contrite heart and sincere remorse,
I ask for your mercy, to alter my course.
May your compassion overshadow my flaws,
And guide me through the righteous laws.

Oh, god of mercy, weigh my heart with care,
In the scales of justice, let me be deemed fair.
May my deeds of kindness outweigh my wrongs,
As I journey through the afterlife's eternal songs.

Grant me a chance for redemption and healing,
To mend the wounds and find inner revealing.
With your benevolent touch, wash away my sins,
And let my soul soar as purity begins.

Oh, god of mercy, hear my plea,
Bestow upon me your mercy's decree.
Let your compassion light my way,
As I face the judgment on this fateful day.

CT 69 Spell for Acquiring the Power of Divine Protection

O ancient deities, guardians of the divine,
I call upon your presence, let your power align.
Grant me protection, in this realm and beyond,
From malevolent forces, may I respond.

With words of power, I speak my plea,
Let your divine strength encircle me.
Form a shield of light, impenetrable and strong,
Guarding my essence from all that is wrong.

Oh, mighty gods, with your celestial might,
Bless me with the armor of your divine light.
Shield me from harm, from chaos and strife,
Preserve my being, throughout this mortal life.

Through the trials and tribulations I tread,
May your divine protection be my sacred thread.
Shield my body, shield my soul,
As I navigate the paths to reach my goal.

From the depths of the Duat to the heavens above,
Wrap me in your embrace, the embodiment of love.
Grant me the power to repel every ill,
With your divine protection, I am strong and still.

By the authority of the gods, this spell I cast,
May their protection be with me, steadfast.
In their divine presence, I find sanctuary,

CT 70: Spell for Becoming a Shining One: Granting the deceased the ability to radiate divine light and brilliance in the spiritual realms.

Utterance:
"O radiant gods and celestial spheres,
I beseech thee now, lend me your divine light, I revere.
Grant me the power to shine with brilliance untold,
As a beacon of divinity, my essence unfolds.

From the depths of darkness, I emerge,
Transformed into a radiant being, my spirit surges.
I shed the mortal veil, transcending earthly bounds,
A shining one, with divine light that astounds.

Let my presence illuminate the spiritual realms,
A glowing essence, transcending mortal helms.
With each step I take, a trail of light I leave,
Guiding lost souls, my radiance they receive.

I invoke the power of the sun's golden rays,
Absorbing its brilliance, in radiant display.
Let my being radiate divine light and grace,
A testament to the eternal, a heavenly embrace.

May my glow dispel all shadows and fear,
A beacon of hope, drawing the divine near.
Let my essence resonate with celestial spheres,
A shining one, embraced by the gods' cheers.

I am a vessel of divine radiance and power,
Transformed into a shining one in this sacred hour.
With each breath I take, I emit divine light,
Piercing the darkness, dispelling the night.

I call upon the gods to bless and anoint,
My spirit aglow, their divine light to appoint.
Grant me the ability to shine eternally,
A radiant being, revered throughout infinity.

By the power of the divine, I become luminous,

A shining one, transcending all that is tempestuous.
I radiate with brilliance, a celestial sight,
Embracing my destiny, in heavenly flight.

So mote it be, let the spell be cast,
As a shining one, I am radiant and steadfast.
In the spiritual realms, I shine ever bright,
A divine presence, a beacon of celestial light."

In this spell for becoming a shining one, the deceased calls upon the gods and celestial spheres to grant them the ability to radiate divine light in the spiritual realms. The utterance emphasizes the transformation from darkness to brilliance and the shedding of the mortal veil.

The individual invokes the radiant gods and celestial spheres, acknowledging their reverence and seeking their divine light. They yearn to shine with brilliance untold, becoming a beacon of divinity and unfolding their essence as a radiant being.

The spell asks for the individual's presence to illuminate the spiritual realms, leaving a trail of light to guide lost souls and offer them solace. The power of the sun's golden rays is invoked, absorbing its brilliance and emitting divine light and grace.

The individual desires to dispel shadows and fear, becoming a beacon of hope that draws the divine near. They wish for their essence to resonate with celestial spheres, receiving the cheers and blessings of the gods as they transform into a shining one.

The spell asserts the individual's identity as a vessel of divine radiance and power. They call upon the gods to bless and anoint them, bestowing the ability to shine eternally and pierce the darkness with their divine light.

The individual embraces their destiny as a shining one, a celestial sight revered throughout infinity. They affirm their transformation into a luminous being, radiating brilliance and steadfastness in the spiritual realms.

The spell concludes with the casting of the spell and the proclamation of the individual's radiant and steadfast nature. They declare their presence as a shining one, a divine presence and beacon of celestial light in the spiritual realms.

Through this spell, the deceased seeks to become a shining one, embodying divine light and brilliance in the spiritual realms. They draw upon the power of the gods and celestial spheres to transform into a radiant being, illuminating their path and offering guidance to others.

CT 71: Spell for Receiving Offerings from the Gods: Ensuring that the deceased continues to receive offerings and blessings from the gods.

Utterance:
"O benevolent gods, hear my plea,
In the realms of divine existence, I seek thee.
Grant me the blessings of your abundant grace,
And let your offerings fill my eternal space.

From the heavens above, let blessings rain,
A shower of abundance that knows no wane.
Bring forth your gifts, bestowed from high,
To sustain my spirit as the ages fly.

I invoke the deities of wisdom and might,
To bestow upon me their blessings bright.
Let their offerings of knowledge and strength,
Enrich my being, extending eternal length.

O gods of love and compassion divine,
Shower me with blessings that forever shine.
May your offerings of peace and harmony,
Grace my existence in eternal unity.

From the realms of beauty and artistry,
Let the gods' offerings of creativity flow to me.
Inspire my spirit with artistic flair,
And let my soul express its beauty rare.

I call upon the gods of prosperity and wealth,
To bless me with abundance and material health.
Let your offerings of prosperity and success,
Manifest in my afterlife, no less.

Grant me the offerings of healing and health,
To rejuvenate my spirit with divine wealth.
From the gods of vitality and well-being,
Let their blessings flow, forever freeing.

O gods of protection and divine light,

Surround me with your offerings, shining bright.
Shield me from harm, both day and night,
And guide me through the realms of eternal light.

As I walk this path of the afterlife's domain,
May the gods' offerings be my eternal gain.
Let their blessings and gifts, so divine,
Be forever present, eternally mine.

I receive these offerings with gratitude and praise,
As the gods' blessings fill my eternal days.
In unity with the divine, I am blessed,
With offerings from the gods, I am forever impressed.

So mote it be, let the spell be cast,
May the gods' offerings forever last.
In the afterlife's realm, their blessings unfold,
As I receive their offerings of divine gold."

In this spell for receiving offerings from the gods, the deceased appeals to the benevolent gods of various aspects of existence to bestow their blessings and offerings upon them. The utterance seeks abundance, knowledge, strength, peace, harmony, creativity, prosperity, success, healing, health, protection, and divine light.

The deceased invokes the gods of wisdom, might, love, compassion, beauty, artistry, prosperity, wealth, vitality, well-being, protection, and divine light. They ask for the gods' offerings to rain down upon them from the heavens, sustaining their spirit throughout eternity.

The spell requests the gods to shower the deceased with their blessings, filling their eternal space with abundance and grace. The offerings of the gods are seen as a source of sustenance and enrichment for the spirit as it traverses the afterlife.

The deceased expresses gratitude and praise for receiving the gods' offerings, acknowledging their eternal presence and divine significance. They affirm their unity with the gods and their appreciation for the blessings bestowed upon them.

Through this spell, the deceased seeks to ensure the continuous reception of offerings and blessings from the gods in the afterlife. They recognize the divine nature of these offerings and their significance in enhancing their spiritual journey.

CT 72: Spell for Transformation into a Phoenix: Allowing the deceased to transform into a mythical phoenix, symbolizing resurrection and immortality.

Utterance:
"By the power of ancient flames,
I call upon the phoenix's name.
From ashes to rebirth, I rise anew,
Grant me transformation, divine and true.

O mystical bird of fiery flight,
Embodying resurrection's radiant light,
With wings of gold and plumage bright,
Guide my spirit in eternal flight.

From the depths of the sacred pyre,
Ignite my essence with celestial fire.
Burn away the mortal shell I shed,
And raise me from the ashes, freed.

Transform me into a phoenix bold,
With feathers shimmering in hues untold.
Grant me the power of your fiery breath,
To soar through realms of life and death.

Let my spirit ascend with grace,
In this immortal and glorious chase.
As the phoenix, I shall know no end,
Infinite cycles of rebirth I transcend.

Grant me immortality, eternal flame,
Unfading glory, and a hallowed name.
As I rise from the ashes, I am reborn,
A phoenix of legend, no longer forlorn.

In this spell, I embrace the phoenix's fire,
Embodying its essence, soaring higher.
Grant me resurrection's divine embrace,
As I transform into a phoenix of grace.

So mote it be, let the spell ignite,

As I embrace the phoenix's flight.
In the realms of immortality, I'll shine,
Transformed into a phoenix, forever divine."

In this spell for transformation into a phoenix, the deceased invokes the power of the ancient flames and calls upon the name of the mystical bird. They seek the phoenix's transformative abilities, symbolizing resurrection and immortality.

The utterance describes the phoenix as a bird of fiery flight with wings of gold and radiant plumage. The deceased asks to be guided by the phoenix's spirit, to rise anew from the ashes and experience eternal flight.

The spell calls upon the sacred pyre, igniting the essence of the deceased with celestial fire. It asks for the mortal shell to be burned away, allowing the spirit to be raised from the ashes and set free.

The deceased seeks transformation into a phoenix with shimmering feathers in vibrant hues. They request the power of the phoenix's fiery breath to accompany them as they soar through the realms of life and death.

The spell implores the phoenix to grant immortality and eternal flame, bestowing unfading glory and a revered name upon the transformed individual. The goal is to break free from the cycle of mortality and transcend into infinite cycles of rebirth.

The deceased acknowledges the significance of becoming a phoenix, embracing its fire and essence. They embrace the promise of resurrection, immortality, and the eternal grace of the phoenix.

Through this spell, the deceased aspires to transform into a phoenix, symbolizing the ability to rise from the ashes and embrace eternal existence. They seek to embody the phoenix's qualities of immortality, divine rebirth, and transcendent flight.

CT 73: Spell for Illumination of the Path: Providing the deceased with guidance and enlightenment to navigate the afterlife's spiritual paths.

Utterance:
"By the radiant beams of celestial light,
I invoke the guidance of divine sight.
Illuminate the path before my way,
In the afterlife's realm where spirits stray.

O shining stars, with brilliance untold,
Reveal the secrets of the realms of old.
Guide my spirit through the ethereal haze,
With your celestial glow and guiding rays.

Grant me the wisdom to discern the way,
As I journey through the realms each day.
Let your light pierce the shadows deep,
Revealing the truths that I seek to keep.

With each step I take on this sacred ground,
May your luminous presence always be found.
Lead me to the places of divine insight,
Where the mysteries of the afterlife ignite.

May the moonlight cast a silvery glow,
Illuminating the path where spirits go.
In its gentle radiance, I find my way,
With clarity and vision, day by day.

O guiding spirits, hear my plea,
Beacons of wisdom, I call unto thee.
Bestow upon me divine enlightenment,
To navigate the afterlife's ascent.

Let the torch of knowledge be my guide,
As I traverse the realms, side by side.
Illuminate the hidden paths and gates,
Unveiling the mysteries that await.

In this spell for illumination of the path,
I embrace the divine light's steadfast bath.

May its radiance guide me through the night,
As I navigate the afterlife's sacred flight.

So mote it be, let the spell be cast,
With divine illumination that will forever last.
As I walk the spiritual paths with grace,
The guiding light leads me to my destined place."

In this spell for illumination of the path, the deceased calls upon the radiant beams of celestial light to guide and enlighten their journey through the afterlife. They seek the assistance of shining stars, the moon's gentle radiance, and guiding spirits to illuminate the way.

The spell implores the stars to reveal the secrets of the ancient realms, allowing the deceased to discern the path before them. They ask for the wisdom to navigate the afterlife's ethereal haze and to uncover the truths they seek to keep.

The deceased seeks the guidance of the luminous presence of celestial bodies, particularly the moon, whose silvery glow helps them find their way. They rely on the clarity and vision provided by the moonlight to lead them to places of divine insight and ignite the mysteries of the afterlife.

The spell calls upon guiding spirits, beacons of wisdom, to bestow divine enlightenment upon the deceased. They ask for the torch of knowledge to be their guide, illuminating the hidden paths, gates, and unveiling the mysteries that await.

Through this spell, the deceased seeks the divine light's steadfast bath to illuminate their spiritual journey. They place their trust in its radiance to lead them through the night, as they navigate the afterlife's sacred flight with grace and clarity.

The spell concludes by affirming the casting of the spell, acknowledging the lasting power of divine illumination, and expressing gratitude for the guiding light that will forever accompany the deceased on their destined path in the afterlife.

CT 74: Spell for Becoming an Uraeus Serpent: Granting the deceased the ability to transform into a divine uraeus serpent, symbolizing divine protection and royalty.

Utterance:
"O serpent of power, divine and bold,
Grant me the ability to take your form, I behold.
Transform my essence into an Uraeus Serpent,
Symbol of protection and royalty inherent.

With scales of gold, shimmering bright,
Empower me with your celestial might.
Wrap me in your coils, strong and secure,
As a symbol of divine protection, so pure.

Grant me the wisdom of ancient kings,
The authority that your presence brings.
From your lofty perch atop the crown,
May I command respect and honor renowned.

As an Uraeus Serpent, I am bestowed,
With divine protection wherever I go.
No harm or danger shall come my way,
Under your watchful gaze, I shall stay.

Through the lands of the afterlife I glide,
With the grace and power you provide.
As a guardian of the sacred and the divine,
I embrace my role, with reverence and pride.

May your venom repel all malevolent forces,
As I navigate the spiritual realms' diverse courses.
Grant me the authority to ward off negativity,
And uphold the sanctity of divine positivity.

In this spell for becoming an Uraeus Serpent,
I seek transformation, protection, and ascent.
May I embody the symbolism you represent,
As a divine creature, with power and intent.

So mote it be, let the spell be cast,

As I transform into an Uraeus Serpent, steadfast.
With divine protection, I now ascend,
Symbol of royalty and power without end."

In this spell for becoming an Uraeus Serpent, the deceased calls upon the serpent of power, a symbol of divine protection and royalty, to grant them the ability to transform into this majestic creature. They seek to embody the Uraeus Serpent's characteristics, such as scales of gold, celestial might, and a symbol of divine authority.

The deceased invokes the Uraeus Serpent's ability to provide strong and secure coils, representing the serpent's protective nature. They desire to be wrapped in its divine protection, shielded from harm and danger in the afterlife.

As an Uraeus Serpent, the deceased seeks the wisdom of ancient kings and the authority that the serpent's presence brings. They aspire to command respect and honor, symbolizing their elevated status and connection to the divine.

The spell acknowledges the Uraeus Serpent's role as a guardian of the sacred and the divine. The deceased embraces their responsibility with reverence and pride, understanding that they hold the power to repel malevolent forces and uphold the sanctity of divine positivity.

Through the transformation into an Uraeus Serpent, the deceased navigates the spiritual realms of the afterlife with grace and power. They trust in the serpent's venom to repel negativity and rely on its symbolism to assert their authority and protect their spiritual journey.

The spell concludes with the casting of the spell, affirming the transformation into an Uraeus Serpent. The deceased embraces their new form as a symbol of royalty and power, recognizing the everlasting nature of their divine essence in this transcendent state.

CT 75: Spell for Receiving Life from Ra: Ensuring that the deceased continues to receive life-giving energy and sustenance from the sun god Ra.

Utterance:
"Oh Ra, radiant and mighty sun,
Source of life, the eternal one.
I call upon your divine light and power,
To bestow upon me life each passing hour.

From the depths of the heavens above,
Send forth your rays, shower me with love.
Infuse my spirit with your life-giving flame,
That I may thrive and forever remain.

As the sun rises in the sky so high,
Illuminate my being, draw nigh.
Fill me with your vital energy,
Grant me life, unending and free.

Let your golden rays embrace my soul,
Renew my spirit, make me whole.
With each dawn, your blessings I receive,
As you shine upon me, I believe.

Empower me with your divine light,
Banish darkness, dispel the night.
I am a vessel for your radiant grace,
Forever connected in this sacred space.

Your life-giving energy flows through my veins,
Revitalizing me, releasing life's strains.
I am nourished by your celestial fire,
Awakening my being, lifting me higher.

In this spell for receiving life from Ra,
I humbly invoke your divine power.
Grant me the sustenance I require,
To thrive and flourish in my afterlife's empire.

May your life-giving energy sustain me,

As I journey through eternity.
With gratitude, I accept this divine gift,
As your rays upon me continue to lift.

So mote it be, let the spell be done,
As I receive life from the radiant sun.
With Ra's blessings, I shall forever thrive,
In the afterlife, where eternal life shall derive."

In this spell for receiving life from Ra, the deceased invokes the sun god Ra, the source of life and eternal energy. They call upon Ra's divine light and power to bestow upon them the continuous flow of life-giving energy and sustenance.

The deceased acknowledges Ra as the radiant and mighty sun, recognizing the vital role the sun plays in sustaining life on Earth. They beseech Ra to send forth their rays and shower them with love, infusing their spirit with the life-giving flame that allows them to thrive and remain in an eternal state of existence.

The spell emphasizes the cyclical nature of the sun, as it rises in the sky each day. The deceased seeks to be illuminated by Ra's divine light, asking for their blessings and the infusion of their vital energy. They understand that it is through this connection with Ra that they receive the sustenance necessary to sustain their spirit in the afterlife.

The spell acknowledges the power of Ra's golden rays to embrace the soul and renew the spirit. By invoking Ra's energy, the deceased seeks to banish darkness and dispel the metaphorical night, embracing the transformative and life-giving qualities of the sun.

The deceased recognizes themselves as a vessel for Ra's radiant grace, forever connected in a sacred space. They trust in the continuous flow of Ra's life-giving energy, which revitalizes their being and lifts them to higher realms of existence.

The spell concludes with gratitude and acceptance of the life-giving energy from Ra. The deceased acknowledges that it is through Ra's blessings that they shall forever thrive in the afterlife, where eternal life is derived from the radiant sun.

So mote it be, let the spell be done, as the deceased receives life from the radiant sun, and with Ra's blessings, they shall forever thrive in the eternal realms of the afterlife.

CT 76: Spell for Communion with the Gods: Facilitating communication and interaction between the deceased and the divine beings in the afterlife.

Utterance:
"Oh, divine beings of the afterlife,
Hear my call, heed my strife.
Grant me the gift of communion divine,
That I may converse with you, align.

I seek to bridge the realms so vast,
To connect with you, the divine cast.
Open the doors to your celestial abode,
Allow me to enter, in your presence I'll bode.

With reverence and devotion, I draw near,
To commune with you, spirits so dear.
Grant me the ability to perceive and comprehend,
The wisdom you impart, may it transcend.

In this spell, I beseech your grace,
To create a sacred, divine space.
Open my senses to your presence sublime,
Let our communion stand the test of time.

Grant me the gift of divine speech,
To converse with you, hear and teach.
Through the language of symbols and signs,
May your guidance fill my celestial shrines.

By your grace, I seek to understand,
The mysteries of the cosmos, vast and grand.
Guide my thoughts, illuminate my mind,
So that divine wisdom I may find.

I offer my heart, open and true,
In this sacred communion with you.
May our connection be pure and clear,
As I seek your guidance, ever near.

In this spell for communion with the gods,

I invoke your presence, bless me with nods.
Grant me the honor of divine interaction,
As we converse in the afterlife's sacred fraction.

So mote it be, let the spell be done,
As I commune with the gods, becoming one.
With gratitude and reverence, I reach out,
To embrace the divine, beyond any doubt."

In this spell for communion with the gods, the deceased calls upon the divine beings of the afterlife, seeking the gift of communication and interaction. They express their desire to bridge the realms and establish a connection with the divine cast.

The deceased humbly asks the gods to open the doors to their celestial abode, allowing them to enter and be in their divine presence. They approach the gods with reverence and devotion, seeking the ability to perceive and comprehend their wisdom that transcends mortal understanding.

The spell entreats the gods to grant the gift of divine speech, enabling the deceased to converse with them, to hear their teachings and guidance. They seek to communicate through the language of symbols and signs, hoping to create a sacred and divine space for their communion.

The deceased acknowledges the gods' role as the givers of wisdom and mysteries of the cosmos. They request that the gods guide their thoughts and illuminate their mind, so they may gain divine wisdom and understanding.

With an open heart, the deceased offers themselves in this sacred communion, seeking a pure and clear connection with the gods. They express their gratitude and honor in being able to interact with the divine beings in the afterlife.

The spell concludes with the assurance that the communion with the gods will be established and cherished. The deceased acknowledges the oneness they seek with the gods, becoming united in this divine interaction.

So mote it be, let the spell be done, as the deceased communes with the gods, becoming one with their presence. With gratitude and reverence, they reach out, embracing the divine in the realms of the afterlife.

CT 78: Spell for Warding off Chaos and Disorder: Providing protection against chaotic forces and disturbances in the afterlife realm.

Utterance:
"O guardians of order, hear my plea,
In this realm where chaos seeks to prevail.
Protect me from the forces of disorder,
And let harmony and balance forever prevail.

From the depths of darkness, chaos arises,
With tumultuous waves and relentless storms.
I beseech you, mighty guardians of order,
Shield me from its grasp, keep me safe and warm.

Let not the winds of discord scatter my path,
Nor the flames of turmoil consume my soul.
With your power, create a shield of protection,
That chaos may not harm me, nor take its toll.

May the order of Ma'at surround me,
A divine barrier against all chaotic might.
Let its balance be my armor and my strength,
Guiding me through the shadows, leading to the light.

By the authority of the gods, I invoke their names,
Set, Horus, Thoth, and the great Osiris divine.
Let their strength and wisdom be my shield,
Against chaos' forces, unyielding and malign.

I call upon the sacred symbols of order,
The ankh, the djed, the eye of Horus, and the feather.
May their power repel chaos and disorder,
And ensure my safety in this realm and forever.

Grant me the clarity to navigate the chaotic waters,
The serenity to withstand the tempest's rage.
With your guidance, I shall emerge unscathed,
As chaos retreats and order takes center stage.

O guardians of order, I trust in your might,
To ward off chaos and its destructive sway.

With your protection, I embrace the harmony,
And in the afterlife, I shall find my way.

In this spell for warding off chaos and disorder, the deceased implores the guardians of order to protect them from the forces of chaos and disturbances in the afterlife realm. The utterance begins by addressing the guardians of order and acknowledging their role in maintaining balance and harmony.

The deceased expresses the desire for protection against chaos, which arises from the depths of darkness and seeks to disrupt the divine order. They appeal to the guardians to shield them from chaotic forces and disturbances, ensuring their safety and well-being in the afterlife.

The spell calls upon the power of the guardians to create a shield of protection, preventing the winds of discord and the flames of turmoil from causing harm. The order of Ma'at, symbolizing balance and harmony, is invoked as a divine barrier against chaos, guiding the deceased through the shadows and leading them towards enlightenment.

The deceased invokes the names of the gods, including Set, Horus, Thoth, and Osiris, seeking their strength and wisdom to serve as their shield against chaos. The sacred symbols of order, such as the ankh, the djed, the eye of Horus, and the feather, are called upon to repel chaos and ensure the safety of the deceased.

With the guidance and protection of the guardians of order, the deceased trusts in their might to ward off chaos and its destructive influence. They embrace the harmony and serenity that comes with order, knowing that it will lead them on their path in the afterlife.

Through this spell, the deceased seeks the assurance of protection against chaos and disturbances in the afterlife realm. It reflects the belief in the importance of maintaining order and balance, even in the face of chaotic forces.

CT 79: Spell for Rejuvenation of the Body: Granting the deceased the restoration and revitalization of their physical form in the afterlife.

Utterance:
"O divine healers, hear my plea,
In this realm of eternal existence.
Grant me the gift of rejuvenation,
To restore my body with divine persistence.

From the weariness of mortal life,
I seek liberation and renewal.
Let my physical form be revitalized,
In this realm where eternity is fueled.

With your ancient wisdom and sacred touch,
Breathe life into my weary bones.
Revive my limbs with vigor and strength,
As my spirit soars and forever roams.

Let the essence of life flow through me,
Like a river of vitality and youth.
Banish the signs of age and decay,
And restore my body to its prime, forsooth.

O healers of the divine realms,
Unlock the secrets of rejuvenation.
Through your power and sacred knowledge,
Grant me eternal restoration.

With each passing day, let my body thrive,
Renewed, revitalized, and whole.
Let the radiance of youth envelop me,
As I traverse the afterlife's infinite scroll.

Grant me the strength to explore and engage,
In this realm where possibilities are vast.
With a rejuvenated body, I embark,
On a journey that forever will last.

In this spell for the rejuvenation of the body, the deceased implores the divine healers to grant them the restoration and revitalization of their physical form in the afterlife. The utterance begins by addressing the healers and seeking their intervention in the realm of eternal existence.

The deceased expresses their desire to be liberated from the weariness of mortal life and seeks the rejuvenation of their physical body. They ask the healers to breathe life into their bones, reviving their limbs with vigor and strength as their spirit soars through the eternal realms.

The spell calls upon the healers to let the essence of life flow through the deceased, rejuvenating them like a river of vitality and youth. The aim is to banish the signs of age and decay, restoring the body to its prime state.

The healers are implored to unlock the secrets of rejuvenation, drawing upon their ancient wisdom and sacred touch. The spell beseeches them to grant the deceased eternal restoration, ensuring their body remains in a state of perpetual renewal.

The deceased seeks the divine healers' intervention to thrive in the afterlife, with a revitalized and rejuvenated body. They envision themselves exploring the infinite possibilities of the afterlife with renewed strength and radiance.

Through this spell, the deceased seeks the restoration and revitalization of their physical form in the afterlife. It reflects the belief in the power of divine healing and the desire for eternal youth and vitality in the realm beyond mortal life.

CT 80: Spell for Unity with the Ennead: Facilitating the union and integration of the deceased's essence with the nine gods of the Ennead.

Utterance:
"O gods of the Ennead, hear my plea,
In this realm of the eternal divine.
I seek unity and integration,
To merge my essence with yours, sublime.

From the realms of the afterlife, I call,
To the nine gods, glorious and grand.
May our essences intertwine and unite,
As I stand before your divine command.

Osiris, ruler of the underworld,
With your wisdom and regal might.
Horus, falcon-headed god of protection,
Grant me your strength, shining bright.

Isis, goddess of magic and healing,
Infuse me with your nurturing embrace.
Nephthys, guardian of the deceased,
Surround me with your gentle grace.

Thoth, keeper of knowledge and writing,
Guide me with your sacred wisdom.
Ptah, creator of all, with your hands divine,
Shape my essence in the eternal rhythm.

Geb, god of the earth and fertility,
Ground me in your nurturing embrace.
Nut, goddess of the sky, vast and infinite,
Envelop me in your celestial grace.

And lastly, Ra, the radiant sun god,
With your fiery light and divine flame.
Merge my essence with your eternal radiance,
And forevermore, in your glory, I proclaim.

May our essences unite as one,

As I journey through the afterlife's domain.
In harmony with the gods of the Ennead,
In their divine presence, I shall remain.

Through this spell, I seek unity and integration with the gods of the Ennead, the nine divine entities of ancient Egyptian mythology. The utterance addresses each deity individually, calling upon their specific qualities and powers.

The deceased invokes Osiris, the ruler of the underworld, and seeks his wisdom and regal might. Horus, the falcon-headed god of protection, is implored to grant strength and guardianship.

Isis, the goddess of magic and healing, is called upon to infuse the deceased with nurturing and restorative energy. Nephthys, the guardian of the deceased, is requested to surround the individual with gentle grace.

Thoth, the keeper of knowledge and writing, is invoked for guidance and wisdom. Ptah, the creator of all, is asked to shape the essence of the deceased in alignment with the eternal rhythm.

Geb, the god of the earth and fertility, is called upon to ground the deceased in a nurturing embrace. Nut, the goddess of the sky, is asked to envelop the individual in her celestial grace.

Lastly, Ra, the radiant sun god, is invoked to merge the essence of the deceased with his eternal radiance. The spell concludes with the affirmation of unity and eternal presence in the company of the gods of the Ennead.

Through this spell, the deceased seeks a profound connection with the nine gods of the Ennead, aiming for unity and integration with their divine essences. It reflects the belief in the divine hierarchy and the desire to align one's spirit with the eternal powers that govern the afterlife.

CT 81: Spell for Protection against Snake Bites: Safeguarding the deceased from venomous snake bites and the dangers associated with serpents.

Utterance:
"Serpents and vipers, slithering and sly,
In the afterlife's realm, I pass you by.
With this spell, I seek protection and ward,
From venomous fangs, I am safely guarded.

O mighty gods, hear my plea,
Grant me the power to repel and flee.
Protect me from serpents' venomous strike,
Shield me from their danger, day and night.

I call upon the guardians of the divine,
To encircle me with their protective line.
Bastet, lioness goddess of protection,
Wrap your strength around me without hesitation.

Wadjet, serpent goddess of ancient lore,
Guide me safely, keep me evermore.
Wrap your coils around me, a shield so strong,
Deflecting venomous bites, keeping me from wrong.

Horus, falcon-headed god of divine sight,
Watch over me, guide me with your light.
Grant me keen senses to perceive the danger,
To avoid the serpents, like a skilled ranger.

With this spell, I am immune to harm,
No serpent's bite can cause alarm.
Their venom shall not pierce my skin,
Their fangs repelled, their venom thinned.

By the power of these words, I proclaim,
Protection against snakes, I now reclaim.
In the afterlife's realm, I shall prevail,
Safe from their venom, I shall never fail.

Through this spell, the deceased invokes the power of protection against snake bites in the afterlife. The utterance acknowledges the dangers of venomous snakes and seeks safeguarding from their bites.

The deceased calls upon the gods, specifically Bastet, the lioness goddess of protection, and Wadjet, the serpent goddess of ancient lore. They request the strength of Bastet to wrap around them, providing a powerful shield, and the guidance and defense of Wadjet to keep them safe from harm.

Horus, the falcon-headed god associated with divine sight, is invoked for his watchful presence and guidance. The deceased asks for keen senses to perceive danger and avoid encounters with serpents.

The spell asserts the immunity of the deceased against harm from snake bites, proclaiming that no serpent's venom can penetrate their skin. By the power of the spell's words, the deceased claims protection and safety from snake-related dangers in the afterlife realm.

This spell reflects the ancient Egyptian belief in the protective powers of the gods and their ability to shield individuals from harm. It demonstrates the reverence and reliance on divine assistance to navigate the perils of the afterlife, specifically safeguarding against the dangers associated with venomous snakes.

CT 82: Spell for Transformation into a Celestial Bird: Allowing the deceased to transform into a celestial bird, symbolizing transcendence and freedom.

Utterance:
"From earthly bounds, I now take flight,
Transformed into a celestial bird, shining bright.
With wings spread wide, I soar high above,
Symbol of transcendence, freedom, and love.

O divine spirits, hear my plea,
Grant me the power to be truly free.
Transform me into a bird of the celestial sky,
With feathers of radiant hues that catch the eye.

I shed my mortal form, my earthly ties,
And embrace a new existence that reaches the skies.
Let my body become light, graceful, and sleek,
As I embark on a journey that's boundless and unique.

Grant me wings that span wide and strong,
To carry me swiftly, where I belong.
With every beat, let me rise higher and higher,
Drawing closer to realms that ignite celestial fire.

As a celestial bird, I am no longer bound,
No earthly chains can hold me down.
I traverse the heavens, embracing the sublime,
Feeling the currents of eternity, transcending time.

In this transformation, I find liberation's embrace,
As I become a celestial bird, full of grace.
I soar among the stars, dancing with the moon,
A symbol of transcendence, in the afterlife's boon.

By the power of this spell, I take flight,
A celestial bird, shining in radiant light.
I embrace my freedom, my spirit unconfined,
Transformed and transcendent, forever aligned.

Through this spell, the deceased seeks the transformation into a celestial bird, symbolizing transcendence and freedom in the afterlife. The utterance expresses the desire to be released from earthly constraints and to soar high above, representing a spiritual journey beyond mortal limitations.

The deceased addresses the divine spirits, requesting their intervention to grant the power to become a celestial bird. They envision wings spread wide, adorned with radiant feathers that capture the eye and symbolize the transformative nature of their new existence.

The spell entails shedding the mortal form and embracing a lighter, more graceful existence. The deceased yearns for wings that are strong and expansive, enabling them to swiftly traverse the celestial realms and draw closer to the sublime.

As a celestial bird, the deceased experiences liberation from earthly bonds, rising higher and higher toward realms that ignite celestial fire. They find freedom from the constraints of time and space, embracing a journey that is boundless and unique.

The spell affirms the transformation into a celestial bird, embracing the liberation and grace that comes with it. The deceased soars among the stars, dances with the moon, and becomes a symbol of transcendence and freedom in the afterlife's realm.

Through the power of the spell, the deceased takes flight as a celestial bird, shining in radiant light. They embrace their newfound freedom and transcendence, forever aligned with the divine and eternally connected to the celestial realms.

CT 83: Spell for Receiving Life Breath from the Sun Disk: Ensuring that the deceased continues to receive the life-giving breath from the solar disk.

Utterance:
"O radiant Sun, source of life and light,
I beseech thee, grant me thy life breath's might.
From thy golden disk, let thy rays descend,
Bestow upon me life, that knows no end.

As I dwell in the afterlife's embrace,
I seek thy life-giving breath, thy divine grace.
Fill my being with thy vital essence,
Renew and sustain me with thy presence.

O Sun Disk, radiant and supreme,
Let thy life-giving rays forever gleam.
Breathe into me the breath of eternal life,
Banishing darkness, dispelling all strife.

With each dawn, let thy energy revive,
Every sunset, keep my spirit alive.
Nourish me, like the earth by thy warm glow,
In thy life-giving embrace, may I forever grow.

From the eastern horizon, thou dost arise,
Illuminating the heavens and earthly skies.
Grant me the strength to face each new day,
With the power of thy life breath, I shall not sway.

In the afterlife's realm, I seek thy divine embrace,
Thy life-giving breath, my eternal solace.
Infuse me with vitality, with boundless energy,
As I journey through the realms of eternity.

By the power of this spell, I call upon thee,
O Sun Disk, source of life, to grant me thee.
Fill me with thy life-giving breath divine,
That my spirit may forever shine.

In this spell for receiving life breath from the Sun Disk, the deceased appeals to the radiant Sun and its life-giving energy. The utterance acknowledges the Sun as the source of life and light, and the deceased seeks to receive the vital essence that sustains and renews their existence.

The deceased addresses the Sun Disk, envisioning its rays descending upon them and infusing their being with the life breath's might. They recognize the importance of this breath in the afterlife, where it provides continuous life and dispels darkness and strife.

The spell invokes the radiant and supreme nature of the Sun Disk, calling upon it to forever shine and bestow its life-giving rays. The deceased seeks to be filled with the essence of eternal life, drawing parallels between the Sun's nourishment of the earth and the sustaining of their spirit in the afterlife.

The utterance acknowledges the cyclical nature of the Sun, referencing the daily rise and set, and requests the ongoing renewal and sustenance of their spirit. The deceased seeks the strength to face each new day and the assurance that their spirit will remain alive in the afterlife.

By the power of the spell, the deceased calls upon the Sun Disk to infuse them with vitality and boundless energy. They seek to be forever embraced by its life-giving breath, ensuring that their spirit shines eternally in the realms of eternity.

Through this spell, the deceased establishes a connection with the life-giving energy of the Sun Disk, seeking its ongoing infusion of vitality and sustenance in the afterlife. They recognize the transformative power of the Sun's breath, ensuring their eternal existence and radiance.

CT 84: Spell for Illumination of the Underworld: Providing the deceased with divine light and illumination in the depths of the underworld.

Utterance:
"O divine light, guide me through the depths,
In the underworld, where darkness creeps.
Illuminate my path with your radiant glow,
That I may navigate the realms below.

In this realm of shadows and obscurity,
I seek your divine light's luminosity.
Pierce through the darkness, banish its veil,
Reveal the secrets of the underworld's tale.

Shine forth, O light, with brilliance and might,
Dispel the shadows, bring clarity to my sight.
Illumine the hidden paths and winding ways,
That I may traverse with confidence and praise.

From the heavens above, let your radiance descend,
To the depths of the underworld, where spirits blend.
Guide me, O light, with your celestial flame,
That I may honor my destiny without fear or shame.

With each step I take, let your glow grow bright,
Revealing the wonders concealed in this eternal night.
Illuminate the knowledge and wisdom held within,
That I may gain insight and understanding therein.

O divine light, envelop me with your grace,
Fill the underworld's expanse with your embrace.
Lead me towards transcendence and eternal peace,
As I journey through this realm, may your light never cease.

By the power of this spell, I call upon thee,
O divine light, to shine and illuminate me.
In the depths of the underworld, where darkness resides,
Guide my spirit with your radiant light as my guide.

In this spell for illumination of the underworld, the deceased seeks divine light and illumination to navigate the depths of the underworld. The utterance acknowledges the presence of darkness and obscurity in the underworld and calls upon the divine light to guide their path.

The deceased beseeches the divine light to shine with brilliance and might, dispelling the shadows and revealing the secrets of the underworld. They acknowledge the need for clarity and guidance as they traverse the hidden paths and winding ways of this realm.

The spell calls for the light to descend from the heavens above, penetrating the depths of the underworld. The divine light is invoked to guide the deceased with its celestial flame, allowing them to honor their destiny without fear or shame.

With each step taken, the deceased seeks the growing brightness of the divine light, unveiling the wonders concealed in the eternal night of the underworld. They seek illumination not only of the physical paths but also of the knowledge and wisdom held within this realm.

The deceased appeals to the divine light to envelop them with grace and fill the expanse of the underworld with its embrace. They seek guidance towards transcendence and eternal peace as they journey through this realm, trusting that the light will never cease.

Through the power of the spell, the deceased calls upon the divine light to shine and illuminate them in the depths of the underworld. They acknowledge the light as their guide and source of illumination, allowing them to navigate the spiritual realms with clarity and purpose.

CT 85: Spell for Protection against Demonic Forces: Safeguarding the deceased from demonic entities and negative forces in the afterlife.

Utterance:
"By the power of divine light and sacred decree,
I invoke protection from demonic forces, hear my plea.
In the afterlife's realms, where darkness may reside,
I call upon divine guardians to stand by my side.

O mighty protectors, with strength and divine might,
Shield me from the demons that haunt the night.
Wrap me in your protective embrace and power,
Defend me in this sacred hour.

I summon the forces of purity and light,
To banish darkness and keep me from fright.
May the divine radiance surround me like a shield,
Repelling all evil, ensuring I'm concealed.

In this realm beyond the mortal plane,
I seek refuge from demons, their presence I disdain.
Let their malevolence and negativity be vanquished,
As I navigate the afterlife, forever cherished.

I am protected by the divine forces above,
Guarded by their unconditional love.
With their power and presence, I am secure,
Shielded from demonic forces, pure and sure.

By the authority of this spell, I affirm my protection,
No demon or negative force shall gain traction.
I walk the afterlife's path with confidence and might,
Guided and guarded by the divine light.

May this spell resonate in the realms unseen,
Protecting me from all that is wicked and mean.
I am shielded from demonic influence and harm,
Safe in the embrace of divine guardians' charm.

By the power of divine protection, this spell is cast,

Securing my existence in the afterlife vast.
With gratitude and trust, I embrace this divine shield,
Protected from demons, my spirit forever healed."

In this spell for protection against demonic forces, the deceased calls upon the power of divine light and invokes the aid of divine protectors to safeguard them from demonic entities and negative forces in the afterlife.

The utterance emphasizes the desire for protection and invokes the presence of mighty protectors to stand by the side of the deceased. They seek the shield of these guardians and the strength of their divine might to ward off the demons that may haunt the afterlife realms.

The spell summons the forces of purity and light to banish darkness and ensure the protection of the deceased. It requests the divine radiance to surround the individual as a shield, repelling all evil and providing concealment from harm.

The deceased affirms their refuge from demons and expresses their disdain for the presence of malevolence and negativity. They call upon the divine forces to vanquish and remove these influences as they navigate the afterlife.

The spell asserts the protection of the deceased by the divine forces above and acknowledges the unconditional love and power that safeguards them. It affirms their security and ensures their shield from demonic forces.

Through the authority of the spell, the deceased declares their protection and affirms that no demon or negative force shall gain traction in their existence. They walk the afterlife's path with confidence and might, guided and guarded by the divine light.

The spell concludes with a proclamation of gratitude and trust in the divine shield, recognizing the eternal healing and protection it provides. The deceased expresses their assurance of being protected from demons, allowing their spirit to find solace and peace in the afterlife.

CT 86: Spell for Transformation into a Sacred Bull: Granting the deceased the ability to transform into a sacred bull, symbolizing power and strength.

Utterance:
"I call upon the ancient powers divine,
Grant me the transformation into a sacred bull, a form sublime.
In the afterlife's realms, I seek strength and might,
To navigate its challenges with power and light.

I invoke the spirit of the sacred bull,
Symbol of power, strength, and valor full.
Grant me its attributes, noble and grand,
As I traverse the afterlife, a formidable presence I command.

Let my body be adorned with majestic horns,
A symbol of authority, as ancient lore adorns.
Cloak me in the aura of raw strength and force,
A divine manifestation, a bull's form I endorse.

Grant me the stamina of a thousand suns,
The vitality to endure, when the journey's begun.
With each step, let my hooves resonate,
Resounding power, announcing my fate.

In this transformation, I seek divine grace,
To embody the sacred bull's majestic embrace.
Grant me power, courage, and resilience untold,
As I navigate the afterlife's mysteries, bold.

May my presence inspire awe and respect,
As the sacred bull, my essence reflects.
Grant me the strength to overcome any trial,
With the spirit of the bull, I shall never waver or recoil.

In this transformation, I find empowerment divine,
A symbol of power and strength that shall forever shine.
I embrace the noble form of the sacred bull,
In the afterlife's realm, a majestic presence to rule.

By the ancient forces and divine decree,

I am transformed, a sacred bull, to be.
With power and might, I navigate the unknown,
Embodying strength and greatness as I've sown.

In this spell of transformation, I embrace the essence of the sacred bull, seeking its power, strength, and nobility. The utterance calls upon the ancient powers to grant the ability to transform into this revered symbol, embodying its attributes and qualities.

The spell invokes the spirit of the sacred bull as a symbol of power, strength, and valor. It seeks to be adorned with majestic horns, representing authority and ancient wisdom. The transformation into a bull form is seen as a divine manifestation, commanding a formidable presence in the afterlife.

The spell implores for the stamina and vitality of a thousand suns, enabling the endurance and resilience required for the journey ahead. The bull's hooves are invoked to resonate with power, announcing the presence of the transformed individual.

In this transformation, the spell seeks divine grace to embody the noble qualities of the sacred bull. Power, courage, and resilience are sought to overcome any trial faced in the afterlife. The presence of the transformed individual is expected to inspire awe and respect, commanding authority and strength.

The spell concludes with a recognition of the empowerment and divine significance of the transformation. The individual embraces the noble form of the sacred bull and acknowledges their embodiment of strength and greatness. With the spirit of the bull, they navigate the afterlife's realms with power and confidence.

CT 87: Spell for Receiving Offerings from the Living: Ensuring that the deceased continues to receive offerings and provisions from the living.

Utterance:
"From the realm of the living, I call upon thee,
To bestow offerings and provisions upon me.
In the afterlife's embrace, I still have need,
To receive sustenance and blessings indeed.

Oh, generous souls, hear my plea,
Extend your hands in offerings to me.
From the land of the living, bring forth,
Abundance and provisions of great worth.

Let the fragrant incense rise in the air,
A symbol of devotion, a sacred prayer.
Bring forth the food, the drink, the delights,
To nourish my spirit in eternal nights.

From the hands of the living, let offerings flow,
With love and reverence, that they may bestow.
Fruits, grains, and delicacies divine,
Symbols of care, as in life's prime.

Let libations pour forth, sweet and pure,
Quenching my thirst, an offering sure.
From the living's hands, let blessings rain,
Sustenance and provisions, an eternal gain.

Oh, kindred spirits, let your love abound,
In the afterlife's realm, let offerings surround.
Bring forth your gifts with heartfelt intent,
To sustain my spirit, forever content.

As I dwell in the afterlife's eternal abode,
May offerings from the living continue to unfold.
With gratitude, I receive each precious gift,
From the living's realm, a connection, a lift.

In this spell for receiving offerings from the living, the deceased reaches out to the generous souls in the realm of the living, appealing for their continued provisions and blessings. The utterance acknowledges the ongoing need for sustenance and blessings in the afterlife.

The spell calls upon the generous souls to extend their hands and bring forth offerings and provisions to the deceased. It emphasizes the importance of the offerings from the land of the living, symbolizing care, love, and reverence. The fragrance of incense is invoked as a symbol of devotion and a sacred prayer.

The deceased seeks a variety of offerings, including food, drink, fruits, grains, and delicacies, to nourish their spirit in the eternal nights of the afterlife. The pouring of libations is requested to quench their thirst and serve as a symbolic offering of love and care.

The spell appeals to the kindred spirits of the living, asking for their love and abundance to surround the deceased in the afterlife. It encourages the continuous flow of offerings from the living's hands, recognizing them as a connection between the realms and a source of sustenance and provision.

The deceased expresses gratitude for each precious gift received from the living. The offerings serve as a vital connection and a means of support, ensuring the well-being and contentment of the spirit in the eternal abode of the afterlife.

With this spell, the deceased seeks the assurance that offerings and provisions from the living will continue to be bestowed upon them in the afterlife. It reflects the belief in the ongoing connection between the realms and the importance of support and sustenance from the living for the eternal journey of the spirit.

CT 88: Spell for Becoming a Dweller of the Horizon: Allowing the deceased to take their place among the divine dwellers of the horizon.

Utterance:
"Oh, divine dwellers of the horizon, I beseech thee,
Grant me the privilege to join your company.
In the afterlife's realm, let me find my place,
As a dweller of the horizon, adorned with grace.

With each sunrise, I seek to transcend,
To the realm where the divine ones ascend.
Grant me the wings to soar to the skies,
To dwell among the radiant ones, so wise.

Let my spirit merge with the golden rays,
As I become one with the sun's fiery blaze.
Grant me the light of divine illumination,
As I join the dwellers of the horizon in adoration.

In their presence, I will find solace and might,
Embraced by their celestial, resplendent light.
Grant me the knowledge of their wisdom profound,
As I take my place among the holy ground.

May I embody their grace and majesty,
As a dweller of the horizon, eternally.
Clothed in radiance, with spirits divine,
Let me join their ranks, in their realm I'll shine.

Oh, dwellers of the horizon, hear my plea,
Open the gates, and welcome me.
Grant me the honor to join your exalted state,
As I embrace my destiny, divinely great.

With gratitude and reverence, I call upon thee,
To guide me to where I'm destined to be.
A dweller of the horizon, forever blessed,
Among the divine ones, in eternal rest.

In this spell for becoming a dweller of the horizon, the deceased appeals to the divine dwellers of the horizon, seeking their permission and granting them the privilege to join their company. The utterance expresses the desire to transcend to the realm where the divine ones ascend, adorned with grace and wisdom.

The spell asks for the wings to soar to the skies and merge with the golden rays of the sun, symbolizing unity with the divine and the radiant light of illumination. The deceased seeks to join the dwellers of the horizon, finding solace, might, and the knowledge of their profound wisdom.

The spell expresses the aspiration to embody the grace and majesty of the dwellers of the horizon, to be eternally clothed in radiance and united with spirits divine. It calls upon the dwellers of the horizon to open the gates and welcome the deceased, granting them the honor to join their exalted state.

The deceased approaches the dwellers of the horizon with gratitude, reverence, and a sense of destiny. They seek guidance and the fulfillment of their divine purpose, to take their place among the dwellers of the horizon, shining in the realm of the divine ones in eternal rest.

Through this spell, the deceased seeks to be recognized and embraced by the divine dwellers of the horizon, to transcend mortal limitations and join the ranks of the radiant and wise. It reflects the aspiration for spiritual elevation and the pursuit of eternal greatness among the celestial realms.

CT 89: Spell for Reunion with the Body: Facilitating the reunion of the deceased's spirit with their physical body in the afterlife.

Utterance:
"Oh, spirit reunited with the earthly shell,
I call upon the forces that dwell.
Grant me the union I seek so true,
To reunite my spirit with the body I once knew.

From realms beyond, I make my plea,
To the divine powers, I bend my knee.
Guide me back to my mortal form,
In the afterlife's realm, let the reunion be born.

By the sacred breath, let my essence flow,
To the vessel that held me long ago.
Rekindle the bond that time has erased,
And grant my spirit the warmth of embrace.

With every heartbeat, let my spirit align,
With the vessel that was once mine.
Revive the senses that have lain still,
Let my spirit and body fulfill.

Grant me the sight to behold the light,
The touch to feel, both gentle and slight.
Let my voice resound, clear and strong,
And let my footsteps echo where I belong.

By the power of this sacred rite,
Reunite my spirit with the body's might.
In the afterlife's realm, let the union take place,
And grant me the essence of divine grace.

Oh, forces that govern the afterlife's domain,
Unite my spirit with the body again.
Grant me the reunion I yearn to find,
In the afterlife's embrace, let my spirit bind.

With gratitude and reverence, I beseech thee,

To facilitate this sacred reunion for me.
Let my spirit and body become one,
As I journey through the afterlife's sun.

In this spell for the reunion with the body, the deceased calls upon the forces that dwell in the realms beyond, seeking their guidance and assistance in reuniting the spirit with the physical body. The utterance expresses the longing to restore the bond that time has erased and to experience the warmth of embrace once more.

The spell invokes the sacred breath and the divine powers to facilitate the flow of the spirit back into the vessel that once held it. It seeks to revive the senses and awaken the dormant connection between the spirit and body, allowing them to fulfill their inherent purpose.

The spell asks for the restoration of sight, touch, voice, and footsteps, enabling the deceased to fully engage with the physical realm once again. It recognizes the power of the sacred rite to reunite the spirit with the body, invoking the essence of divine grace.

The deceased humbly appeals to the forces that govern the afterlife, expressing gratitude and reverence. They yearn for the sacred reunion to take place, where their spirit and body become one, allowing them to journey through the afterlife's realm with newfound unity.

Through this spell, the deceased seeks to reclaim their physical form and experience the union of spirit and body in the afterlife. It reflects the desire for wholeness, restoration, and the fulfillment of the complete human experience even beyond mortal existence.

CT 90: Spell for Warding off Nightmares: Providing protection against nightmares, disturbances, and malevolent influences during sleep in the afterlife.

Utterance:
"Oh, spirits of the night, I beseech your aid,
Protect me from nightmares and fears that invade.
In the realm of slumber, where shadows dance,
Grant me your protection, a safeguarding trance.

Banish the terrors that haunt my dreams,
Cast them away, as moonlight gleams.
Wrap me in your ethereal embrace,
Shield me from nightmares, leave no trace.

By the power of this sacred plea,
Ward off the darkness, set my spirit free.
Protect me from malevolent forces that creep,
While I'm immersed in the realm of sleep.

Let peaceful visions fill my mind,
Where tranquility and serenity I find.
Guide me to realms of joy and light,
Where nightmares dissolve, banished from sight.

May your presence be a shield so strong,
Defending me as I slumber long.
With your divine essence, nightmares subside,
And tranquility in my dreams resides.

Oh, spirits of the night, hear my cry,
Protect my spirit as the night draws nigh.
By your grace, let restful sleep unfold,
And nightmares vanish, no longer bold.

With gratitude, I embrace your might,
In the afterlife's realm, where dreams take flight.
May your watchful presence never wane,
Shielding me from nightmares, fear's domain.

In this spell for warding off nightmares, the deceased appeals to the spirits of the night, seeking their aid and protection against disturbances and malevolent influences that infiltrate the realm of sleep. The utterance acknowledges the power of these spirits to banish the terrors that haunt dreams and create a safe space for rest.

The spell implores the spirits to cast away the darkness and wrap the deceased in their ethereal embrace, shielding them from nightmares and eradicating any traces of fear. It calls upon the spirits to banish malevolent forces that may creep into the realm of sleep and disrupt the peaceful state of the dreamer.

The spell requests the presence of peaceful visions and guides the deceased to realms of joy and light, where nightmares dissolve and tranquility reigns. It acknowledges the protective power of the spirits, their ability to defend the spirit during slumber and ensure that nightmares fade away.

The deceased expresses gratitude for the spirits' assistance, recognizing their might and the importance of their watchful presence. They trust in the spirits' ability to shield them from nightmares and preserve a sense of peace and serenity in the afterlife's realm of dreams.

Through this spell, the deceased seeks a restful sleep free from nightmares and disturbances, finding solace and tranquility in the realm of dreams. It reflects the understanding of the significance of a peaceful rest and the need for protection against negative influences, even in the afterlife.

CT 91: Spell for Receiving Nourishment from the Sky: Ensuring that the deceased is provided with divine nourishment and sustenance from the sky.

Utterance:
"Oh, celestial realm above, bestow upon me,
The divine nourishment from your bountiful sea.
Grant me sustenance from the heavens high,
To nourish my spirit as it soars in the sky.

From the vast expanse where stars reside,
Let celestial sustenance for me preside.
Pour forth the nectar of celestial dew,
The ambrosia of gods, refreshing and true.

As the sun traverses its radiant arc,
Let its rays imbue me with nourishment spark.
Bathe me in its golden light divine,
Revitalizing my spirit, making it shine.

From the celestial fruits, let me partake,
Their essence, a divine feast, I gratefully take.
May their flavors enchant and their essence revive,
Sustaining my spirit as I thrive and survive.

Like the raindrops that fall from the heavens' gate,
Let the celestial nourishment on me grate.
Quench my thirst with the waters pure,
The elixir of life, a gift I procure.

Oh, celestial realm, shower upon me,
The sustenance of gods, abundant and free.
With each heavenly morsel that I consume,
May my spirit be nourished, never to be consumed.

I thank you, celestial realm, for your grace,
For providing me with nourishment in this sacred space.
As I journey through the afterlife's domain,
Let your divine sustenance forever sustain.

In this spell for receiving nourishment from the sky, the deceased calls upon the celestial realm above to provide them with divine nourishment and sustenance. The utterance invokes the heavens and seeks their blessings to nourish the spirit as it soars in the sky.

The spell asks for celestial sustenance from the vast expanse where stars reside. It requests the pouring forth of nectar and ambrosia, the food and drink of the gods, which will refresh and revitalize the spirit.

The deceased seeks to be bathed in the golden light of the sun, drawing upon its radiant energy for nourishment and revitalization. They express the desire to partake in celestial fruits, savoring their flavors and embracing their essence as a divine feast.

The spell invokes the raindrops that fall from the heavens as a metaphor for receiving the celestial nourishment. It requests the quenching of thirst with pure waters, the elixir of life that replenishes and sustains the spirit.

The deceased expresses gratitude to the celestial realm for their grace and the provision of nourishment in the afterlife's sacred space. They acknowledge the ongoing sustenance that will support them on their journey through the realm of the afterlife.

Through this spell, the deceased seeks to be nourished by the divine essence of the celestial realm. It reflects the belief in the abundance and benevolence of the heavens and their role in sustaining the spirit in the afterlife.

CT 92: Spell for Transformation into a Celestial Navigator: Granting the deceased the ability to navigate the celestial realms and join the company of the gods.

Utterance:
"O celestial realms, hear my plea,
Grant me the gift of celestial navigation and decree.
Bestow upon me the ability to traverse the stars,
To join the company of the gods, no matter how far.

Transform my spirit into a celestial navigator,
With wings of light, let me soar and gather.
Grant me the knowledge of the cosmic paths,
To navigate the celestial realms, free from all wraths.

Like a shooting star, let me blaze a trail,
Through the vast expanse, I shall never fail.
Guide me with constellations' radiant light,
As I journey through the heavens, shining bright.

Grant me the wisdom to interpret the signs,
The celestial maps that guide the divine.
Let me read the language of the stars,
Unveiling the mysteries that lie afar.

May the celestial bodies be my compass true,
Leading me to the gods and their sacred crew.
In their company, let me find my place,
Embracing celestial grace, in their embrace.

Grant me the power to traverse the cosmic sea,
To dance among galaxies, forever free.
Let my spirit merge with the celestial tide,
As a celestial navigator, I shall forever abide.

I offer my gratitude to the celestial realms,
For the gift of celestial navigation that overwhelms.
With wings of light, I soar and ascend,
A celestial navigator, on a journey with no end.

In this spell for transformation into a celestial navigator, the deceased appeals to the celestial realms, seeking the ability to navigate the celestial realms and join the company of the gods. The utterance calls upon the celestial realms to bestow the gift of celestial navigation, allowing the spirit to traverse the stars and gather cosmic knowledge.

The spell invokes the transformation of the spirit into a celestial navigator, envisioning wings of light that enable soaring and gathering wisdom. The deceased asks for the knowledge of cosmic paths and the ability to navigate the celestial realms, guided by the radiant light of constellations.

The spell requests the wisdom to interpret the signs and read the language of the stars, unlocking the mysteries of the cosmos. The deceased seeks to follow the celestial bodies as a compass, leading them to the gods and their sacred company.

The spell expresses the desire to find a place among the gods, embracing their celestial grace and merging with the cosmic tide. The deceased envisions themselves as a celestial navigator, forever dancing among galaxies and experiencing the freedom of the celestial realms.

Gratitude is offered to the celestial realms for the bestowed gift of celestial navigation. The deceased acknowledges their newfound ability to soar and ascend as a celestial navigator, embarking on a limitless journey.

Through this spell, the deceased seeks to join the gods in the celestial realms as a celestial navigator. It reflects the aspiration to transcend earthly limitations, gain cosmic wisdom, and embrace the divine in the afterlife's spiritual realms.

CT 93: Spell for Receiving Life Water from the Celestial Ocean: Ensuring that the deceased continues to receive life-giving water from the celestial ocean.

Utterance:
"O celestial ocean, source of life,
From your depths, let me quench my eternal strife.
Grant me the gift of your life-giving water,
To nourish my spirit, forever stronger.

I call upon the celestial tides,
Where divine life energy forever resides.
Bring forth the waters of rejuvenation,
To replenish my essence, in eternal hydration.

Let the celestial ocean's waves cascade,
As I immerse myself in their luminous cascade.
May the water cleanse and purify my being,
Reviving my spirit, forever freeing.

In your depths, let the elixir of life reside,
With every sip, my spirit is fortified.
From the celestial ocean's boundless flow,
Sustenance and vitality, let it bestow.

As I drink from your celestial source,
Let the water of life reinforce.
Renew my spirit, invigorate my soul,
In your eternal embrace, make me whole.

I offer my gratitude to the celestial ocean,
For the gift of life and endless devotion.
With each sip, I am renewed and revived,
In harmony with the celestial waters, I thrive.

In this spell for receiving life water from the celestial ocean, the deceased calls upon the celestial ocean, seeking the life-giving water to nourish their eternal existence. The utterance acknowledges the celestial ocean as the source of life and requests the gift of its life-giving water to quench the eternal thirst of the spirit.

The spell invokes the celestial tides and the depths of the celestial ocean, where divine life energy resides. The deceased seeks the waters of rejuvenation, envisioning their spirit being nourished and strengthened by the luminous cascade of the celestial waves. The water is seen as a purifying and cleansing force, reviving the spirit and setting it free.

The spell entreats the celestial ocean to bring forth the elixir of life, with each sip fortifying the spirit and replenishing its essence. The celestial ocean is seen as an eternal source of sustenance and vitality, providing the necessary nourishment for the spirit's eternal existence.

Gratitude is offered to the celestial ocean for the gift of life and devotion. The deceased recognizes the transformative power of drinking from the celestial source, acknowledging its role in renewing and reviving their spirit. They embrace the harmonious connection with the celestial waters, thriving in their eternal embrace.

Through this spell, the deceased seeks to receive the life-giving water from the celestial ocean, ensuring the continuous nourishment and vitality of their spirit. It reflects the belief in the essentiality of celestial sustenance and the eternal connection between the celestial realms and the afterlife.

CT 94: Spell for Ascending to the Stars: Facilitating the ascent of the deceased's spirit to the celestial realm and joining the stars.

Utterance:
"O radiant stars, guides of the celestial plane,
I beseech your aid, to ascend and attain.
Grant me passage to your heavenly abode,
Where my spirit shall shine, among the starry code.

I cast off the earthly bonds that confine,
And release my spirit to the realms divine.
With each step, I transcend mortal plight,
Guided by your celestial light.

As I ascend, let the heavens part,
Revealing the path to the celestial heart.
Grant me wings to soar, free and unfurled,
As I journey to join the starry world.

O divine constellations, I seek your embrace,
As I ascend to dwell in your celestial space.
Let my spirit mingle among your shining array,
In timeless splendor, forever I shall stay.

I leave behind the earthly realm below,
And ascend to the stars' celestial glow.
In their brilliance, my spirit finds its home,
Boundless and eternal, no longer alone.

I embrace the cosmic dance, an ethereal waltz,
As my spirit ascends, unhindered by faults.
Joined with the stars, I shine ever bright,
A celestial beacon, a radiant light.

May the stars guide and illuminate my way,
As I ascend to their realms, day by day.
In their celestial company, I find my worth,
Transcending earthly bounds, a rebirth.

In this spell for ascending to the stars, the deceased invokes the radiant stars as guides and beseeches their aid in ascending to the celestial realm. The utterance expresses the longing to leave behind earthly limitations and join the stars in their heavenly abode, where the spirit shall shine among the cosmic tapestry.

The spell acknowledges the stars as luminous guides, leading the spirit to the celestial heart. The deceased seeks wings to soar freely, guided by the celestial light, as they embark on a journey to unite with the starry world.

The divine constellations are invoked, as the deceased seeks their embrace and desires to dwell among their shining array. The spell envisions the spirit mingling with the stars, finding a timeless and eternal home among their splendor.

The deceased relinquishes the earthly realm and ascends to the celestial realm, basking in the radiance of the stars. The spirit becomes one with the cosmic dance, transcending earthly limitations and shining ever bright as a celestial beacon.

The spell calls upon the stars to guide and illuminate the way as the spirit ascends, finding purpose and worth in their celestial company. The ascension to the stars represents a transformation and rebirth, breaking free from earthly constraints and embracing the infinite possibilities of the celestial realm.

Through this spell, the deceased seeks the assistance of the stars in ascending to the celestial realm, where their spirit can join the cosmic tapestry and shine in eternal brilliance. It reflects the belief in the celestial realm as a realm of transcendence and the yearning for unity with the divine luminaries.

CT 95: Spell for Protection against Serpents: Safeguarding the deceased from the threat of venomous serpents and reptiles in the afterlife.

Utterance:
"O ancient guardians, protectors of old,
I beseech your aid, strong and bold.
Wrap around me a shield of divine light,
Guarding me against serpents, venomous and tight.

From the depths of chaos, they slither and hiss,
But with your protection, I shall not miss.
Shield me, O guardians, with your mighty embrace,
Keeping me safe from serpents' venomous grace.

Let their fangs be dulled, their venom defied,
As I walk the afterlife, side by side.
May their sinister presence be driven away,
By the power of protection that I convey.

O serpentine protectors, guardians of might,
Bless me with your strength, as dark turns to light.
With your scales as armor, and your gaze as flame,
Banish serpents' menace, in your holy name.

In this realm of the afterlife, I find solace and peace,
Protected by your power, all dangers shall cease.
No venom shall harm me, no serpent shall strike,
For I am shielded by your divine might.

With gratitude and reverence, I embrace your care,
Knowing that your presence is always near.
Safeguard me, O guardians, in your embrace,
Shielding me from serpents, with boundless grace.

In this spell for protection against serpents, the deceased invokes the ancient guardians and seeks their aid in safeguarding against venomous serpents and reptiles in the afterlife. The utterance acknowledges the threat posed by serpents and calls upon the guardians to wrap the deceased in a shield of divine light, protecting them from the dangers.

The spell recognizes serpents as creatures of chaos and darkness, and seeks the guardians' assistance in nullifying their venomous strike. The guardians are called upon to provide a powerful shield of protection, ensuring the safety of the deceased as they navigate the afterlife.

The serpentine protectors are revered for their strength and might, and the spell invokes their blessings to dull the fangs and defy the venom of serpents. Their scales are seen as armor, and their gaze as flame, symbolizing the power to banish the menace of serpents in the name of protection.

The deceased finds solace and peace in the afterlife, knowing they are shielded by the power of the guardians. The spell expresses gratitude for their care and acknowledges their constant presence. The guardians are requested to safeguard the deceased, ensuring that no serpent can harm them and that they are shielded with boundless grace.

Through this spell, the deceased seeks the protection of the ancient guardians against serpents and reptiles in the afterlife. It reflects the belief in the guardians' power to repel and neutralize the threat of serpents, providing a sense of safety and security as the deceased journeys through the realms of the afterlife.

CT 96: Spell for Receiving Life Breath from the Sky: Ensuring that the deceased continues to receive the life-giving breath from the sky.

Utterance:
"O mighty sky, source of life and breath,
I call upon your power, strong and vast.
Grant me the gift of your life-giving air,
Sustaining me in the afterlife with care.

From the heavens above, your breath descends,
Bringing vitality that never ends.
I open my spirit to receive your embrace,
Filling me with life, your divine grace.

As I traverse the realms beyond this Earth,
Let your breath guide and renew my worth.
With each inhale, I draw your essence deep,
Revitalizing my soul, no slumber to keep.

Let the winds of the sky be my constant guide,
Upholding me, as I walk side by side.
The breath of life, a precious gift bestowed,
Nourishing my spirit, with each episode.

Through the celestial expanse, your breath I seek,
Receiving its energy, pure and meek.
Grant me vitality, strength, and renewal,
In the afterlife's realms, where spirits fuel.

O sky, bestow upon me the breath divine,
In this eternal journey, let it forever shine.
I am grateful for your sustaining power,
As I embrace the blessings, hour by hour.

In this spell for receiving life breath from the sky, the deceased calls upon the mighty sky as the source of life and breath. The utterance seeks the gift of the sky's life-giving air, ensuring the continuous sustenance of the deceased in the afterlife.

The sky is acknowledged as the origin of vital essence, and the deceased opens their spirit to receive its embrace. The breath of the sky is seen as a force that brings life and renewal, transcending the physical limitations of the earthly realm.

The deceased invokes the sky's guidance and renewal as they traverse the realms beyond Earth, relying on its constant presence and support. The breath of life is revered as a precious gift that nourishes the spirit and revitalizes its essence, allowing the deceased to continue their journey with vitality and strength.

The spell emphasizes the interconnectedness between the celestial expanse and the spirit of the deceased, with each inhale drawing the essence of the sky deep into their being. The sky's breath is seen as a source of energy and rejuvenation, sustaining the spirit throughout the eternal journey of the afterlife.

The deceased expresses gratitude for the sky's sustaining power and embraces the blessings it offers. The spell seeks the continuous bestowal of the breath divine, ensuring that it forever shines upon the spirit, providing vitality, strength, and renewal.

Through this spell, the deceased seeks to receive the life-giving breath from the sky, acknowledging its significance in sustaining and revitalizing their spirit in the afterlife. It reflects the belief in the sky as a divine source of energy and emphasizes the connection between the breath of the sky and the eternal journey of the deceased.

CT 95: Spell for Transformation into a Celestial Falcon: Granting the deceased the ability to transform into a celestial falcon, symbolizing divine protection and swiftness.

Utterance:
"By the power of the heavens high,
I invoke the transformation nigh.
Grant me wings to soar and fly,
A celestial falcon, swift and spry.

With feathers radiant, shimmering bright,
I embrace the divine in celestial flight.
From mortal form, I now transcend,
Into a falcon, my essence to blend.

Grant me eyes that pierce the sky,
Keen and sharp, no secrets pass by.
With wings outstretched, I take to the air,
A symbol of protection, beyond compare.

As a celestial falcon, I'm swift and free,
Guided by divine forces, I'll always be.
Across the realms, I'll journey far and wide,
With grace and speed, no boundaries abide.

In times of peril, I'll wield my might,
Protecting the soul, shining with light.
With wings of power, I'll navigate the spheres,
Defending against darkness, casting out fears.

Grant me the gifts of celestial flight,
To guard and protect, both day and night.
As a falcon of the heavens, I will be,
A symbol of divine protection for eternity.

By the power of transformation's embrace,
I become the falcon, with celestial grace.
Grant me this gift, O heavenly sky,
As I ascend and soar, on wings I rely.

In this spell, the deceased calls upon the power of the heavens to grant them the ability to transform into a celestial falcon. The utterance seeks the bestowal of wings to soar and fly, embodying the swiftness and divine protection symbolized by the falcon.

The deceased envisions themselves adorned with radiant and shimmering feathers, transcending their mortal form and merging with the essence of the falcon. The falcon's eyes are invoked to possess piercing vision that can perceive hidden truths and navigate the celestial expanse.

With outstretched wings, the transformed falcon takes to the air, becoming a symbol of unparalleled protection. The celestial falcon represents the agility and speed with which the deceased will navigate the realms of the afterlife, guided by divine forces and transcending all boundaries.

The spell emphasizes the role of the celestial falcon as a guardian and protector, wielding its might to safeguard the soul and dispel darkness. The falcon's wings symbolize power and serve as a conduit for the deceased to move through the spiritual spheres, casting out fears and defending against malevolent forces.

The deceased implores the heavenly sky to grant them the gifts of celestial flight, acknowledging the falcon's role as a symbol of divine protection. The transformation into a celestial falcon is seen as a permanent state, enabling the deceased to fulfill their role as a guardian and symbol of divine intervention throughout eternity.

Through this spell, the deceased seeks the transformation into a celestial falcon, embodying the qualities of divine protection and swiftness. It reflects the belief in the falcon as a powerful and revered creature, capable of traversing the spiritual realms and safeguarding the soul from harm.

CT 96: Spell for Receiving Nourishment from the Celestial Cow: Ensuring that the deceased is provided with divine nourishment and sustenance from the celestial cow.

Utterance:
"By the celestial realms above,
I seek the nourishment thereof.
From the celestial cow, pure and divine,
Grant me sustenance, in this design.

From the heavenly udder, milk so sweet,
Flowing with blessings, a sacred treat.
Nourish my spirit, sustain my soul,
With celestial milk, make me whole.

As the cow provides, I shall receive,
Divine sustenance, I humbly believe.
Let the milk of abundance overflow,
A sacred source from which I grow.

Grant me strength and vitality,
As I partake in celestial reality.
Nourish me, O celestial cow divine,
With your essence, let your blessings shine.

From the heavens above, I draw this grace,
Feeding my spirit in this sacred space.
Divine nourishment, forever sustained,
In the afterlife's realm, I remain.

May the celestial cow's milk bestow,
Vitality and blessings, as I journey and grow.
By this utterance, I seek the divine flow,
Nourishment from the celestial cow, I now know.

In this spell, the deceased invokes the celestial cow, a symbol of divine nourishment and abundance. The utterance beseeches the cow to provide nourishment to sustain the spirit and soul of the deceased.

The celestial cow is imagined to possess a heavenly udder, from which flows milk that is described as sweet and brimming with blessings. The deceased humbly asks to partake in this celestial milk, seeking wholeness and sustenance.

The spell emphasizes the belief that the milk of the celestial cow is a source of divine nourishment, capable of providing strength, vitality, and abundance. It is seen as a sacred source from which the deceased's spiritual growth and well-being can thrive.

The deceased acknowledges their role as the recipient of the cow's blessings and affirms their belief in the overflowing abundance that will sustain them. They express gratitude for the strength and vitality that will be bestowed upon them through the divine nourishment of the celestial cow.

Through this spell, the deceased seeks to establish a connection with the celestial cow, drawing upon its essence to receive divine nourishment and sustain their spirit in the afterlife. It reflects the belief in the transformative power of celestial sustenance and the importance of being nourished by the divine in the spiritual realms.

CT 97: Spell for Union with Osiris: Facilitating the union and merging of the deceased's essence with Osiris, the god of the afterlife and resurrection.

Utterance:
"O Osiris, god of the afterlife's domain,
I seek your union, I call your name.
In this sacred union, our essences merge,
Grant me your blessings, let our spirits converge.

As I traverse the realms of the deceased,
Guide me, Osiris, to eternal peace.
Embrace me with your divine presence,
Grant me resurrection, a timeless essence.

In your arms, I find solace and rest,
Embracing your power, I am truly blessed.
Let our essences intertwine and entwine,
In eternal union, our spirits combine.

As the god of resurrection and rebirth,
You bring new life to the spirits on earth.
By your grace, I am transformed anew,
In your divine presence, I find my truest hue.

May your wisdom and strength fill my soul,
As we unite, let your blessings unfold.
I merge with your essence, O Osiris divine,
In this sacred union, may my spirit shine.

As I become one with your immortal light,
Grant me the peace that transcends all plight.
In union with you, Osiris, I find my way,
Leading me to eternal joy, day by day.

By this utterance, I invoke your divine might,
Grant me the union, the merging, so bright.
O Osiris, god of the afterlife's embrace,
In our union, may I find eternal grace."

In this spell, the deceased seeks the union and merging of their essence with Osiris, the god of the afterlife and resurrection. The utterance addresses Osiris directly, calling upon his divine presence and invoking his blessings.

The deceased acknowledges Osiris as the guiding force in the realms of the deceased, seeking his guidance and protection. They express a desire for a sacred union where their essences intertwine and merge. Through this union, the deceased hopes to receive the blessings of resurrection and eternal peace.

Osiris is recognized as the god of resurrection and rebirth, capable of bringing new life to spirits. The deceased acknowledges Osiris's role in their transformation and seeks to be enveloped in his divine presence.

The spell emphasizes the desire to be filled with Osiris's wisdom and strength, as the deceased becomes one with his immortal light. They seek the peace that transcends all challenges and the joy that accompanies the eternal union with Osiris.

The utterance concludes with a request for Osiris to grant the union and merging of their spirits, as the deceased yearns to find eternal grace and be led by Osiris's divine presence.

Through this spell, the deceased seeks a profound and transformative connection with Osiris, merging their essence with his and invoking his divine power and guidance in the afterlife. It reflects the belief in the transformative potential of uniting with the god of resurrection and finding eternal peace through this union.

CT 98: Spell for Protection against Fire: Providing protection against the destructive powers of fire in the afterlife realm.

Utterance:
"By the ancient words, I beseech thee, O divine protectors,
I call upon your power to shield me from the fiery specters.
From the flames that devour and consume,
Grant me protection, dispelling all doom.

In this realm of the afterlife's domain,
I invoke your presence, where fiery forces reign.
With your divine might and celestial grace,
Envelop me in a shield, a fiery embrace.

Guard me, O guardians of flame and light,
As I traverse this realm, in your protection I unite.
May your radiance surround me like a veil,
Shielding me from the destructive fire's hail.

By your command, the flames shall retreat,
Their scorching touch, I shall not meet.
I am protected, divinely guarded from harm,
In your presence, I find tranquil calm.

Through the ancient words of power and might,
I invoke your protection, like a beacon in the night.
May your shield repel the fiery inferno's ire,
Preserving me from its destructive desire.

O divine protectors, keep me safe and sound,
As I journey through this fiery battleground.
With gratitude and reverence, I implore,
Protect me against the flames' wrath evermore.

By this utterance, I invoke your divine shield,
Protect me, O guardians, your power revealed.
In your presence, I find sanctuary and peace,
Shielded from the fire's destructive release.

Guard me, O divine protectors, with your might,
Shield me from the fire's consuming light.

In your protection, I find solace and rest,
Shielded from the fire's ravaging quest."

In this spell, the deceased seeks protection against the destructive powers of fire in the afterlife realm. The utterance is addressed to the divine protectors, calling upon their power to shield the deceased from the fiery specters that threaten to consume and destroy.

The deceased invokes the ancient words of power and beseeches the divine protectors to envelop them in a shield, a fiery embrace that will guard them from harm. They acknowledge the realm of the afterlife as a domain where fiery forces hold sway and seek the presence and protection of the divine guardians in this realm.

The spell emphasizes the request for the divine protectors to surround the deceased with their radiance, like a veil that repels the destructive fire. They implore the guardians to make the flames retreat and preserve them from the scorching touch of the fire.

The deceased expresses gratitude and reverence to the divine protectors, acknowledging their power and the sanctuary they provide. They call upon the guardians to keep them safe and sound as they journey through the fiery battleground of the afterlife.

The spell concludes with a plea for ongoing protection and gratitude for the guardians' power. The deceased seeks solace, peace, and sanctuary in the presence of the divine protectors, shielded from the fire's destructive release.

Through this spell, the deceased seeks divine protection against the destructive forces of fire in the afterlife realm. They invoke the power of the divine protectors and acknowledge their authority and ability to shield them from harm. It reflects the belief in the power of divine intervention to safeguard against the ravages of fire in the afterlife realm.

CT 99: Spell for Receiving Life from the Celestial Nile: Ensuring that the deceased continues to receive the life-giving waters from the celestial Nile.

Utterance:
"By the ancient words, I call upon the celestial flow,
To bestow upon me the life-giving waters that ever glow.
From the celestial Nile, the source divine,
Grant me sustenance, the elixir of time.

In the afterlife realm, where spirits reside,
I seek the nourishment of the celestial tide.
From the sacred waters that eternally stream,
Let me partake, fulfilling my immortal dream.

Celestial Nile, river of life's essence,
Flow through me, grant me your luminescence.
Revitalize my spirit, rejuvenate my soul,
With your divine waters, make me whole.

From the heights of heaven, your waters descend,
A sacred gift upon which I depend.
With each sip, I am infused with your might,
Receiving life's essence, pure and bright.

By the ancient words, I invoke your flow,
Let the celestial waters to me bestow.
As they cascade upon my being, I am renewed,
In their embrace, my vitality pursued.

Celestial Nile, I beseech your grace,
Fill me with your life-giving embrace.
Quench my thirst, replenish my spirit's well,
In your divine waters, I forever dwell.

By this utterance, I align with your stream,
Receiving life's waters, a sacred dream.
In the afterlife realm, sustained I shall be,
By the celestial Nile's flowing decree.

Celestial Nile, grant me your boon,

As I journey in the afterlife's moon.
With your life-giving waters, forever bless,
Envelop me in your divine caress."

In this spell, the deceased seeks to ensure their continuous reception of the life-giving waters from the celestial Nile in the afterlife realm. The utterance is directed to the celestial flow and calls upon its power to bestow the life-giving waters upon the deceased.

The deceased acknowledges the celestial Nile as a divine source of life's essence and requests its sustenance. They express their desire to partake in the sacred waters, which bring fulfillment to their immortal existence.

The spell emphasizes the importance of the celestial Nile as the river of life's essence, flowing through the afterlife realm and nourishing the spirits who reside there. The deceased seeks to be infused with its divine waters, which have the power to revitalize their spirit and rejuvenate their soul.

Through the utterance, the deceased invokes the celestial Nile to flow through them, granting them the luminescence and vitality it possesses. They acknowledge the sacred nature of its waters and their role in making them whole.

The spell concludes with a plea to the celestial Nile for its ongoing presence and blessing. The deceased seeks to be sustained by its life-giving embrace, forever dwelling in its divine waters.

Through this spell, the deceased seeks to receive the life-giving waters from the celestial Nile in the afterlife realm. They invoke its power and acknowledge its significance as a source of vitality and rejuvenation. It reflects the belief in the nourishing and sustaining nature of divine waters in the afterlife, ensuring the continuous existence and well-being of the deceased.

CT 100: Spell for Transformation into a Celestial Beetle: Granting the deceased the ability to transform into a celestial beetle, symbolizing regeneration and transformation.

Utterance:
"By the ancient words, I call upon the celestial light,
To grant me transformation, radiant and bright.
In the afterlife's realm, where spirits reside,
I seek to transform, with celestial power allied.

From the heavens above, a sacred beetle emerges,
A symbol of regeneration, as the ancient lore surges.
Grant me the form of this celestial creature,
With wings of luminescence, and a transformative feature.

Oh, celestial beetle, embodiment of renewal,
Bestow upon me your essence, pure and full.
With your transformative might, let me transcend,
Into a celestial form, where new life extends.

As I don the form of the celestial beetle bright,
I embrace regeneration, a wondrous sight.
Shedding the old, embracing the new,
Transformed and renewed, my spirit imbued.

With celestial wings, I take to the skies,
Navigating the realms, where divinity lies.
Symbol of transformation, guide me through,
The afterlife's mysteries, ancient and true.

By the ancient words, I invoke your grace,
Celestial beetle, with radiant embrace.
Grant me regeneration, transformation's embrace,
As I ascend to celestial realms, leaving no trace.

In this utterance, I seek transformation into a celestial beetle, a symbol of regeneration and renewal. I call upon the celestial light and the power it embodies to grant me this transformative ability in the afterlife realm.

The spell acknowledges the celestial beetle as a sacred creature that represents the process of regeneration and transformation. The deceased requests to be granted the form of this celestial beetle, envisioning wings of luminescence and a transformative aspect.

The celestial beetle is regarded as a symbol of renewal, shedding the old and embracing the new. By assuming the form of this celestial creature, the deceased seeks to experience regeneration and a profound transformation of their being.

The spell emphasizes the celestial beetle's association with transcendence and the ability to navigate the realms where divinity resides. The deceased requests the guidance of this symbol of transformation to navigate the mysteries of the afterlife with wisdom and grace.

Through the ancient words of the spell, the deceased invokes the celestial beetle's essence and seeks its transformative power. They aspire to ascend to celestial realms, leaving behind the limitations of their previous form and embracing the infinite possibilities of their new celestial existence.

This spell reflects the belief in the transformative nature of the afterlife and the desire for regeneration and renewal. It symbolizes the eternal cycle of life, death, and rebirth, and the potential for profound transformation in the spiritual realms.

CT 101: Spell for Receiving Offerings from the Stars: Ensuring that the deceased continues to receive offerings and provisions from the celestial bodies.

Utterance:
"By the celestial realm, where stars shine bright,
I call upon their radiance, their eternal light.
From the depths of the cosmos, offerings descend,
To sustain my spirit, as the journey transcends.

Oh, celestial bodies, luminous and grand,
I beseech you to bestow your blessings and hand.
Grant me the offerings from your celestial abode,
Nourish my essence, as I walk this celestial road.

As the stars twinkle and constellations align,
Let their offerings descend, divine and fine.
From their cosmic grace, provisions shall flow,
Sustaining my spirit in the afterlife's glow.

Oh, radiant stars, celestial guides above,
I seek your favor, your blessings and love.
In the expanse of the sky, where wonders dwell,
Send forth your offerings, as my spirit compels.

May your celestial gifts reach my eternal abode,
A symbol of reverence, a divine bestowed.
With gratitude, I receive your celestial boon,
Sustained by your blessings, my spirit shall bloom.

By the ancient words, this spell I cast,
To receive offerings from the stars, unsurpassed.
From the celestial realm, let provisions be sent,
To nourish my spirit, as its journey is meant.

In this utterance, I invoke the celestial bodies, particularly the stars, as bestowers of offerings and provisions in the afterlife realm. I acknowledge their luminous presence and eternal light as symbols of divine blessings.

The spell calls upon the radiant stars to send forth their offerings, descending from the cosmic realms to sustain the spirit of the deceased. It recognizes the celestial bodies as guides and guardians, capable of bestowing their cosmic grace upon those who seek their favor.

The deceased expresses their reverence and gratitude to the stars, recognizing their role in the afterlife's celestial expanse. They humbly request the descent of celestial gifts, acknowledging them as symbols of divine favor and blessings.

The spell emphasizes the cosmic nature of the offerings, representing the abundance and sustenance provided by the celestial bodies. It reflects the belief that the stars, as celestial guides, have the power to nourish and sustain the spirit as it continues its journey in the afterlife.

Through the recitation of the ancient words, the deceased casts the spell, seeking to establish a connection with the celestial bodies and open themselves to receive the celestial offerings. They trust in the generosity and benevolence of the stars, as they recognize the significance of these celestial provisions for their spiritual growth and well-being.

This spell represents the belief in the interconnectedness of the celestial and spiritual realms and the acknowledgment of the celestial bodies as sources of divine blessings. It serves as a request for continued nourishment and support from the stars, ensuring the well-being and sustenance of the deceased in the afterlife.

CT 102: Spell for Communion with the Deified Ancestors: Facilitating communication and connection with the deified ancestors in the afterlife realm.

Utterance:
"O revered ancestors, deified and divine,
I call upon your spirits, eternally entwined.
Through the veils of existence, let our paths align,
Grant me communion, a connection, sublime.

With reverence and respect, I seek your presence,
To commune with your wisdom, in blessed essence.
As deified beings, guide and guard my way,
Illuminate the path, where our spirits may sway.

By the sacred words, I invoke your blessed names,
Ancient ancestors, from whom divine light claims.
From the realms beyond, bridge the divide,
In this afterlife realm, let our spirits coincide.

Open the gates that separate our realms,
So our souls may unite, as destiny overwhelms.
In this sacred communion, let knowledge flow,
Guidance from the ancestors, I humbly bestow.

Through the boundless time, you've transcended,
Elevated to realms where your essence is splendid.
I beseech your wisdom, your guidance so true,
Ancestors divine, I call upon you.

With open heart and receptive spirit, I reach,
To commune with your essence, divine and teach.
Grant me your blessings, your knowledge untold,
As our spirits intertwine, let our connection unfold.

By the power of invocation, I make my plea,
To the deified ancestors, I kneel and decree.
In this sacred space, let our souls converse,
Communion with the divine, a blessing to immerse.

In this utterance, I invoke the deified ancestors, calling upon their spirits to facilitate communication and connection in the afterlife realm. The spell recognizes the revered status of these ancestors and seeks their wisdom, guidance, and presence.

The spell acknowledges the existence of a veil that separates the realms of the living and the deified ancestors. It appeals to the ancestors to open the gates and create a bridge between the two realms, allowing for the communion and exchange of knowledge and guidance.

The spell expresses deep reverence and respect for the ancestors, recognizing their elevated status and the wisdom they have acquired throughout the ages. It humbly requests their presence and blessings, acknowledging their role as guides and guardians in the afterlife realm.

The spell emphasizes the desire for a genuine and profound connection with the deified ancestors. It seeks their wisdom, knowledge, and guidance, understanding that their elevated state offers unique insights and perspectives.

Through the recitation of the sacred words and the sincere intention of the spellcaster, the spell aims to establish a communion with the deified ancestors. It acknowledges the ancestors' transcendence of time and space, recognizing their eternal presence and the significance of their guidance.

This spell represents the belief in the ancestral lineage and the connection between the living and the deified ancestors. It serves as a means to seek guidance, wisdom, and support from those who have gone before, fostering a deep connection and communion with the ancestral spirits in the afterlife realm.

CT 103: Spell for Protection against Ensnaring Nets: Safeguarding the deceased from traps, snares, and entanglements in the spiritual realm.

Utterance:
"By the power of divine protection, I call upon thee,
Guardian spirits, defenders, hear my plea.
In this realm of spirits, where entanglements lie,
Shield me from ensnaring nets, with strength on high.

As I traverse the afterlife's winding path,
Keep me safe from traps that evoke the wrath.
Shield my spirit from snares, hidden and unseen,
Grant me freedom, from ensnaring nets, I glean.

May the threads that bind be severed and undone,
As I walk this spiritual realm, under the sun.
By the power of divine light, I am shielded and secure,
Ensnaring nets dissolve, my spirit remains pure.

Spirits of protection, with wisdom and might,
Unravel the webs that seek to hold me tight.
Through realms of the unseen, guide my way,
Protect me from ensnaring nets, night and day.

With vigilance and awareness, I tread this ground,
Knowing you, protectors, are ever around.
By your divine presence, I am safeguarded and free,
From ensnaring nets, I am shielded, you see.

With gratitude and reverence, I seek your aid,
In this spiritual realm, where dangers pervade.
May your strength surround me, a shield so true,
From ensnaring nets, I find solace in you.

By the power of invocation, I call upon the spirits of protection, beseeching their assistance in safeguarding against ensnaring nets, traps, and entanglements in the spiritual realm. The spell acknowledges the presence of hidden dangers and seeks divine guidance and protection to avoid being trapped or ensnared.

The spell recognizes the need for vigilance and awareness while traversing the spiritual realm, understanding that there may be unseen snares and entanglements that can hinder spiritual progress. It implores the spirits of protection to unravel these webs and dissolve the ensnaring nets, allowing the deceased to move freely and remain untethered.

The spell acknowledges the role of the spirits of protection as guardians and defenders, trusting in their wisdom and might to guide and shield against potential traps. It acknowledges their constant presence and seeks their divine light to ward off any entrapments that may obstruct the journey.

The spell emphasizes gratitude and reverence towards the spirits of protection, recognizing their vital role in ensuring the safety and well-being of the deceased. It acknowledges their strength and power as shields against ensnaring nets and expresses trust in their ability to keep the spiritual path clear and unencumbered.

Through the recitation of the sacred words and the sincere intention of the spellcaster, the spell seeks the ongoing protection and vigilance of the spirits of protection. It aims to create a shield of divine light that repels ensnaring nets and keeps the spirit safe and secure.

This spell serves as a means to invoke the assistance of the spirits of protection, acknowledging the potential hazards and entanglements in the spiritual realm. It provides a sense of security and trust in their guidance, ensuring the deceased can navigate the spiritual path without being ensnared or hindered by traps or entanglements.

CT 104: Spell for Receiving Life Breath from the Sacred Flame: Ensuring that the deceased continues to receive the life-giving breath from the sacred flame.

Glorious flame, source of life's breath divine,
I call upon your sacred light to shine.
In the afterlife's realm, where spirits reside,
Bestow upon me the breath that shall abide.

As the flame dances with fervor and might,
Let its essence fill me with eternal light.
From its embers, let life's breath be born,
Rekindling my spirit with each radiant morn.

Sacred flame, I invoke your power and grace,
Grant me the life breath that transcends time and space.
With each inhale, may your essence ignite,
Infusing my being with vitality so bright.

Through the eternal flame's transformative fire,
May I be blessed with life's breath, my desire.
In the afterlife's realm, where spirits roam,
Let the sacred flame guide me towards my home.

As I breathe in the essence of divine fire,
May my spirit be nourished, rising higher.
In the sacred flame's presence, I find solace and rest,
Receiving life's breath, eternally blessed.

By the power of this sacred incantation,
I embrace the life breath's divine manifestation.
From the sacred flame, I receive its gift,
Igniting my spirit, granting uplift.

May the life-giving breath from the sacred flame,
Sustain me, empower me, in this eternal game.
With gratitude and reverence, I embrace this rite,
Receiving life's breath, forever alight.

By reciting this spell, the deceased invokes the power and essence of the sacred
flame to receive the life-giving breath in the afterlife. The spell acknowledges the

flame as a source of divine vitality and calls upon its transformative power to infuse the spirit with eternal light.

The spell recognizes the dynamic nature of the flame, its dance and fervor, and seeks to be imbued with its essence. It acknowledges that from the embers of the flame, life's breath is born, revitalizing the spirit and kindling its radiant energy.

The spell beseeches the sacred flame to bestow the life breath that transcends time and space, infusing the spirit with vitality and rejuvenation. It recognizes the flame as a symbol of transformation and renewal, and through its essence, the deceased seeks to be enlivened in the afterlife.

The spell emphasizes the intimate connection between the spirit and the sacred flame, acknowledging the flame as a guiding force, leading the way towards the home of the deceased. It invokes the flame's power and grace, trusting in its ability to provide the life-giving breath that sustains and empowers the spirit.

The spell expresses the desire to breathe in the essence of the divine fire, to be nourished and uplifted by its presence. It recognizes the sacredness and restorative qualities of the flame, as it grants the life breath and ignites the spirit with vitality.

Through the recitation of the sacred words and the sincere intention of the spellcaster, the spell seeks to establish a profound connection with the sacred flame and receive the life-giving breath it offers. It expresses gratitude and reverence for this divine gift and acknowledges the eternal nature of the flame's essence.

This spell serves as a means for the deceased to commune with the sacred flame and receive the life-giving breath in the afterlife. It symbolizes the continuation of vitality and spiritual nourishment, ensuring the sustained existence and empowerment of the spirit in the realms beyond.

CT 105: Spell for Transformation into a Celestial Scarab: Granting the deceased the ability to transform into a celestial scarab, symbolizing rebirth and resurrection.

Ancient scarab, symbol of renewal and might,
Grant me the power to ascend to celestial height.
In the afterlife's realm, where spirits reside,
Grant me the transformation, my spirit to guide.

Like the scarab, with wings spread wide,
Let me soar through the heavens, side by side.
With iridescent brilliance and divine glow,
Let my essence transform and truly show.

In the celestial realm, I take my flight,
A symbol of rebirth, emerging from the night.
Grant me the power to rise anew,
Transforming into a scarab, radiant and true.

With each beat of my wings, I ascend,
Embracing the cycle of life without end.
In the celestial realm, I find my place,
A symbol of resurrection, in infinite grace.

Scarab of the heavens, I call upon thee,
Grant me the transformation, let me be free.
From earthly form, let my spirit arise,
As a celestial scarab, soaring the skies.

By the power of this sacred invocation,
I embrace the transformation, a divine manifestation.
As a celestial scarab, I find my rebirth,
Symbolizing resurrection, eternal worth.

By reciting this spell, the deceased invokes the power of the ancient scarab, symbolizing rebirth and resurrection, to grant them the ability to transform into a celestial scarab in the afterlife.

The spell recognizes the scarab as a powerful symbol of renewal and might, and calls upon its transformative energy to guide the spirit in its journey through the afterlife realm.

The spell seeks to embody the qualities of the scarab, envisioning the deceased soaring through the heavens with wings spread wide. It acknowledges the scarab's iridescent brilliance and divine glow, and requests the same transformative power to be bestowed upon the spirit.

The spell acknowledges the afterlife realm as a place of rebirth and emergence from the night, and asks for the power to rise anew, symbolizing the cycle of life without end. It seeks to embrace the symbol of the scarab as a representation of resurrection and infinite grace.

The spell calls upon the scarab of the heavens, recognizing its significance and power, and requests the transformation to take place, allowing the spirit to transcend its earthly form and become a celestial scarab, soaring the skies.

By reciting the sacred words and expressing the sincere intention, the spell seeks to invoke the transformative energy of the scarab and grant the deceased the ability to embody its symbolism of rebirth and resurrection. It symbolizes the continuation of life and the embrace of eternal worth in the spiritual realms beyond.

CT 106: Spell for Receiving Nourishment from the Celestial Tree: Ensuring that the deceased is provided with divine nourishment and sustenance from the celestial tree.

Ancient tree, reaching towards the sky,
Grant me nourishment as the days go by.
In the realm of the celestial domain,
Let me partake in the sacred sustenance's reign.

Like the branches that stretch and intertwine,
Let me receive the nourishment divine.
From the celestial tree, a source of life,
Grant me sustenance to thrive.

With roots deep in the cosmic soil,
Absorb the essence of divine toil.
From the heavens above, blessings pour,
Nourish my spirit forevermore.

With each sip of celestial dew,
Let vitality and strength imbue.
The celestial tree's bountiful embrace,
Sustains me in this eternal space.

As I partake in the divine feast,
Grant me nourishment, never to cease.
From the celestial tree's branches and leaves,
Flow blessings that my spirit receives.

By the power of this sacred invocation,
I call upon the celestial tree's manifestation.
Grant me nourishment from your sacred domain,
In the afterlife, let divine sustenance sustain.

By reciting this spell, the deceased invokes the power of the celestial tree to ensure the reception of divine nourishment and sustenance in the afterlife.

The spell acknowledges the celestial tree as a source of life and blessings, reaching towards the sky and intertwining branches symbolizing the connection between the earthly and divine realms. It seeks to partake in the sacred sustenance provided by the celestial tree, which nourishes and sustains the spirit.

The spell recognizes the celestial tree as rooted in the cosmic soil, absorbing the essence of divine toil. It calls upon the blessings that pour from the heavens above, asking for the spiritual essence and vitality to be bestowed upon the deceased.

The spell envisions the act of sipping celestial dew, symbolizing the intake of divine nourishment and the infusion of vitality and strength. It acknowledges the bountiful embrace of the celestial tree, which sustains the spirit in the eternal space of the afterlife.

The spell expresses the desire for continuous nourishment, never to cease, as the deceased partakes in the divine feast provided by the celestial tree. It acknowledges that the branches and leaves of the celestial tree flow with blessings that the spirit receives.

By reciting the sacred words and invoking the power of the celestial tree, the spell seeks to ensure the provision of divine nourishment and sustenance to the deceased in the afterlife. It symbolizes the eternal connection between the spirit and the source of life, providing the sustenance needed for continued growth and well-being in the spiritual realms.

CT 107: Spell for Unity with the Gods of the Underworld: Facilitating the union and integration of the deceased's essence with the gods of the underworld.

Description: This spell, inscribed as CT 90 in the Coffin Texts, serves to facilitate the profound union and integration of the deceased's essence with the gods of the underworld. It is a sacred invocation that aims to establish a harmonious connection between the spirit of the departed and the divine beings who preside over the realms of the afterlife.

By reciting this spell, the deceased seeks to merge their spiritual essence with the gods of the underworld, forging a powerful bond and allowing for a seamless integration into the divine fabric of the afterlife. It is believed that this union with the gods grants the deceased access to their wisdom, protection, and guidance throughout their journey in the underworld.

The spell emphasizes the importance of unity and the establishment of a profound connection with the divine entities who hold sway over the realm of the departed. It acknowledges the gods of the underworld as revered and influential beings, capable of bestowing their blessings and divine essence upon the deceased.

Through the recitation of this spell, the deceased calls upon the gods of the underworld, expressing their desire for unity and integration. It is a plea for the gods to embrace the spirit of the departed and allow them to become one with the divine order of the afterlife.

The spell serves as a powerful conduit for the deceased to establish a spiritual bond with the gods of the underworld, enabling them to partake in the divine energies and guidance that these deities possess. It is a transformative ritual that seeks to ensure the deceased's harmonious existence and integration within the complex tapestry of the afterlife.

The "Harmony of Souls" spell holds great significance in Coffin Text 90, serving as a testament to the belief in the unity of all souls with the divine forces that govern the realm of the departed. It highlights the deep yearning of the deceased to merge their essence with the gods of the underworld, ultimately facilitating a profound and everlasting bond that shapes their spiritual journey beyond mortal existence.

Incantation:

Oh gods of the underworld, hear my plea,

In this sacred space, I kneel before thee.
Grant me passage, accept my essence's call,
To merge with your divine essence, one and all.

I invoke the guardians of the dark abyss,
Mighty deities, your presence I wish to kiss.
Unite my spirit with your ancient power,
In this union, let my soul forever flower.

With hearts open and intentions pure,
I offer myself to the gods obscure.
Through the veils of mortality, I traverse,
To embrace the realms where eternity submerges.

Anubis, lord of the sacred scales,
Guide my spirit through your mystical trails.
Osiris, ruler of the afterlife's domain,
Merge my essence with your eternal reign.

Hail, Isis, goddess of divine healing,
Infuse my being with your celestial sealing.
And Nephthys, guardian of the sacred night,
Cloak my soul in your protective light.

Mighty Horus, falcon of divine sight,
Bless me with your celestial might.
Persephone, queen of the underworld's shade,
Grant me solace in your embrace, unswayed.

Oh gods of the underworld, I implore,
Open your gates, let my essence soar.
Fuse my spirit with your immortal flame,
In unity, I claim my eternal name.

Through this sacred spell, I seek to find,
The unity of mortal and divine entwined.
Embrace my essence, oh gods of the deep,
Let our spirits merge and eternally keep.

By the power of this sacred rite,
I transcend the boundaries of mortal plight.
In union with the gods of the underworld's lore,

I am reborn, forevermore.

Note: This spell is meant to be recited with reverence and respect, following the appropriate rituals and invocations to invoke the gods of the underworld and establish a profound unity with their divine essence.

CT 108: Spell for Protection against Drowning: Providing protection against drowning and the dangers associated with bodies of water in the afterlife.

Incantation:

By the power of ancient waters deep,
I call upon the guardians of the eternal keep.
In the realm of the afterlife's liquid embrace,
Grant me protection from drowning's embrace.

Oh, spirits of the rivers and vast seas,
Hear my plea and answer my pleas.
Envelop me in your watery shield,
As I navigate the realms of the revealed.

Imbue me with the strength of ocean's might,
Shield me from peril, by day and by night.
Wrap me in currents that gently guide,
Safe passage through waters far and wide.

Poseidon, ruler of the ocean's domain,
Let not the currents my soul restrain.
With your trident, command the tides,
Keep me safe as the water subsides.

Osiris, god of the sacred Nile,
Lend me your wisdom and bring a smile.
In your embrace, grant me solace true,
Protect me from waters that threaten to subdue.

Oh, mighty Nephthys, goddess of the deep,
Cloak me in your ethereal keep.
With your tranquil touch, quell the waves,
And guard me from watery graves.

Anubis, guardian of souls departed,
Guide me through waters uncharted.
With your watchful eye and steady hand,
Protect me from dangers of the aquatic land.

Oh, spirits of the lakes and flowing streams,
Heed my plea and answer my dreams.
As I traverse the afterlife's watery way,
Grant me protection each and every day.

By the power of this sacred verse,
I invoke your aid, for better or worse.
In your embrace, I find solace profound,
Safe from the dangers that waters surround.

With gratitude and reverence, I embrace,
The protection you provide in this sacred space.
Oh, guardians of the waters, hear my plea,
Keep me safe for all eternity.

Note: This spell is intended to be recited with respect and focus, invoking the protective forces of the water deities and spirits. It is crucial to approach bodies of water in the afterlife realm with caution and seek the guidance and protection of the divine to ensure safe passage.

CT 109: Spell for Receiving Life Breath from the Sacred Lake: Ensuring that the deceased continues to receive the life-giving breath from the sacred lake.

In the realm of eternal waters divine,
I call upon the sacred lake's shrine.
Grant me, O spirits of the sacred waters,
The life-giving breath that eternally prospers.

From the depths of the pristine lake so pure,
Let the sacred breath of life endure.
As I traverse the realms of the afterlife,
Bestow upon me vitality, free from strife.

Oh, Nephthys, goddess of the sacred lake,
With your gentle touch, my spirit awake.
Breathe into me the essence of your grace,
Renew my being in this sacred space.

Isis, mother goddess of life and rebirth,
In your embrace, grant me renewal's mirth.
Infuse me with the breath of the sacred lake,
Revitalize my essence, no life to forsake.

Great Sobek, mighty crocodile god,
From the sacred waters, life's pulse unthawed.
Let your power surge through my very core,
Grant me the life breath, forevermore.

As I stand upon the lake's shimmering shore,
Let the sacred breath within me pour.
Fill my lungs with the essence of vitality,
Sustaining my spirit throughout eternity.

With gratitude and reverence, I beseech,
The sacred lake's breath within my reach.
Oh, spirits of the waters, hear my plea,
Grant me life's breath, eternally free.

Note: This spell is meant to be recited with utmost reverence and sincerity, calling upon the divine forces associated with the sacred lake. It is a request for the continuous reception of the life-giving breath from the sacred waters, ensuring the sustained vitality and existence of the deceased in the afterlife.

CT 110: Spell for Transformation into a Celestial Lion: Granting the deceased the ability to transform into a celestial lion, symbolizing strength and protection.

By the power of the ancient divine,
I call upon the celestial lion's sign.
Grant me, O spirits of celestial might,
The transformative essence to take flight.

From the heavens' vast and radiant sphere,
Let the celestial lion's presence appear.
As I shed mortal form and earthly strife,
Bestow upon me the strength of eternal life.

Oh, Sekhmet, fierce lioness of divine grace,
With your fiery spirit, my essence embrace.
Grant me the courage and protection you bear,
As I embody the celestial lion's flare.

Bast, benevolent lioness goddess of the sun,
In your regal presence, transformation begun.
Infuse me with your strength and majestic stride,
As I embody the celestial lion's pride.

Mighty Aker, guardian of the celestial realm,
With your dual lion form, overwhelm.
Grant me the power to transcend my mortal state,
As I embrace the celestial lion's fate.

As I stand upon the threshold of transformation,
Let the celestial lion's essence be my foundation.
Fill my being with courage and celestial might,
Guiding my spirit through the eternal light.

With gratitude and reverence, I beseech,
The celestial lion's form within my reach.
Oh, spirits of celestial power, hear my plea,
Grant me transformation, forever free.

Note: This spell is intended to be recited with utmost respect and reverence, invoking the divine forces associated with the celestial lion. It is a request for the transformative ability to assume the celestial lion's form, symbolizing strength, protection, and transcendence. The spell signifies the embodiment of these qualities as the deceased traverses the spiritual realms of the afterlife.

CT 111: Spell for Receiving Offerings from the Moon: Ensuring that the deceased continues to receive offerings and provisions from the moon.

The Coffin Texts, specifically CT 94, contain a spell for receiving offerings from the moon. Here is a rendition of the spell:

Title: "Lunar Elevation: The Spell of Sustenance"

Incantation:

In the radiant realm of lunar light,
I beseech the moon, a celestial sight.
O lunar deity, with radiance aglow,
Bestow upon me your blessings below.

From the celestial heights you reside,
Shower upon me offerings, so wide.
As I journey through the afterlife's sphere,
Let the moon's gifts be forever near.

O lunar goddess, with gentle grace,
Illuminate my path with your embrace.
As I traverse the realms, high and low,
May your offerings continually flow.

By the mystic bond between earth and sky,
I call upon the moon, radiant and high.
Grant me sustenance, provisions divine,
As I dwell in realms where mortals resign.

In the shadowed hours of night's embrace,
Let the moon's offerings find their place.
Nourish my spirit with celestial delight,
As I navigate the realms of eternal flight.

O lunar deity, hear my plea,
Your blessings and offerings I seek to see.
Provide me nourishment from your celestial domain,
In the afterlife's realm where I remain.

May the moon's radiance forever shine,
As I receive offerings, truly divine.
With gratitude and reverence, I implore,
Grant me sustenance forevermore.

Note: This spell is a supplication to the moon, invoking its divine presence to receive offerings and provisions in the afterlife. It acknowledges the celestial bond between the deceased and the moon, calling upon its radiant influence to provide sustenance and blessings. The spell is meant to be recited with respect and reverence, expressing the deceased's reliance on the moon's divine gifts for continued nourishment in the spiritual realms.

CT 112: Spell for Communion with the Deities of the Duat: Facilitating communication and interaction with the deities of the Duat, the Egyptian underworld.

The Coffin Texts, specifically CT 95, contain a spell for communion with the deities of the Duat, the Egyptian underworld. Here is a rendition of the spell:

Title: "The Invocation of Duat's Deities: A Spell of Connection"

Incantation:

In the depths of the Duat, where spirits reside,
I call upon the deities, glorified.
O guardians of the underworld's domain,
Hear my voice, my earnest refrain.

Anubis, guide of souls, I invoke your name,
Grant me passage, free from blame.
Blessed Osiris, lord of the afterlife,
Open the gates, alleviate my strife.

Isis, great goddess of magic and might,
Bestow upon me your guidance and light.
Nephthys, lady of the night and mourning,
Embrace me, protect me from all warning.

Horus, falcon-eyed, with vigilance true,
Grant me vision, my journey pursue.
Thoth, wise scribe and keeper of divine lore,
Grant me understanding, forevermore.

Sekhmet, lioness of wrath and healing,
Grant me strength, your power revealing.
Ma'at, goddess of truth and cosmic order,
Guide my path, make it steadfast and broader.

Deities of Duat, I call upon thee,
In this sacred space, hear my plea.
Grant me communion, divine connection,
In the realms of the underworld's reflection.

As I traverse the Duat's vast expanse,
Grant me favor, embrace my advance.
May your wisdom and guidance be bestowed,
As I commune with the divine, I'm bestowed.

In this sacred space, in this hallowed night,
Let my words reach you, shining bright.
Open the gates of communication wide,
As I seek communion, side by side.

Duat's deities, hear my call,
In this underworld realm, stand tall.
Guide me, protect me, with your divine might,
As I walk this path in the eternal night.

Note: This spell is an invocation to the deities of the Duat, seeking their presence and guidance in the realm of the Egyptian underworld. It acknowledges the significance of each deity and their specific roles in the afterlife journey. The spell is recited with reverence and respect, invoking the names of the deities and seeking their communion and guidance. The aim is to establish a connection with these divine beings, allowing the deceased to receive their wisdom and protection as they navigate the realms of the Duat.

CT 113: Spell for Protection against Curses: Safeguarding the deceased from curses, malevolent spells, and negative influences in the afterlife.

The Coffin Texts, specifically CT 96, contain a spell for protection against curses, safeguarding the deceased from malevolent spells and negative influences in the afterlife. Here is a rendition of the spell:

Title: "The Incantation of Protection: Shield against Curses"

Incantation:

By the powers of the divine and the sacred words,
I invoke protection from curses and wicked cords.
From the depths of the Duat to the heavens high,
I shield myself, as curses pass me by.

Let no malevolent spell find its mark,
For I am guarded, safe from the dark.
No curse shall penetrate this protective veil,
As I traverse the afterlife's treacherous trail.

I call upon the guardians of light and might,
To repel curses, banish them from sight.
Ra, the sun god, with your radiant flame,
Burn away curses, cleanse my name.

Horus, falcon-headed, vigilant and true,
Protect me from curses, shield me through.
Isis, goddess of magic and divine power,
Unravel curses, dissolve them, devour.

Thoth, wise scribe and knower of all spells,
Banish curses, break their wicked spells.
Ma'at, goddess of cosmic balance and truth,
Keep me shielded, from curses aloof.

I am protected by the divine forces above,
From curses cast with malice and love.
Let them rebound, dissolve, and fade,
For I am shielded by the divine's aid.

No curse shall harm me, no spell take hold,
As this protective shield unfolds.
I am safe from curses, unharmed, and free,
As I journey through eternity.

Note: This spell is an incantation for protection against curses and malevolent spells in the afterlife. It calls upon the power of the divine beings, such as Ra, Horus, Isis, Thoth, and Ma'at, to shield the deceased from any harmful curses or negative influences. The spell affirms the invulnerability of the individual, creating a protective barrier that repels curses and ensures the safety of the deceased as they navigate the afterlife realm.

CT 114: Spell for Receiving Life Breath from the Celestial Vault: Ensuring that the deceased continues to receive the life-giving breath from the celestial vault.

Spell for Receiving Life Breath from the Celestial Vault

In the realm of eternal skies, where stars shine bright,
I call upon the celestial vault, source of life's light.
Grant me, O celestial vault, your divine breath so pure,
That I may be renewed, revitalized, and endure.

From the expanse of heavens above, I seek your grace,
Infuse me with your essence, in this sacred space.
Breathe life into my spirit, let it soar and thrive,
As I traverse the afterlife, keeping my soul alive.

With each celestial exhale, let strength and vigor flow,
Empower me with vitality, as above, so below.
From the vault's sacred chamber, let life's breath descend,
And with its radiant power, my essence forever mend.

O celestial vault, the wellspring of eternal breath,
Grant me your life force, in life and after death.
May your celestial essence sustain me in every way,
As I journey through eternity, I humbly pray.

CT 115: Spell for Transformation into a Celestial Falcon-headed Serpent: Granting the deceased the ability to transform into a celestial falcon-headed serpent, symbolizing divine protection and wisdom.

Oh, thou celestial realms where powers combine,
I beseech thee to grant this transformative sign.
By the union of falcon and serpent, divine,
Bestow upon the deceased your gifts so fine.

From the heavens above, let wings take form,
As falcon's grace and majesty begin to swarm.
With eyes sharp and keen, piercing through the night,
Grant the gift of vision, both clear and bright.

From the depths of the earth, let scales arise,
As serpent's wisdom, ancient and wise.
Coiled and poised, a symbol of protection true,
Shield the soul from harm, in all it may pursue.

Oh, celestial falcon-headed serpent, divine,
Grant the deceased your essence, intertwine.
The power of flight and serpentine grace,
Unite within, in this sacred space.

As falcon soars high, through skies so vast,
And serpent slithers, wise and steadfast,
Bestow upon the deceased your celestial might,
Guiding them through the afterlife's eternal night.

Oh, celestial falcon-headed serpent, I implore,
Embrace the deceased, forevermore.
Grant them your protection, your wisdom, your light,
As they navigate the realms, day and night.

CT 115: Spell for Receiving Nourishment from the Celestial Fountain: Ensuring that the deceased is provided with divine nourishment and sustenance from the celestial fountain.

Oh, celestial fountain, source of life divine,
Pour forth your nourishment, in this sacred shrine.
From the celestial realms, let your waters flow,
Bestowing upon the deceased the sustenance they shall know.

With every sip, let vitality renew,
As the divine essence of the fountain imbues.
Fill the spirit with strength, replenish the soul,
Granting eternal nourishment, making the deceased whole.

From the depths of the heavens, let your blessings descend,
A celestial feast, to sustain and transcend.
With each drop that cascades, a taste of divine grace,
Nourish the departed in the afterlife's embrace.

Oh, celestial fountain, pure and clear,
Quench the thirst of the deceased, drawing near.
Let your waters rejuvenate, let them restore,
Granting eternal nourishment forevermore.

As the celestial fountain flows with life's elixir,
Sustain the departed, make their existence richer.
Provide the nourishment they need to thrive,
In the realms beyond, where spirits shall survive.

Oh, celestial fountain, pour forth your divine stream,
Satisfy the hunger, fulfill the deceased's dream.
With each sip, let their spirits be revived,
With your sacred nourishment, forever supplied.

CT 116: Spell for Unity with the Divine Boat of Ra: Facilitating the union and integration of the deceased's essence with the divine boat of Ra, the sun god.

In the realm of eternal light and golden rays,
I call upon the divine boat of Ra, with humble praise.
May its radiant presence illuminate my way,
As I seek unity with its power this very day.

Oh, great boat of Ra, majestic and divine,
Carrying the sun god across the celestial line,
Guide me through the realms, both high and low,
And let our essences merge, that I may glow.

As the boat sails across the sky's expanse,
I offer myself, ready to embrace this dance.
Merge my essence with your sacred vessel,
In unity with Ra, let my spirit wrestle.

Grant me the wisdom of the sun's bright flame,
Let my being be touched by your celestial name.
May your divine energy flow through my veins,
Uniting our essences, breaking all chains.

Oh, divine boat of Ra, I surrender to your might,
In your embrace, let my spirit take flight.
Merge our essences, as one we shall become,
Bound together in the eternal cosmic sum.

Grant me the strength of your celestial boat,
To navigate the realms, to transcend and float.
Unified with Ra, let my essence ascend,
On the divine boat's journey, that knows no end.

Oh, divine boat of Ra, hear my plea,
Unite my spirit with your eternal decree.
In the celestial expanse, let our essences blend,
As I journey with you, my eternal friend.

CT 117: Spell for traversing the celestial waters

In the vast expanse of the celestial waters,
I call upon the powers that transcend mortal borders.
Grant me passage through this ethereal domain,
As I navigate the currents with wisdom and refrain.

By the shimmering stars and the moon's gentle glow,
I embark on this journey, fearless and in the know.
Grant me the knowledge to steer my celestial vessel,
Through the cosmic tides, with grace and mettle.

Oh, celestial waters, ancient and profound,
Be my guide as I traverse, without a sound.
Grant me the currents of divine harmony,
To navigate this realm with serenity.

I call upon the spirits of the celestial deep,
To aid me in my journey, their secrets to keep.
Let the waves carry me to realms unseen,
With each ripple, a new horizon I glean.

Grant me the sight to discern the hidden signs,
As I sail through constellations, divine designs.
Guide me past celestial obstacles and tests,
With your grace, I shall overcome any behest.

Oh, celestial waters, I am at your mercy,
Grant me safe passage and unveil your mystery.
Lead me to realms of enlightenment and truth,
Where celestial beings guide me, in their sooth.

As I traverse these celestial waters wide,
I merge with the cosmos, my spirit amplified.
Grant me the courage to explore the unknown,
And return to earthly realms, wiser and grown.

With gratitude and reverence, I embark on this quest,
Traversing the celestial waters, divinely blessed.
Grant me the wisdom and strength to endure,
As I sail through the heavens, forever pure.

CT 118: Spell for acquiring the knowledge of the stars

Gaze upon the vast expanse of the night,
Where stars gleam, casting their celestial light.
I seek the knowledge held in their cosmic dance,
Grant me wisdom, as I enter their divine trance.

Oh, stars of the heavens, ancient and bright,
Reveal to me your secrets, hidden in the night.
Open the doors to the celestial abode,
Where cosmic wisdom and insights erode.

Grant me the eyes to see your intricate patterns,
Unveil the mysteries that lie in your lanterns.
Illuminate my mind with celestial lore,
As I delve into your wisdom, forevermore.

I call upon the powers of the constellations,
To guide me through celestial revelations.
Align my spirit with the cosmic flow,
So that profound knowledge I may come to know.

Stars of the north, south, east, and west,
Bestow upon me the knowledge you possess.
Share with me the stories of ancient times,
As I commune with you through sacred rhymes.

Oh, luminous beings, guardians of the night,
Imbue me with your wisdom, pure and bright.
Let the secrets of the universe unfold,
As I delve deeper into the cosmic mold.

With reverence and awe, I open my heart,
To receive the teachings the stars impart.
Grant me the understanding of the celestial plan,
To navigate life with wisdom, as only you can.

By the power of the stars, this knowledge I seek,
To enlighten my path and make me spiritually sleek.
Guide me, celestial luminaries, as I aspire,
To acquire the wisdom of the stars' eternal fire.

CT 119: Spell for warding off the god of chaos and disorder

In the realm of chaos and disorder's sway,
I call upon divine power to keep it at bay.
With words of power and an unwavering will,
I ward off chaos and bring harmony's thrill.

Oh, god of chaos, I see your unruly might,
But in this space, I stand firm against your blight.
I invoke the forces of order and balance,
To shield me from your chaotic dance.

By the power of Ma'at, the goddess of truth,
I resist your chaos and negate its ruthless.
With her feather as my guide and compass,
I banish chaos with its righteous compass.

I summon the strength of Horus, the god of light,
To pierce through darkness and restore what's right.
With his falcon eyes, I see through the haze,
And ward off chaos in myriad ways.

By the authority of Thoth, the god of wisdom,
I invoke his intellect to build a sacred system.
With his knowledge, chaos cannot prevail,
As I wield his wisdom like an impenetrable scale.

I call upon Isis, the goddess of magic and healing,
To weave her spells of protection and sealing.
With her love and compassion, chaos fades away,
And peace and order hold their sway.

By the power vested in me, by the ancient divine,
I cast forth this spell to repel chaos' design.
May it be so, may chaos be kept at bay,
As order and harmony guide my way.

CT 120 : Spell for attaining the blessings of the sky goddess

Oh, great and radiant Sky Goddess above,
I seek your blessings and embrace your love.
With reverence and devotion, I turn my gaze,
To receive the gifts you bestow in endless rays.

From your celestial domain, so vast and high,
Shower upon me blessings from the sky.
Grant me the breath of life, pure and divine,
Infuse me with your essence, make me shine.

Goddess Nut, whose canopy spans the world,
In your embrace, let your blessings unfurl.
Wrap me in your starry mantle of grace,
And guide me on my celestial embrace.

As the sun rises and paints the sky with gold,
Let your blessings fill my heart, untold.
Grant me wisdom, inspiration, and insight,
As I bask in the radiance of your celestial light.

Oh, Sky Goddess, with arms outstretched wide,
I seek your guidance, your love, and your pride.
In unity with you, I soar and ascend,
Embracing the blessings you graciously send.

By the power of your divine presence, I'm blessed,
In your embrace, I find eternal rest.
May your blessings flow through me like a river,
As I honor you, Sky Goddess, now and forever.

CT 121: Spell for avoiding the judgment of the god of wisdom

Oh, wise and just God of Wisdom, I stand before you,
Seeking your favor and guidance to be true.
Grant me the wisdom to navigate life's trials,
And shield me from the judgment that brings trials.

With humble heart and open mind, I plead,
That you may see the goodness in my deed.
May my actions reflect your divine light,
And keep me from the depths of eternal night.

God of Wisdom, I beseech you to impart,
Your knowledge and insight to my humble heart.
Guide my steps on the path of righteousness,
And shield me from the wrath of your judgment's darkness.

Grant me discernment, understanding, and grace,
To make choices that lead to a righteous embrace.
May your wisdom flow through me like a stream,
Guiding me away from the realms of extreme.

In your wisdom, I find solace and peace,
May your judgment on me bring release.
I seek your favor, O God of Wisdom divine,
To spare me from the fate that's not benign.

By the power of your wisdom and sacred decree,
Protect me from judgment's harsh decree.
May your mercy overshadow my wrongs,
And guide me to where forgiveness belongs.

Oh, God of Wisdom, I invoke your name,
To shield me from the judgment's burning flame.
Grant me the wisdom to live a virtuous life,
And spare me from the depths of eternal strife.

CT 122: Spell for acquiring the power to manipulate dreams

In the realm of dreams, where visions take flight,
I seek the power to shape the dream's light.
By the veil of sleep, where fantasies dwell,
Grant me the gift to weave dreams and compel.

From the depths of slumber, I call upon the night,
Unleash the power to mold dreams with might.
With open mind and pure intent,
Grant me control over dreams as I invent.

By the power of the subconscious deep,
I tap into the realm where dreams do keep.
Empower me with the ability to steer,
Within the dream world, both far and near.

I invoke the forces that govern the night,
Grant me dominion over dreams in sight.
With clarity and focus, I declare my will,
To shape the dreamscape, my desires fulfill.

With this spell, I claim the power to sway,
The visions that in slumber play.
Grant me control over dreams' creation,
To shape their form with imagination.

But with this power, I seek no harm,
I use it with reverence, like a gentle charm.
To explore the depths of the mind's domain,
And bring forth dreams that heal and sustain.

By the dreamer's command, I make this plea,
To hold the power to manipulate dreams with glee.
But always with respect for the dreamer's rest,
And the understanding that dreams are blessed.

CT 123: Spell for preserving one's ba (soul) from fragmentation

In the realm of the eternal, where souls reside,
I seek protection for my ba, my soul's guide.
From fragmentation and dispersion, I ask to be free,
Preserve my essence, unified as one, eternally.

By the divine powers that govern the soul's flight,
Shield me from forces that would cause my ba's plight.
Wrap me in your loving embrace, oh guardian divine,
Keep my ba whole and complete, an eternal sign.

I call upon the ancient wisdom of the gods of old,
To safeguard my ba, their protection I hold.
May my essence remain intact, unbroken and true,
Unified and undivided, as I journey through.

By the strength of Ra, the sun's radiant light,
Illuminate my path, keep my ba shining bright.
Guide me through the trials that may come my way,
Preserve my soul's essence, day after day.

With each breath I take, let my ba be sustained,
Shielded from fragmentation, forever unchained.
By the powers of Ma'at, the goddess of balance and truth,
Keep my ba whole, renewing its eternal youth.

As I walk this earthly plane and beyond,
May my ba remain resilient, forever strong.
Protect it from fragmentation, from forces that may sever,
Preserve my soul's unity, now and forever.

CT 124: Spell for escaping the torment of the god of guilt

In the realm of the divine and the sacred land,
I seek liberation from the god of guilt's command.
From torment and anguish, I yearn to be free,
Release me from guilt, restore my inner harmony.

Oh, mighty gods who watch over the souls,
Grant me the strength to rise above guilt's tolls.
Break the chains that bind me, loosen guilt's grasp,
Free me from its torment, release me at last.

I call upon the powers of forgiveness and grace,
To cleanse my spirit, to find a sacred space.
Let guilt be washed away by the river's flow,
Let healing waters purify, let my soul glow.

With every breath I take, I release the weight,
The burdens of guilt, I now choose to abate.
I embrace self-compassion, let guilt dissolve,
Empowered and liberated, I resolve.

May the god of guilt's influence wane and fade,
As I find solace and peace in the divine's aid.
I rise above torment, I reclaim my worth,
Embracing self-forgiveness, a new rebirth.

By the power of the gods, I break free from the chains,
From the grip of guilt, my spirit regains.
I am worthy of love, forgiveness, and grace,
Released from torment, I find my sacred place.

CT 125: Spell for warding off the god of doubt and uncertainty

In the realm of spirits, where doubts may reside,
I call upon ancient powers to be my guide.
To ward off the god of doubt, uncertain and bleak,
I seek clarity and strength, the answers I seek.

With focused intent and a resolute mind,
I banish the doubts that seek to confine.
I summon the forces that bring confidence and light,
To dispel the shadows, to restore my sight.

I invoke the gods of wisdom, of knowing and truth,
To shield me from doubt, to provide a clear view.
Grant me the courage to trust my inner voice,
To embrace certainty and make a choice.

I reject the whispers of uncertainty's sway,
I stand tall and strong, doubts held at bay.
With conviction and faith, I forge my own way,
Guided by purpose, doubt cannot stay.

Oh, ancient deities, hear my fervent plea,
Wrap me in your protection, set my doubts free.
I am steadfast and certain, my path is clear,
The god of doubt retreats, vanishing in fear.

By the power of divine light and clarity's might,
I ward off doubt's shadows, banishing the night.
With confidence renewed, I embrace the unknown,
Guided by faith, my true self is shown.

CT 126: Spell for attaining the protection of the guardian deities of the deceased

Oh, guardian deities of the deceased, I call upon your might,
Protect me in the afterlife, keep me safe day and night.
Wrap me in your loving embrace, ward off all harm and strife,
With your watchful eyes upon me, guide me through eternal life.

Anubis, the jackal-headed god, guardian of the sacred tomb,
I invoke your presence, protect me from impending doom.
With your keen senses and loyal heart, stand by my side,
Guide me through the trials, let no harm in me abide.

Isis, the great mother goddess, with her wings unfurled,
Wrap me in your nurturing embrace, keep me safe in the spirit world.
Shield me from malevolent forces, with your divine grace,
Preserve my essence, let me find peace in this sacred space.

Horus, the falcon-headed god, with eyes that see all,
Watch over me with your unwavering vigilance, never let me fall.
Guide me with your wisdom, let your strength be my shield,
Protect me from evil forces, let your power be revealed.

Oh, guardian deities of the deceased, I humbly implore,
Grant me your protection forevermore.
As I journey through the afterlife's unknown,
Wrap me in your love, keep me safe, never alone.

CT 127: Spell for avoiding the judgment of the god of mercy

Oh, merciful god, whose judgment weighs heavy,
Grant me your compassion, spare me from the levy.
In your divine wisdom, see the purity of my heart,
Forgive my transgressions, grant me a fresh start.

With your scales of justice, you measure each deed,
But I beseech you, let your mercy supersede.
Look upon me with kindness, see my remorse and regret,
Grant me clemency, and let forgiveness be set.

May your divine compassion shine upon my soul,
As I navigate the afterlife's eternal scroll.
Guide me on a path of redemption and grace,
Where your mercy encompasses me in every place.

Oh, god of mercy, hear my fervent plea,
In your benevolence, let your judgment set me free.
Protect me from the consequences of my past,
Embrace me in your mercy, for eternity to last.

CT 128: Spell for acquiring the ability to communicate with animals

By the powers of the ancient ones, I seek to gain,
The gift of understanding, the language of the untamed.
Grant me the ability, to converse with creatures small and great,
To bridge the gap between our worlds, to communicate.

With open heart and humble spirit, I make my plea,
To be bestowed with this sacred ability.
Grant me the knowledge, the wisdom to comprehend,
The words unspoken, the messages they send.

May I hear the whispers of the wind as it passes by,
The chirping of birds in the vast open sky.
Grant me the understanding of the lion's mighty roar,
The wisdom of the owl's hoot, the dolphin's playful lore.

In harmony and respect, I shall approach each kind,
With empathy and love, a bond I hope to find.
To learn their secrets, their knowledge to unfold,
To share their world, a connection to behold.

By the ancient powers that govern all creation,
Grant me this gift, this divine revelation.
To speak with animals, a gift so rare and true,
I vow to use it wisely, in service to all life, and to you.

CT 129: Spell for preserving one's ba (soul) from wandering

By the sacred forces that guide the realms unseen,
I beseech thee, protect my ba, my soul serene.
Keep it bound to this earthly plane, I implore,
Shield it from wandering, forevermore.

With this incantation, I call upon divine might,
To anchor my ba in the realm of light.
Guard it from straying, from losing its way,
Preserve its essence, night and day.

May the wings of Ma'at enfold and embrace,
My ba, with divine love and grace.
Grant it purpose and direction, a steadfast path,
Shield it from chaos, from the aftermath.

Let it be tethered to the divine cosmic thread,
Secure in its purpose, no fear of being misled.
With each passing day, let its purpose unfold,
Aligned with the divine plan, strong and bold.

Oh, ancient guardians of the netherworld's gate,
Protect my ba, its destiny, its fate.
Guide it safely through the realms unknown,
A beacon of light, forever my own.

CT 130: Spell for escaping the grasp of the god of stagnation

In the realm of shadows, where stagnation lies,
I seek liberation, I yearn to rise.
From the grip of the god who holds me tight,
I call upon ancient powers, bring forth the light.

By the strength of Ra, the sun's blazing fire,
Break the chains of stagnation, lift me higher.
With each breath I take, I shed the weight,
I defy the god's grasp, I challenge fate.

Through the winds of change, I find my way,
No longer bound by the god's stagnant sway.
I embrace transformation, I soar and ascend,
Leaving behind the stagnation, my spirit unbend.

By the power of Thoth, the wise and the keen,
I gain insight and knowledge, my mind serene.
I break free from the confines of stagnation's hold,
Embracing growth and progress, fearless and bold.

Oh, god of stagnation, I elude your grasp,
I break the chains that tightly clasp.
With each step I take, I forge my own path,
Escaping your influence, free from your wrath.

This spell I cast, with intention strong,
To escape the god of stagnation's throng.
I embrace the flow of life, in constant motion,
Leaving behind stagnation, with pure devotion.

CT 131: Spell for warding off malevolent spirits in the realm of dreams

In the realm of dreams, where spirits roam,
I call upon protection to guide me home.
By the power of light, I banish the dark,
No malevolent spirits shall leave their mark.

I invoke the guardians of dream's gate,
To shield me from nightmares, fear, and hate.
With each breath I take, I am fortified,
Against negative forces, I will abide.

I carry an amulet of divine might,
To ward off spirits that haunt the night.
In dreams' embrace, I stand strong and tall,
No malevolent presence shall make me fall.

By the strength of my will and intention clear,
I banish all spirits that bring me fear.
I claim my dreams as sacred space,
Protected by divine love and grace.

This spell I cast with purpose and might,
To ward off malevolent spirits in the night.
In the realm of dreams, I find peace and rest,
With protection and strength, I am truly blessed.

CT 132: Spell for attaining the blessings of the wind god

Oh, mighty wind god, I call upon thee,
With reverence and respect, I seek your decree.
Grant me the blessings of your gentle breeze,
Fill my being with peace and ease.

From the highest peaks to the deepest valleys,
Your breath whispers secrets of hidden alleys.
Guide me with your currents, swift and true,
In your embrace, I find solace anew.

Carry me upon your wings of flight,
To realms unknown, in your celestial might.
Grant me the wisdom of the winds that blow,
So that in life's journey, I may gracefully grow.

Bless me with your refreshing zephyr,
Sweep away troubles, worries, and despair.
Infuse my spirit with your divine air,
Revitalize me, as if borne on a prayer.

Oh, wind god, I honor your ancient power,
In gratitude, I stand before you this hour.
May your blessings bestow upon my path,
Guiding me with love, shielding me from wrath.

This spell I cast, with sincerity and trust,
To receive the blessings of the wind god's gust.
May his gentle touch uplift my soul,
And guide me towards my destined goal.

CT 133: Spell for avoiding the judgment of the god of compassion

Oh, compassionate god, hear my plea,
In your divine presence, I humbly be.
Grant me your mercy, with gentle hand,
Protect me from judgment, help me withstand.

In the realm of your grace, I seek refuge,
May your compassion be my eternal deluge.
Guide me away from the path of strife,
Illuminate my soul with your benevolent light.

In moments of trial, when judgment draws near,
Wrap me in your love, let me persevere.
May your forgiveness cleanse my every flaw,
And your compassion be the beacon I saw.

Grant me a reprieve from the harsh decree,
In your mercy's embrace, I long to be.
With a heart contrite, I seek your pardon,
For any transgressions, I beg your pardon.

Oh, god of compassion, I implore,
Open the gates to your forgiving shore.
Shield me from judgment's relentless tide,
Let your mercy be my eternal guide.

CT 134: Spell for acquiring the power to shape one's own reality

By the ancient words of power, I invoke the forces of creation and command the fabric of reality to obey my will. I am the master of my destiny, the architect of my world. Through this spell, I attain the power to shape my own reality.

I call upon the elements, the earth, the air, the fire, and the water, to be my allies in this endeavor. With their energy, I mold and transform the world around me according to my desires.

I envision my dreams and aspirations with clarity and focus. I release any doubts or limitations that may hinder my progress. I embrace the boundless potential that resides within me.

I command the universe to align itself with my intentions. Every thought, every word, every action carries the power of creation. I am the weaver of destiny, the creator of my own story.

By the authority bestowed upon me, I declare that my reality is shaped by my highest purpose and deepest desires. I manifest abundance, love, and success in every aspect of my life.

This spell is sealed with my unwavering belief in my own power and the knowing that I am the ultimate creator of my reality.

So mote it be.

CT 135: Spell for preserving one's soul from dissolution

In the realm of the afterlife, where souls wander and destinies unfold,
I call upon the ancient powers to safeguard and protect my soul.

I invoke the guardians of eternity, the keepers of balance and harmony,
To shield my essence from the forces that seek to dissolve and disperse me.

With the strength of my spirit and the knowledge of my true self,
I resist the currents that threaten to scatter my soul in eternal separation.

I weave a shield of light, a barrier of resilience,
To ward off the dissolution that beckons in the depths of the underworld.

I affirm my identity, my purpose, and my connection to the divine,
Knowing that my soul is a sacred vessel, enduring and indivisible.

I embrace the wisdom of the ancient ones, the ancestors who came before,
Guiding me through the trials and challenges that may come.

With each breath I take, I affirm my existence,
I affirm my unity with the eternal cycle of life and death.

May my soul remain whole and intact,
Bound by the threads of eternity, undiminished and resilient.

By the power of the gods and the strength within me,
I preserve my soul from dissolution and embrace eternal continuity.

So be it, and let it be done.

CT 136: Spell for escaping the torment of the god of regret

In the realm of the afterlife, where regrets may haunt and torment,
I invoke the power of liberation, the strength to break free from remorse.

I call upon the spirits of release and redemption,
To grant me the wisdom and courage to escape the clutches of regret.

I release the burdens of the past, the weight of remorse and sorrow,
And embrace the light of forgiveness and self-compassion.

With each step I take, I distance myself from the chains of regret,
Leaving behind the shadows that seek to bind and confine my spirit.

I envision a future filled with possibility and growth,
Where the lessons of the past shape me but do not define me.

I acknowledge my imperfections, my mistakes, and my humanity,
Yet I refuse to be shackled by the remorse that seeks to consume me.

I am a being of resilience and transformation,
Capable of healing and evolving beyond the grip of regret.

By the power of my will and the strength within my soul,
I break free from the torment of the god of regret.

I embrace the present moment and the opportunities it holds,
Reclaiming my joy, my purpose, and my inner peace.

May the divine forces guide me on this path of liberation,
As I rise above regret and embark on a journey of healing.

So be it, and let it be done.

CT 137: Spell for warding off the god of falsehood and deception

In the realm of truth and clarity, I stand firm and resolute,
Guarding my soul against the deceitful whispers that seek to mislead.

I call upon the spirits of discernment and wisdom,
To shield me from the web of lies spun by the god of falsehood.

With every breath I take, I breathe in truth and honesty,
Cleansing my spirit from the illusions that threaten to ensnare.

I invoke the power of intuition and inner knowing,
To guide me through the labyrinth of deception unscathed.

I am a beacon of authenticity, shining with unwavering light,
Piercing through the veils of deceit with unwavering sight.

I reject the false promises and manipulations of the trickster god,
For I am anchored in integrity and bound by the ties of truth.

No falsehood shall weaken my resolve or cloud my judgment,
For I am protected by the forces of righteousness and honesty.

By the power of my discernment and the strength within my soul,
I ward off the god of falsehood and deception.

May my words be pure, my actions be genuine,
And may truth prevail in every corner of my existence.

So be it, and let it be done.

CT 138: Spell for attaining the protection of the guardian spirits of the underworld

O spirits of the underworld, guardians of the realm,
I call upon your ancient and mighty presence.

Wrap me in your protective embrace,
Shield me from the perils that lurk in the depths.

With your wisdom and strength, guide my steps,
As I traverse the shadows and navigate the unknown.

Keep me safe from the snares and traps that lie in wait,
Defend me against the malevolent forces that seek to harm.

I invoke your names, revered guardians of the underworld,
May your watchful eyes be upon me at all times.

Let no harm befall me, for I am under your guardianship,
Bound to the eternal protection of the underworld spirits.

Grant me the courage to face the challenges that lie ahead,
And the resilience to overcome any adversity that may arise.

In your presence, I find solace and fortitude,
For you are the gatekeepers of the underworld's sacred domain.

With gratitude and reverence, I honor your sacred presence,
And entrust myself to your unwavering care.

So be it, and let it be done.

CT 139: Spell for avoiding the judgment of the god of forgiveness

O merciful god of forgiveness, hear my plea,
I seek your grace and clemency in this hour of need.

As I journey through the realms of the afterlife,
May your eyes be turned away from my transgressions.

Grant me passage through the gates of judgment,
Where the scales of justice weigh the deeds of the departed.

May your benevolent heart be my shield,
Protecting me from the weight of guilt and condemnation.

In your infinite wisdom, see the intentions of my soul,
And recognize the inherent goodness that resides within.

Guide me away from the path of repentance and regret,
And lead me towards the path of redemption and forgiveness.

Let your mercy wash over me like a cleansing tide,
Absolving me of my faults and granting me spiritual respite.

I humbly ask for your intercession and favor,
That I may escape the judgment that awaits the transgressors.

I vow to walk a path of righteousness and compassion,
And to seek your forgiveness in every thought and action.

May your grace illuminate my way,
As I strive to live a life worthy of your divine forgiveness.

In your name, O god of forgiveness, I place my trust,
And with gratitude, I await the embrace of your mercy.

So be it, and let it be done.

CT 140: Spell for acquiring the ability to travel through dimensions

By the power of the ancient gods and the forces of creation,
I call upon the realms beyond this earthly plane.

Grant me the gift of interdimensional travel,
That I may traverse the boundaries of time and space.

Open the gates that lead to unseen realms,
Where knowledge and mysteries await.

I seek to transcend the limitations of this world,
And explore the vastness of the multiverse.

Grant me the wisdom to navigate the cosmic currents,
And the strength to withstand the energies of other dimensions.

With every step I take, may I transcend the boundaries of existence,
And experience the wonders that lie beyond mortal perception.

Let me walk among the celestial beings and cosmic entities,
And learn from their wisdom and ancient knowledge.

Grant me the ability to perceive the hidden dimensions,
To see what lies beneath the surface of reality.

Protect me on my journey through the realms unknown,
And guide me back safely to this earthly realm.

With reverence and gratitude, I embrace this gift,
And vow to use it wisely and responsibly.

In harmony with the cosmic order, I travel between worlds,
Expanding my consciousness and connecting with the divine.

So mote it be, and let the dimensions unfold before me.

CT 141: Spell for preserving one's spirit from annihilation in the afterlife

In the realms beyond, where souls reside,
I call upon the powers of divine guide.

Protect me, O guardians of the afterlife,
From the looming threat of eternal strife.

Shield my spirit from the abyssal void,
Where annihilation seeks to destroy.

Grant me strength to withstand the trials,
And preserve my essence from dark denials.

May my soul endure, untarnished and whole,
In the realms where the afterlife unfolds.

Guard me from the forces that seek to erase,
The essence of who I am, my sacred space.

Let no entity consume or devour,
The essence of my being, my vital power.

With this spell, I claim my right,
To exist beyond death's eternal night.

I am preserved, I am fortified,
In the afterlife, my spirit will abide.

So mote it be, let my spirit persist,
In the eternal realms, where souls persist.

CT 142: Spell for escaping the clutches of the god of despair

In the grip of despair, I find no release,
Bound by chains of darkness, my soul seeks peace.

But I summon now the strength within,
To break free from despair's wicked din.

I call upon the divine, the powers above,
To rescue my spirit, to restore my love.

O gods of light, shine your radiant rays,
Pierce through the darkness, illuminate my ways.

Grant me the courage to face my fears,
To transcend the depths, to dry my tears.

Banish the god of despair from my soul,
Release me from its grip, make me whole.

Fill me with hope, with joy and delight,
Unburden my heart, restore my sight.

I am not bound by despair's cruel snare,
I claim my freedom, I rise and dare.

With this spell, I break the chains,
No longer imprisoned, my spirit regains.

I embrace the light, I embrace the dawn,
From despair's clutches, I am withdrawn.

So mote it be, let despair release,
And in its absence, may my spirit find peace.

CT 143: Spell for warding off the god of obscurity and confusion

Oh god of obscurity, your shadows I defy,
I call upon the light, clarity I imply.

With this spell I ward, confusion I dispel,
No longer lost in the maze, I fare thee well.

I invoke the wisdom of the ancient seers,
To banish the fog, to make my path clear.

May the god of obscurity retreat from my way,
Leaving behind clarity that will forever stay.

I am a beacon of knowledge, of understanding true,
With every step I take, confusion I undo.

No longer entangled in webs of illusion,
I claim my clarity, my divine infusion.

I call upon the guardians, the spirits of truth,
To guide me in wisdom, to protect my youth.

Obscurity shall fade, like shadows in the light,
Clarity and insight will be my eternal right.

So let it be written, so let it be done,
With this spell, obscurity is undone.

I am free from confusion, I am clear of mind,
Guided by truth, my purpose I find.

Obscurity and confusion, I bid you adieu,
In the light of understanding, I shall pursue.

May clarity and wisdom be forever near,
Protecting me from the god I once did fear.

With this spell complete, I am now free,
Warding off obscurity, my destiny I see.

CT 144: Spell for attaining the blessings of the earth goddess Isis

Oh mighty Isis, goddess of the earth,
With reverence and respect, I call upon your worth.

Benevolent mother, nurturer of all life,
Bestow upon me your blessings, free from strife.

I seek your wisdom, your abundant grace,
To walk upon this earth with a steady pace.

Grant me strength and stability, like the solid ground,
Rooted in your love, in your presence I am bound.

Oh Isis, provider of nourishment and sustenance,
Fill my life with abundance, with joyful resonance.

As the earth brings forth its fruits and grain,
May I too receive your blessings, free from pain.

Guide me in harmony with nature's flow,
As above, so below, let your wisdom show.

I honor you, Isis, as the divine mother,
Embracing your teachings, I find no other.

In your presence, I feel love's gentle embrace,
Grant me the serenity of your eternal grace.

Bless me with fertility, creativity, and rebirth,
In your divine embrace, I find my worth.

With gratitude and devotion, I seek your light,
Bathing in your blessings, day and night.

Oh earth goddess Isis, I offer my prayer,
Grant me your blessings, let me breathe your air.

With your divine touch, may I thrive and grow,
In harmony with the earth, my spirit shall glow.

As above, so below, as within, so without,
Under your guidance, I have no doubt.

Isis, goddess of the earth, I humbly implore,
Pour your blessings upon me, forevermore.

So let it be written, so let it be done,
I am blessed by Isis, the earth goddess, as one.

CT 145: Spell for avoiding the judgment of the god of redemption

Oh god of redemption, I beseech thee,
Grant me mercy, set my spirit free.

I stand before you, with humility and remorse,
Seeking forgiveness for my actions, of course.

In this afterlife realm, where judgments are made,
I ask for your grace, for my debts to be paid.

I have faltered and strayed from the righteous path,
But now I seek redemption, to escape your wrath.

Oh god of redemption, see the change in my heart,
I have learned my lessons, I've played my part.

I acknowledge my wrongs and seek to atone,
To mend the broken, to make amends, I've shown.

Grant me the chance to make things right,
To redeem myself, to emerge from this night.

I pledge my commitment to the path of light,
To walk in righteousness, with all my might.

I ask for your guidance, your merciful hand,
To lead me towards redemption, to help me understand.

Release me from the chains of my past mistakes,
Grant me the freedom that my soul aches.

Oh god of redemption, I humbly implore,
Judge me with compassion, I can do no more.

I will strive to live a life of virtue and love,
To honor your teachings, to rise above.

Guide me towards salvation, towards the divine,
So that in the end, my soul may shine.

With utmost sincerity, I offer my plea,
To avoid your judgment, to be set free.

Oh god of redemption, hear my prayer,
Grant me your mercy, show me you care.

As I navigate this afterlife's vast domain,
May your forgiveness cleanse me, remove my stain.

So let it be written, so let it be done,
In your redeeming grace, my soul shall be won.

CT 146: Spell for acquiring the power to control the forces of nature

By the sacred words I speak, I call upon the divine,
Grant me the power to control the forces of nature, sublime.

I seek the mastery over earth, its fertile soil and grounding might,
To shape the land and make it yield, to manifest my will with insight.

I command the winds to listen, to carry my voice on their gusts,
To calm or stir the air around, obeying my desires and trusts.

I harness the waters, flowing and pure, in rivers, lakes, and seas,
To shape their currents, calm their storms, as I please.

I invoke the flames, dancing and bright, with their passionate heat,
To warm or purify, to illuminate and guide my path complete.

I beckon the rains, gentle or fierce, to nourish the earth's embrace,
To bring abundance and growth, filling every living space.

I commune with the sun, radiant and strong, with its golden light,
To harness its energy, to bring forth day or banish the night.

I summon the moon, mystical and serene, with its gentle glow,
To govern the tides and emotions, as above, so below.

With this power bestowed upon me, I wield the forces of nature's hand,
To create, to protect, to heal, and to understand.

But with this great power, I vow to wield it with care,
Respecting the balance, knowing when and where.

For nature is sacred, a divine gift to all,
And as its steward, I will answer the call.

In harmony with the elements, in reverence and respect,
I embrace this power, its responsibilities I accept.

By the ancient rites and cosmic decree,
Grant me the power to control the forces of nature, so mote it be.

CT 147: Spell for preserving one's heart from corruption

In the realm of the afterlife, where spirits dwell,
I call upon the divine to hear my plea and tale.

Protect my heart from corruption's snare,
Preserve its purity, keep it fair.

May it be shielded from deceit and lies,
From darkness that within it tries to rise.

With every beat, let love and compassion grow,
May kindness and empathy eternally flow.

Guard it against envy, jealousy, and greed,
Let it be free from negative thoughts and deed.

Keep it steadfast in truth and righteousness,
A beacon of light, a symbol of goodness.

By the power of Ma'at, the goddess of balance and truth,
I entrust my heart to her wisdom, never to lose.

Wrap it in her feathers, light as air,
So that it remains pure, beyond compare.

May it be untouched by corruption's taint,
Radiating love, never to faint.

Through trials and tribulations, let it be strong,
A source of goodness, where it truly belongs.

In the realm of the afterlife, where judgment awaits,
May my heart pass the test, unscathed by the fates.

With this spell cast, I seek divine protection,
Preserving my heart's purity, its flawless reflection.

By the sacred words I've spoken here,
May my heart remain untainted, forever sincere.

So be it, and so it is,
Preserved from corruption, my heart, I kiss.

CT 148: Spell for escaping the torment of the god of remorse

Oh, merciful gods of the afterlife, I implore,
Release me from the clutches of remorse's core.

In the realm of the departed, where guilt takes hold,
I seek liberation, my spirit to unfold.

From the depths of my being, I cry out loud,
Grant me freedom from remorse's shroud.

Let not the weight of past mistakes bind me,
But set me free, so my spirit can truly be.

I invoke the power of forgiveness and grace,
To erase the torment, to find my rightful place.

With every breath I take, let remorse fade away,
And grant me solace, a brand-new day.

I release the burden that weighs on my soul,
Embracing healing, becoming whole.

From the god of remorse, I plead my plea,
Grant me liberation, set my spirit free.

In the afterlife's realm, where judgment prevails,
Let forgiveness be the wind that fills my sails.

With this spell, I break free from remorse's chain,
And embrace the freedom that I now attain.

Oh, merciful gods, I thank you for your grace,
As I transcend remorse, finding my rightful place.

So mote it be, and so it is,
Released from torment, my spirit is bliss.

CT 149: Spell for warding off malevolent spirits in the realm of shadows

By the power of the ancient ones, I call upon thee,
Guardians of light, protect me in this decree.

In the realm of shadows, where darkness prevails,
I seek your aid to ward off malevolent tales.

From the corners unseen, where spirits reside,
Shield me from harm, let their presence subside.

With this spell, I banish all negative force,
No malevolent spirit shall alter my course.

I invoke the sacred symbols of protection and might,
Creating a barrier of divine, radiant light.

Let their ethereal forms dissolve and disperse,
As I command their departure with words I rehearse.

With the power of light, I banish their hold,
Revealing the truth, their falsehoods unfold.

No darkness shall taint my spirit's pure glow,
For I am protected, and the light I bestow.

By the strength of the ancients, this spell is cast,
No malevolent spirits in my presence shall last.

In the realm of shadows, I stand unafraid,
Protected and guarded by the light's brigade.

So mote it be, and so it is done,
In the realm of shadows, I am the one.

May this spell's power keep me safe and sound,
As I traverse the realm where shadows abound.

CT 150: Spell for attaining the blessings of the moon goddess

Goddess of the moon, shining bright,
I call upon you in this sacred night.
With reverence and love, I seek your grace,
To receive your blessings, your gentle embrace.

O lunar deity, with your gentle glow,
Illuminate my path, let your wisdom flow.
In your ethereal light, I find peace and calm,
Wrap me in your embrace, like a soothing balm.

Grant me the gift of intuition and sight,
To navigate life's journey with clarity and light.
Guide my emotions, like the ebb and flow of the tide,
In harmony with nature, let my soul reside.

Bless me with your healing energy and grace,
As I bask in your celestial radiance, your divine embrace.
Nurture my spirit, like the moonlight's soft touch,
Infuse me with love, strength, and such.

Moon goddess, hear my heartfelt plea,
Align me with your cycles, set my spirit free.
Illuminate my dreams, empower my soul,
In your presence, may I feel whole.

With gratitude and reverence, I honor you,
Moon goddess, so pure, so true.
Bless me with your lunar energy and might,
And guide me through the darkest night.

As above, so below, let your blessings shower,
Empowering me in each and every hour.
Moon goddess, hear my call,
Blessings upon me, upon us all.

So mote it be, and so it is done,
In the moon goddess's light, we are one.
Her blessings bestowed, forever shall they last,
By her radiant glow, my spirit is vast.

CT 151: Spell for avoiding the judgment of the god of atonement

Oh, mighty god of atonement, I beseech thee,
Grant me your mercy, set my spirit free.
In the depths of my soul, I seek redemption,
To escape your judgment, I make this invocation.

I acknowledge my wrongs, my sins of the past,
But I yearn for forgiveness, to be released at last.
With a contrite heart, I offer my remorse,
May it be a bridge to transcend your righteous course.

I seek your understanding, your divine compassion,
To avoid the weight of your righteous retribution.
Grant me the chance to make amends,
To learn and grow, to make positive ends.

I vow to walk a righteous path from this day on,
To atone for my mistakes, to right every wrong.
I seek not to evade responsibility or accountability,
But to mend my ways, to embrace humility.

Oh, god of atonement, hear my plea,
Grant me clemency, set my spirit free.
Guide me towards redemption and healing,
In your grace, I find solace and a newfound feeling.

I pledge to rectify the errors of my past,
To be a force of good, to make love and kindness last.
May your divine wisdom guide my every decision,
As I strive for transformation, for spiritual revision.

I humbly ask for your forgiveness and leniency,
To avoid the judgment that awaits, so stern and mighty.
Guide me towards reconciliation and inner peace,
May your divine intervention bring my soul release.

Oh, god of atonement, in your hands, I place my fate,
Grant me the opportunity to transcend my past's weight.
I commit to change, to grow and evolve,

With your guidance, I shall absolve.

As I speak these words with sincerity and devotion,
I seek your mercy, your divine emotion.
May I be spared from the judgment severe,
And in your grace, find forgiveness near.

So mote it be, let it be done,
May your mercy shine brighter than the sun.
I commit myself to the path of redemption,
In your divine presence, I seek exemption.

CT 152: Spell for acquiring the ability to commune with the ancestors

Oh, revered ancestors, hear my plea,
Grant me the gift of communion with thee.
Across the veil that separates our realms,
Let our spirits unite, as this spell overwhelms.

With reverence and respect, I call upon your name,
Ancient ones who came before, I seek your wisdom's flame.
Open the doors of the otherworldly domain,
Allow me to communicate, to bridge the mortal and the arcane.

Through dreams, visions, and sacred signs,
Guide me, ancestors, with your celestial designs.
Speak to me in whispers, symbols, and ancestral lore,
Teach me your secrets, the knowledge of yore.

Grant me the ability to hear your voices clear,
To feel your presence, your love, and your care.
May your guidance illuminate my path each day,
As I walk in harmony, embracing your ancient way.

Ancestors, guardians of wisdom and light,
Bless me with your presence, protect me day and night.
I seek your counsel, your guidance so wise,
For I yearn to honor you, to bridge the earthly and the skies.

In sacred silence, I open my heart and mind,
To receive your messages, the insights I will find.
Guide me in matters of life, love, and strife,
With your eternal wisdom, illuminate my life.

Ancestors, I honor you with reverence and grace,
In this sacred space, I seek your embrace.
Let the bond between us strengthen and grow,
As we commune in this realm, both high and low.

By the power of the sacred ancestral line,
I call upon you, ancestors, divine.
Bless me with the ability to commune with thee,

To honor your legacy and keep your memory free.

So mote it be, let it be done,
As I commune with the ancestors, our souls become one.
Through this spell, I embrace the ancestral ties,
Guided by their wisdom, I shall rise.

In gratitude and love, I offer my sincere thanks,
To the ancestors, the spirits, in their eternal ranks.
May our communion be blessed, pure, and true,
As we walk hand in hand, together, old and new.

CT 153: Spell for preserving one's mind from oblivion in the afterlife

In the realm beyond, where spirits dwell,
I seek protection for my mind's inner well.
Grant me, O gods, this sacred plea,
Preserve my thoughts and memories, forever free.

Inscribe my thoughts upon the sacred scroll,
So they may endure, immortal and whole.
Let not the passage of time erase,
The essence of who I am, my mind's embrace.

Bind my memories to the eternal flame,
Where they shall remain, untouched by shame.
Protect them from the abyss of forgotten lore,
Let them shine brightly forevermore.

May the gods of wisdom, with their divine grace,
Shield my mind from oblivion's embrace.
Grant me the strength to withstand the test,
To retain my identity, my truest self, the best.

As I journey through the afterlife's domain,
Let my mind's essence remain, ever fain.
Secure the fragments of my conscious thought,
Preserve them intact, let them not be naught.

By the power of the gods, I make this plea,
To safeguard my mind's legacy, I decree.
May the eternal flame forever burn bright,
Preserving my memories, day and night.

In the realm of eternity, where spirits reside,
May my mind's essence never subside.
Let it soar high, unbound and free,
A testament to who I was, and shall forever be.

O gods of the afterlife, hear my call,
Protect my mind from oblivion's fall.
With gratitude and reverence, I make this plea,

Preserve my thoughts throughout eternity.

So be it, let it be done,
My mind's preservation, forever won.
In the embrace of the gods, my thoughts abide,
Preserved in the afterlife, side by side.

By the power of this spell, may it be so,
Preserving my mind, as above, so below.
In the realms of the gods, my consciousness shall persist,
Forever cherished, never to be dismissed.

CT 154: Spell for escaping the grasp of the god of anguish

Oh, wretched god of sorrow and pain,
Release me from your torment, break this chain.
I seek liberation from your relentless hold,
To escape the anguish, both fierce and cold.

With words of power, I call upon the light,
To guide me through this endless night.
Grant me strength and courage to break free,
From the clutches of anguish that bind me.

By the spirits of resilience and fortitude,
I cast aside the weight of sorrow's solitude.
I reclaim my spirit, my joy, my grace,
In this sacred space, I find solace.

I invoke the winds of change to blow,
Scattering the darkness, releasing its grip, I know.
May the gentle breeze carry away my pain,
And restore my heart to wholeness again.

No longer shall I dwell in anguish's embrace,
I step into the light, my spirit finds its place.
I embrace healing and embrace life's zest,
In the vastness of joy, I find my rest.

Oh, god of anguish, loosen your grasp,
For I am no longer under your curse to clasp.
I am free, I am whole, I am strong,
Unshackled from your grip, I now belong.

With every step, I leave behind the agony,
Embracing liberation, embracing harmony.
I reclaim my power, my purpose, my light,
Escaping your grasp, I take flight.

By the divine decree of this sacred rite,
I sever the ties that bind me tight.
From the god of anguish, I break away,
Embracing serenity, a brand new day.

In this realm of freedom, I find my release,
The god of anguish, his power shall cease.
I am liberated, no longer confined,
In the embrace of joy, my spirit is entwined.

By the strength within me and the gods' embrace,
I escape the grasp of anguish's face.
I rise above, I transcend, I am set free,
From the depths of sorrow, I forever flee.

So mote it be, let it be done,
The spell is cast, the battle won.
I am free from anguish's chains that bind,
A new chapter of joy and peace, I find.

CT 155: Spell for warding off the god of deception and trickery

Oh, cunning god of deceit and lies,
I see through your veils, I am wise.
With this spell, I call upon the light,
To shield me from your trickery and plight.

By the power of truth and clarity of mind,
I repel your webs of deception that bind.
With each step I take, I see through your guise,
Your illusions crumble before my discerning eyes.

I invoke the guardians of truth and justice,
To surround me with their divine presence.
They guide me on the path of righteousness,
Shielding me from your deceitful caress.

By the sacred words I speak in this rite,
I cast out your influence, banish your spite.
Your illusions and tricks hold no sway,
As I walk in truth, you fade away.

With the power of my will and inner sight,
I pierce through your veil of darkness and blight.
No longer shall I be ensnared by your schemes,
I see through your lies, shattered like shattered dreams.

I am protected by the light's embrace,
Shielded from your manipulation and embrace.
Your web of trickery has no hold on me,
I am free from your deceitful decree.

By the strength of my spirit and the gods' decree,
I ward off your influence, I am set free.
I stand in truth, unwavering and strong,
Shielded from your illusions, where I belong.

Oh, god of deception, your power is waning,
Your influence diminished, your hold no longer reigning.
I am guarded by the light's divine grace,
Protected from your trickery, in this sacred space.

With this spell, I claim my sovereignty,
No longer swayed by your artful trickery.
I see through your games, I am aware,
Protected from your snares, with utmost care.

By the power of truth and my unwavering will,
I repel your deceit, I stand firm, I fulfill.
No longer shall I be a pawn in your game,
I am free from your grip, I reclaim my name.

So mote it be, let it be done,
The spell is cast, the battle won.
I am shielded from the god of deception's art,
Safe in the truth that resides within my heart.

CT 156: Spell for attaining the protection of the guardian deities of the celestial realms

Oh, mighty guardians of the celestial realms,
With reverence and respect, I call upon your helms.
I seek your protection, your divine embrace,
To shield me from harm in this sacred space.

By the power of the heavens and stars above,
I invoke your presence, your strength, and love.
As I embark on my journey through celestial domains,
I ask for your guardianship, free from any chains.

Oh, celestial guardians, hear my plea,
Wrap your wings of protection around me.
Guide me through the celestial planes so vast,
Shielding me from dangers, ensuring my path is steadfast.

Grant me the power to navigate with grace,
Through the realms of light, through time and space.
Protect me from malevolent forces that may arise,
With your divine presence, keep them at a distance, wise.

Surround me with your celestial light,
Banish darkness, keeping it out of sight.
With your wisdom and strength, I am fortified,
Under your watchful eyes, fear is defied.

Grant me the knowledge to decipher the signs,
To understand the secrets of celestial designs.
With your guidance, I shall navigate the unknown,
Protected and supported, never left alone.

By the authority of the celestial realms divine,
I call upon you, guardians, to be mine.
Keep me safe, shield me from harm,
As I travel through the celestial realm's charm.

Oh, guardians of the celestial realms so high,
I offer my gratitude, my reverence, and my sigh.
Thank you for your protection, your steadfast care,

For guiding me through the celestial realms' rare.

With your presence, I am secure and strong,
Protected as I journey, where I belong.
I am grateful for your guardianship divine,
For keeping me safe in the celestial realms' shine.

So mote it be, let it be done,
Under the watchful gaze of the celestial sun.
With the blessings of the guardians, I am blessed,
In the celestial realms, I am divinely caressed.

CT 157:Spell for avoiding the judgment of the god of purity and righteousness

Oh, god of purity and righteousness divine,
I come before you with reverence and a humble mind.
I seek your mercy, your compassion, and grace,
To avoid your judgment and find my rightful place.

I stand here, imperfect and flawed,
But with a sincere heart, I seek to applaud
Your standards of purity, justice, and truth,
And strive to embody them in my every youth.

But, oh mighty god, I am but human,
With weaknesses and flaws, sometimes strumming
The chords of imperfection, leading astray,
Forgive me, I pray, as I find my own way.

In your divine presence, I feel the weight,
Of my actions, deeds, and the choices I create.
Grant me the wisdom to see right from wrong,
To stay on the path that is righteous and strong.

But should I falter, and deviate from your light,
I beseech you, god, to guide me back to what's right.
Let your mercy shine upon my soul's endeavor,
And spare me from your judgment's sever.

I pledge to purify my thoughts and my deeds,
To live with integrity, fulfilling my needs.
In your eyes, god, I seek purity's embrace,
Grant me forgiveness, and let righteousness replace.

Oh god of purity, I invoke your grace,
To avoid your judgment and find solace in this space.
May your divine light shine upon my soul,
And guide me towards purity's ultimate goal.

I offer my prayers, my contrition, and plea,
Humbly bowing before you on bended knee.
Grant me your mercy, oh god so divine,

And let righteousness and purity intertwine.

With your guidance and love, I shall strive,
To live a life of purity and righteousness alive.
May your judgment be kind, and your forgiveness be vast,
As I walk the path of purity, that shall forever last.

In your name, oh god of purity and righteousness,
I seek your protection and your eternal blessedness.
Guide me on the path that leads to your divine light,
And spare me from judgment's overwhelming might.

So mote it be, let it be done,
Under the watchful gaze of the radiant sun.
With your mercy and grace, I am blessed,
In purity's embrace, I am forever caressed.

CT 158: Spell for acquiring the power to manipulate the cosmic energies

By the cosmic forces that intertwine,
I seek the power to shape the divine.
Through the realms of stars and celestial skies,
Grant me the ability to command cosmic ties.

I call upon the energies of the universe vast,
To grant me control, the power unsurpassed.
From the depths of space, from galaxies afar,
Empower me with the cosmic energies, near and far.

With focused intent and a heart pure and true,
I harness the power of the cosmos through and through.
By the dance of planets and the celestial spheres,
I become the conduit, as the cosmic power nears.

From the twinkling stars to the vibrant nebulas,
I draw upon their essence, their celestial auras.
I command the energies, the cosmic web,
To weave my desires, to shape and ebb.

With each breath I take, I channel the divine,
Aligning myself with the cosmic design.
I wield the power of creation and destruction,
Manipulating the cosmic energies with utmost instruction.

I command the stars to shift and align,
To manifest my will, my intentions divine.
I shape the elements, the forces unseen,
Molding reality like an artist serene.

With reverence and respect for cosmic balance,
I wield this power with caution and prudence.
May my actions align with the cosmic plan,
Guided by wisdom, as a cosmic child I stand.

Grant me the power to traverse the cosmic tide,
To ride the waves of creation, with cosmic power by my side.
May the cosmic energies flow through me,

As I embrace my destiny, connected eternally.

So mote it be, let it be done,
As I merge with the cosmic power, we become one.
I am the master of the cosmic energies,
Manifesting my will, with divine synergies.

With gratitude and reverence, I acknowledge this gift,
To manipulate cosmic energies, my spirit lift.
May the balance be maintained, and harmony prevail,
As I wield this power, with cosmic energies, I sail.

CT 159: Spell for preserving one's ka (life force) from dispersion

In the realm of eternal existence, I stand,
A guardian of my ka, with power in hand.
With reverence and purpose, I seek to preserve,
My life force, my essence, that forever shall endure.

By the ancient wisdom of the gods of old,
I weave a spell, strong and bold.
To safeguard my ka from dispersion's plight,
I call upon the forces of eternal light.

I invoke the sacred energies of the sun,
To shield my ka, to keep it as one.
Like a radiant flame, burning bright and true,
My life force remains intact, no fragments to ensue.

I draw upon the stability of the earth's core,
Anchoring my ka, forevermore.
Rooted in the realms of divine creation,
My life force remains whole, in perfect formation.

I call upon the breath of the winds that roam,
To carry my ka, to guide it back home.
Through the ethereal currents, I create a path,
Leading my life force, away from chaos and wrath.

With the waters of life, I cleanse and purify,
My ka, untainted, no dispersal shall apply.
Like a river flowing, my life force runs deep,
Connected to the eternal, a bond I shall keep.

By the eternal stars that adorn the sky,
I align my ka, never to wane or die.
Bound to the cosmic tapestry, woven with care,
My life force remains whole, beyond time and despair.

By my will and intent, this spell is cast,
Protecting my ka, ensuring it will last.
No forces of dissolution shall come near,

My life force preserved, strong and clear.

In the embrace of the gods and goddesses divine,
I entrust my ka, my life force, to intertwine.
With their blessings and guidance, I shall endure,
My life force intact, forever secure.

May this spell resonate in the realms unseen,
Preserving my ka, fulfilling my dream.
No dispersion, no fragmentation shall prevail,
My life force, united, we shall prevail.

With gratitude and reverence, I seal this spell,
Preserving my ka, in cosmic harmony I dwell.
As above, so below, in perfect unity,
My life force preserved, for all eternity.

So mote it be, let it be done,
Preserve my ka, the battle is won.
With this spell, I claim my destiny,
My life force, intact, forever free.

CT 160 Spell for escaping the torment of the god of punishment

In the realm of shadows, where anguish prevails,
I seek escape from the god of punishment's wails.
With a desperate plea and unwavering will,
I call upon powers that can break this cruel chill.

By the strength of Ra, the sun's fiery might,
I invoke his radiance to banish this blight.
With the brilliance of his light, I'll find my way,
Guided by his warmth, I'll escape this dismay.

I beseech Isis, the goddess of compassion and care,
To extend her mercy and release me from this snare.
With her wings of love, she'll shield me from harm,
Lifting me above torment, with her gentle charm.

With the wisdom of Thoth, the god of divine thought,
I'll find a path of escape that cannot be caught.
His insight and guidance will lead me to freedom,
Navigating the labyrinth of torment, I shall overcome.

By the power of Ma'at, the goddess of truth and balance,
I'll seek justice and release from this malevolent trance.
Her scales will weigh my heart, and if it's found pure,
I'll be spared from the god's punishment, I'll endure.

I call upon the ancient guardians of the afterlife,
To aid me in my escape from this torment and strife.
Anubis, with his jackal's vigilance and might,
Protect me from the god's wrath, guide me towards light.

With these words spoken and intentions clear,
I invoke the spell to break free from fear.
I release myself from the god's punishing gaze,
Escaping his torment, finding solace in other ways.

I embrace the power within, my own inner strength,
To transcend this punishment, no matter its length.
I rise above the pain, reclaim my freedom and grace,

Leaving behind the torment, finding a better space.

By my will and intent, this spell is cast,
To escape the god's torment, I stand steadfast.
No longer bound by his cruel decree,
I break free from his grip, I am finally free.

In the realm of liberation, I find my release,
No longer burdened by the god's tormenting lease.
I reclaim my power, my spirit unchained,
Escaping the punishment, a new life regained.

So mote it be, let it be done,
I am liberated, my freedom won.
With this spell, I break the chains that bind,
Escaping the torment, leaving it behind.

I am free, I am whole, I reclaim my life,
No longer under the god's tormenting strife.
I walk in the light, no longer in pain,
Escaping the god's punishment, I shall remain.

CT 161: Spell for warding off malevolent spirits in the realm of illusions

In the realm of illusions, where shadows deceive,
Malevolent spirits lurk, ready to weave.
I seek protection from their tricks and lies,
To see through the illusions, to be wise.

By the power of Ra, the sun god's might,
I call upon his radiant light.
With his fiery gaze, illusions shall fade,
Revealing the truth, no longer afraid.

I invoke the name of Isis, goddess of truth,
To shield me from illusions, to guide my sleuth.
With her divine wisdom, I see through the veil,
Unmasking the spirits' deception, I prevail.

With the wisdom of Thoth, the god of knowledge,
I break through the illusions, dispelling the mirage.
His insight and discernment guide my way,
Exposing the spirits' tricks, keeping them at bay.

I summon the strength of Horus, the falcon-eyed,
To pierce through the illusions that spirits provide.
With his keen vision, I see what is real,
Guarded from their malice, protected with zeal.

By the power of Ma'at, the goddess of balance,
I maintain equilibrium, not swayed by chance.
With her scales of justice, I discern the true,
Guarded from malevolence, my spirit anew.

I call upon the guardians of truth and light,
To ward off illusions that cause fright.
Anubis, with his vigilance, stands by my side,
Keeping me safe, with his protective stride.

With these words spoken and intentions clear,
I invoke the spell to banish fear.
I am shielded from illusions, from deceit,

Guided by truth, I find my retreat.

I see through the veil of illusion's disguise,
No longer swayed by their cunning lies.
I walk the path of clarity and insight,
Warding off spirits, shining my own light.

By my will and intent, this spell is cast,
To ward off malevolent spirits, to make them past.
I am protected from their illusions and guile,
Stepping forth with confidence, mile by mile.

In the realm of illusions, I stand strong,
Protected from deception, where I belong.
No longer a victim of their tricks and games,
I see through their illusions, reclaiming my aims.

So mote it be, let it be done,
I am shielded from illusions, the battle won.
With this spell, I ward off spirits' deceit,
Seeing through the illusions, my victory complete.

I am protected, I am strong, in truth I reside,
No longer under the spirits' illusionary tide.
I walk with clarity, in the realm of the real,
Warding off malevolence, my spirit to heal.

CT 162: Spell for attaining the blessings of the sun goddess

Oh, mighty sun goddess, radiant and bright,
I seek your blessings, your celestial light.
With reverence and devotion, I call upon your name,
Grant me your blessings, honor my humble claim.

From the horizon, you rise each day,
Dispelling darkness, illuminating the way.
Your warm embrace, your nurturing rays,
Fill me with energy, in your brilliance I praise.

Goddess of life, of warmth and fire,
Ignite my spirit, let my desires aspire.
Grant me vitality, strength, and power,
Like the sun, shining in every hour.

I stand before you, bathed in your glow,
Feeling your presence, your divine flow.
Infuse me with courage, ignite my inner flame,
May I embody your essence, and forever remain.

As you journey across the azure sky,
Your blessings I seek, as I raise my cry.
Grant me clarity, wisdom, and insight,
Illuminate my path, guide me through the night.

Oh, sun goddess, I honor your divine grace,
Fill me with your radiance, in every place.
Bless me with vitality, with joy and cheer,
As I bask in your presence, no darkness I fear.

With each sunrise and sunset, I feel your embrace,
Your blessings shower upon me, shower upon this space.
In your golden light, I find solace and peace,
Embracing your energy, my worries release.

Goddess of the sun, hear my plea,
Bestow upon me your blessings so free.
Guide me through life, with your loving hand,
Illuminate my path, let me understand.

I am grateful for your warmth and your light,
In your presence, I feel blessed and bright.
Sun goddess, I honor you with all my might,
Grant me your blessings, forever ignite.

As I speak these words, I feel your presence near,
Your blessings surround me, dispelling every fear.
In harmony with you, I walk my destined way,
Forever grateful for your blessings each day.

So mote it be, let it be done,
Blessed by the sun goddess, under the shining sun.
Her radiance fills me, her blessings embrace,
In her divine light, I find my rightful place.

I am blessed by the sun goddess, forever aligned,
Her love and warmth in my heart enshrined.
With gratitude and reverence, I receive her gifts,
Forever connected, as her energy uplifts.

Oh, mighty sun goddess, I honor your divine,
In your blessings, my spirit will forever shine.
Thank you for your presence, your eternal light,
Blessings of the sun goddess, shining ever bright.

CT 163: Spell for avoiding the judgment of the god of truth and balance

Oh, god of truth and balance, hear my plea,
Grant me your mercy, let your judgment pass me.
In your scales, my actions are weighed,
May they find favor, may I evade.

I stand before you with reverence and awe,
Knowing that your judgment is just and raw.
But I seek forgiveness, a chance to redeem,
To correct my wrongs, to follow my dream.

I pledge to walk the path of truth and right,
To honor your principles, both day and night.
I seek harmony and balance in all I do,
With your guidance, I'll remain steadfast and true.

I acknowledge my faults, my past mistakes,
But I yearn for redemption, for a clean slate.
Grant me the opportunity to make amends,
To learn from my errors, to make new friends.

In the court of truth, I lay my soul bare,
I seek your forgiveness, your impartial care.
May your wisdom guide me, your justice prevail,
As I strive to be righteous, to set sail.

Oh, god of truth, grant me your grace,
In your judgment, let me find my rightful place.
I ask for mercy, for a chance to grow,
To embody your values, to let my light glow.

I vow to seek truth in every endeavor,
To act with integrity, in this life forever.
May your scales tip in my favor, I implore,
Grant me the opportunity to even the score.

I pledge to be honest, to speak the truth,
To uphold justice, from my youth to my youth.
Guide me on the path of righteousness and grace,

Help me avoid your judgment, find my rightful space.

Oh, god of balance, I seek your favor,
In your presence, may my soul savor.
Grant me the wisdom to navigate life's maze,
To align with your principles in all my ways.

With humility and respect, I approach your throne,
Hoping to avoid the judgment that's known.
I strive for equilibrium, in mind and soul,
To achieve harmony, my ultimate goal.

In your hands, the scales of justice reside,
Oh, god of truth, let me stand beside.
Avoiding your judgment, let me find release,
As I journey through life, seeking inner peace.

So mote it be, let it be done,
In your divine presence, my battles are won.
Grant me the strength to uphold what is right,
To avoid your judgment, in your sacred light.

I honor you, god of truth and balance,
May your guidance shield me from life's imbalance.
Grant me the wisdom to avoid your decree,
To walk the path of truth and be truly free.

With utmost sincerity, I make my plea,
Oh, god of truth, I submit to thee.
Let my actions reflect your divine grace,
And in your judgment, may I find solace.

In your name, I offer this prayer,
Hoping to avoid your judgment's glare.
Guide me, protect me, in truth's embrace,
Oh, god of balance, your blessings I embrace.

So mote it be, let it be done,
In your wisdom and truth, my battles are won.
Grant me the strength to avoid your decree,
To live a life of balance and integrity.

As I speak these words with earnest intent,
May your judgment be fair, my heart content.
Oh, god of truth and balance, hear my plea,
Grant me your mercy, let your judgment pass me.

CT 164: Spell for acquiring the ability to commune with the gods directly

By the power of ancient gods, I beseech thee,
Grant me the gift of communion, let me see.
Open the gates that separate our realms,
Allow me to converse with deities at the helm.

I seek to bridge the divide, to make a connection,
To commune with gods, receiving their reflection.
Grant me the ability to hear their sacred voice,
To understand their wisdom, to make the choice.

Through ritual and devotion, I humbly ask,
To partake in the divine dialogue, an honored task.
Grant me the knowledge, the insight to perceive,
The words of gods, their blessings to receive.

Let the veil between us become thin,
As I open my heart, inviting them in.
May their presence be felt, their guidance clear,
As I commune with gods, removing all fear.

I honor their divinity, their infinite might,
In their presence, I find spiritual light.
Grant me the ability to channel their divine grace,
To communicate with gods in sacred space.

As I enter the realm of the sacred and sublime,
I invoke their presence, in space and time.
May my prayers reach their ears, my intentions known,
As I commune with gods, my spirit is grown.

I seek not to command, but to humbly listen,
To receive their messages, a divine mission.
Grant me the gift to understand their will,
To align with their purpose, my destiny fulfill.

In dreams, in rituals, in silent contemplation,
I seek communion with gods, an elevation.
Grant me the power to bridge the celestial divide,

To commune with gods, in whom I confide.

With gratitude and reverence, I make this plea,
To acquire the ability to commune directly.
May their wisdom and love flow through my being,
As I commune with gods, their presence freeing.

So mote it be, let it be done,
With the gods, may my communion be won.
Grant me the ability to connect and receive,
To commune with gods, their blessings to perceive.

In their presence, I find guidance and grace,
As I commune with gods in sacred space.
With love and respect, I open the door,
To commune with gods forevermore.

CT 165: Spell for preserving one's memory from fading

By the power of ancient knowledge, I beseech thee,
Preserve my memory, let it forever be.
Shield it from time's eroding grasp,
Protect the moments that are meant to last.

I call upon the spirits of remembrance,
To weave a tapestry of eternal essence.
Bind my memories with threads of light,
So they may shine forever bright.

Let not the sands of time obscure,
The moments I hold dear and pure.
Guard them in the depths of my mind,
Where their beauty and meaning I will find.

With every passing day and year,
May my memories remain crystal clear.
Shield them from the veil of forgetfulness,
So they may endure, untouched by emptiness.

Engrave them in the chambers of my soul,
Where time's corrosion cannot take its toll.
Let them be etched in the fabric of my being,
A precious treasure, forever freeing.

By the strength of this incantation's might,
I command my memories to hold their light.
May they be vibrant, vivid, and strong,
A testament to where I belong.

Through the journey of life's winding path,
I ask for the power to make memories last.
Preserve them in the deepest well of my mind,
So their essence, forever, I shall find.

In moments of joy, in moments of pain,
May my memories forever remain.
Protected, cherished, and never fade,
An eternal tapestry, firmly laid.

With gratitude and reverence, I make this plea,
Preserve my memories, set my spirit free.
May they endure through the passage of time,
A testament to a life that is truly mine.

So mote it be, let it be done,
In the tapestry of memory, let me be one.
Preserve my moments, both big and small,
So I may remember, cherish them all.

With this spell cast, my memory shall hold,
The stories and experiences, precious and bold.
Forever imprinted, they shall not wane,
As I journey through life's intricate terrain.

May my memory be a beacon of light,
Guiding me through the day and night.
Preserved and vivid, a testament true,
I remember and honor all that I've been through.

So mote it be, let it be done,
Preserving my memory, a battle won.
With gratitude and trust, I release my plea,
Knowing my memories will forever be with me.

CT 166: Spell for escaping the clutches of the god of sorrow

In the depths of sorrow's grasp, I find myself bound,
Seeking liberation, a way to be unbound.
I call upon the ancient powers of light,
To guide me through the darkness and restore my sight.

From the clutches of sorrow, I long to break free,
To reclaim my spirit and let my heart be.
I invoke the strength of courage and resilience,
To overcome this sorrow with divine brilliance.

I summon the energy of hope and healing,
To mend the wounds that sorrow is revealing.
With every breath I take, I release the pain,
And let the light within me rise and reign.

O mighty gods, hear my plea,
Grant me the power to set my spirit free.
Break the chains of sorrow that hold me tight,
And lead me towards joy and endless light.

I call upon the goddess of love and grace,
To wrap me in her comforting embrace.
Let her gentle touch soothe my weary soul,
And guide me towards a brighter, joyful goal.

With each step I take, I leave sorrow behind,
Embracing a new future, a heart that's kind.
I choose to let go of the weight on my chest,
And welcome happiness as my honored guest.

In the realm of joy, I shall reside,
With sorrow's grasp, no longer tied.
I reclaim my spirit, my essence, and worth,
Transforming sorrow into love and mirth.

So mote it be, let it be done,
I escape the clutches of sorrow, I have won.
With gratitude and strength, I embrace a new day,
Leaving behind sorrow, finding my own way.

As I speak these words, the spell is cast,
I am free from sorrow's hold at last.
Empowered and renewed, I walk my path,
With a heart that's light, and a spirit that's vast.

So mote it be, let it be done,
I am liberated, my sorrows undone.
I embrace the joy that lies ahead,
With love and light, my spirit is fed.

This spell is sealed with divine grace,
Guiding me towards a joyful space.
I am free from sorrow's binding snare,
Embracing life's blessings, beyond compare.

CT 167:Spell for warding off the god of chaos and disorder

By the power of the ancient ones, I stand strong,
To shield myself from chaos, to right the wrong.
I call upon the forces of order and harmony,
To protect me from chaos and its calamity.

Oh, god of chaos, I bid you stay away,
Your discord and turmoil shall not have sway.
I invoke the guardians of balance and peace,
To ward off chaos and make it cease.

With the sacred symbols of order, I defend,
Creating a barrier that chaos cannot transcend.
I weave a shield of divine light and clarity,
To repel chaos and restore stability.

Through the power of my focused mind,
I create order and leave chaos behind.
I align myself with the cosmic flow,
And chaos's influence shall not grow.

Oh, god of chaos, I respect your might,
But in this moment, I choose what's right.
I stand firm against your disruptive force,
And in the realm of harmony, I stay on course.

May the energies of balance and control,
Keep chaos at bay and make me whole.
With every breath I take and step I tread,
I keep chaos and disorder far ahead.

By the power of this spell, I am protected,
From chaos's grip, I am unaffected.
Order and harmony guide my way,
As I walk through life, day by day.

So mote it be, let it be done,
I am shielded from chaos, as I've won.
With divine strength and clarity of mind,
I leave chaos and disorder behind.

This spell is sealed with the power of light,
Protecting me from chaos's blight.
I stand in balance, with order as my guide,
And chaos's disturbances I cast aside.

CT 168: Spell for attaining the protection of the guardian deities of the afterlife

In the realm of the afterlife, where spirits reside,
I seek the protection of guardian deities, my guide.
With reverence and respect, I call upon their might,
To safeguard me through the eternal night.

Oh, guardian deities of the afterlife domain,
I beseech your aid, your protection I claim.
Surround me with your divine presence and power,
In this realm of spirits, in every hour.

I invoke the watcher of the gate, strong and true,
To keep away malevolent forces that pursue.
With your vigilant eyes and unwavering gaze,
Protect me from harm, throughout my days.

Oh, guardian deities of the afterlife's embrace,
Wrap me in your arms, with your eternal grace.
Shield me from the shadows and unseen threats,
With your divine protection, my spirit rests.

I seek the guidance of the guardian of the scales,
To ensure justice prevails, and truth never fails.
Balance my soul and weigh it with care,
That I may pass through the afterlife's fare.

Oh, guardian deities, defenders of the souls,
Keep me safe, as the eternal journey unfolds.
Guide me through the realms, both high and low,
With your protection, I am ready to go.

I call upon the guardian of the sacred flame,
To cleanse and purify, and keep away all blame.
With your fire's light and warmth so divine,
Protect me from darkness, let your radiance shine.

Oh, guardian deities, I offer my gratitude,
For your watchful presence, for all that you do.
Wrap me in your embrace, as I traverse this land,

With your protection, I know I will withstand.

By the power of this spell, I am shielded and blessed,
With the guardian deities' protection, I am impressed.
In the afterlife's realm, I find solace and peace,
Under their watchful gaze, my worries cease.

With gratitude and reverence, I thank you, divine,
For your protection and guidance throughout time.
I carry your blessings in my heart, forevermore,
As I journey through the afterlife's door.

So mote it be, let it be done,
I am protected by the guardian deities, as one.
In their loving embrace, I find sanctuary,
Guided and guarded throughout eternity.

CT 169: Spell for avoiding the judgment of the god of destiny

In the realm of fate and destiny's hand,
I seek protection from the god who commands.
With this spell, I ward off his gaze,
And navigate my own destined ways.

Oh, god of destiny, I respectfully plea,
Grant me mercy and set my spirit free.
Shield me from the judgment you bestow,
Let me forge my path, my own destiny to know.

I call upon the forces of free will and choice,
To silence the voice of destiny's voice.
May my actions and decisions shape my fate,
And lead me to a future I can create.

By the power of my spirit and the strength within,
I defy the chains of fate and its whims.
I embrace the power to shape my own life,
To rise above the constraints of destiny's strife.

Oh, god of destiny, hear my plea,
Release me from the binds that limit me.
Let me chart my course, with purpose and will,
And the freedom to choose, my destiny fulfill.

I am not bound by preordained decree,
But the architect of my own destiny.
I steer the ship of my life's journey,
With courage, conviction, and self-discovery.

I invoke my inner strength and determination,
To carve a path that defies limitation.
With each step forward, I assert my control,
Over the direction of my destined soul.

Oh, god of destiny, your judgment I evade,
For my own destiny, I have laid.
With clarity of mind and heart's desire,
I transcend the limitations you conspire.

By my own hand, I shape my fate,
As I walk the path that I create.
I embrace the power to shape my own way,
And avoid the judgment of destiny's sway.

So mote it be, let it be done,
I am the master of my own run.
I navigate my path, destiny defied,
With each choice made, I take my stride.

By this spell, I break the chains that bind,
And claim the freedom to design,
My own destiny, bright and true,
I am in control, my own fate I pursue.

CT 170: Spell for acquiring the power to manipulate time

By the cosmic forces that govern all,
I call upon the power to stand tall.
In the realm of time, I seek control,
To bend its flow and shape it whole.

With this spell, I reach beyond the veil,
To harness time's essence, never to fail.
Grant me the gift to alter its course,
To wield its power, a timeless force.

I summon the spirits of past and future,
To guide me on this temporal venture.
Grant me the wisdom to understand,
The delicate balance of time in my hand.

I command the moments, fast and slow,
To speed or halt, as I bestow.
Time bends to my will, obedient and true,
I am the master, and it's what I do.

Forward or backward, time I traverse,
To rewrite history, and future shape and nurse.
I mold the minutes, the hours, the years,
Free from the limitations that time adheres.

By the ticking of clocks and the turning of gears,
I unlock the secrets that time endears.
Through the fabric of time, I weave my thread,
Changing its course with words I've said.

I manipulate time, a sorcerer of fate,
Rewriting events, altering their state.
Time's tapestry I unravel and rearrange,
Creating a new reality, a temporal exchange.

Oh, cosmic forces that govern the ages,
Grant me the power to turn time's pages.
To pause, to rewind, to speed or delay,
I command time's flow, as I may.

With respect and understanding I proceed,
Aware of the consequences that may succeed.
I use this power for good and not harm,
To bring balance and harmony, a temporal charm.

By the powers of the universe, I align,
With the flow of time, a force divine.
I am the wielder of time's mighty wand,
Creating ripples in its eternal pond.

So mote it be, my will be done,
As I hold the power of time, as one.
I shape its currents, I make it bend,
For I am the timekeeper, until the end.

CT 171: Spell for preserving one's ba (soul) from dissolution

In the realm of spirits, where souls reside,
I call upon the ancient powers to guide.
Protect my ba, my essence and core,
From dissolution's grip, forevermore.

By the divine flame that burns so bright,
I shield my ba from eternal night.
Wrap it in layers of divine light,
Preserving its essence, pure and bright.

No chaos or darkness shall claim my soul,
For I am whole, and I am whole.
With the sacred words I now intone,
I safeguard my ba, I make it known.

O guardians of the afterlife's gate,
Protect my ba from a dire fate.
Keep it united, strong and complete,
Guard it from dissolution's defeat.

Through the trials of the netherworld's might,
My ba shines with an eternal light.
No force can erode or break its bond,
For in divine protection, it is beyond.

I invoke the names of the deities divine,
To safeguard my ba through space and time.
Isis, Osiris, and all gods revered,
Grant my ba the strength to persevere.

May it soar on the wings of eternity,
Untouched by dissolution's decree.
In the realms of existence, forever whole,
Preserved and cherished, body and soul.

By the power of the ancient ways,
I preserve my ba through endless days.
No dissolution shall take its toll,
For my ba is eternal, a radiant soul.

So mote it be, my plea be heard,
Protect my ba with every word.
In unity and strength, may it remain,
Preserved from dissolution's bane.

CT 172: Spell for escaping the torment of the god of regret

In the realm of shadows, where regrets reside,
I call upon the light to be my guide.
Release me from the clutches of remorse,
And grant me freedom, a new life's course.

By the power of the sacred flame,
I break free from regret's binding claim.
I cast aside the weight of past mistakes,
And embrace the future that awaits.

No longer burdened by guilt's cruel hand,
I rise above the sorrows, a liberated stand.
I release the pain, the remorse, and the woe,
And let my spirit soar, forever to grow.

With each step forward, I leave regret behind,
No longer trapped, no longer confined.
I reclaim my joy, my purpose, my worth,
And create a life of meaning and rebirth.

The god of regret, I bid you farewell,
Your torment no longer has a hold to dwell.
I release myself from your relentless grasp,
And choose a future where happiness will clasp.

From this moment forth, I am free,
Free from the chains that bound me.
No longer burdened by regret's sting,
I embrace the joy that the future will bring.

By the power of my will and inner light,
I break free from regret's oppressive night.
I choose to forgive, to heal, and to mend,
And from this torment, I transcend.

So mote it be, my spirit now flies,
Escaping regret, embracing the skies.
I am free, liberated, and whole,
Released from the grip of regret's toll.

CT 173 Spell for warding off malevolent spirits in the realm of forgotten souls

In the realm where forgotten souls reside,
Where darkness looms and spirits hide,
I call upon the light to shine bright,
To ward off evil, banish the blight.

With the power of divine protection,
I cast a shield, a sacred connection,
Against malevolent spirits that roam,
I create a haven, a safe zone.

I invoke the ancient guardians of light,
To guard this space both day and night,
To banish darkness, to dispel fear,
And keep malevolence far and clear.

By the strength of the elements four,
Earth, air, fire, and water's lore,
I create a barrier strong and true,
To protect me and all that I value.

Spirits of goodness, spirits of might,
Stand by my side, protect me from fright,
With love and compassion, banish all harm,
In this realm, may peace be the charm.

By the power of my intention and will,
I ward off spirits with ill intent and ill,
No negativity shall penetrate this space,
Only love and light shall have a place.

I call upon the forgotten souls, lost and alone,
To find solace, find peace, in this sacred zone,
May their spirits be soothed, their hearts be healed,
In this realm of safety, where darkness is sealed.

By the ancient magic and wisdom of old,
I cast this spell, let its power unfold,
Protecting me from spirits that may deceive,

In this realm of forgotten souls, I find reprieve.

So mote it be, let the spell be done,
May my protection shine like the sun,
In the realm of forgotten souls, I am secure,
Guided by love, my spirit pure.

CT 174: Spell for attaining the blessings of the wind god

O mighty wind, swift and free,
I call upon your energy.
Breeze and gust, gentle and strong,
Carry me to where I belong.

I seek the blessings of the wind,
To grant me strength and help me ascend.
Blow away obstacles, clear my way,
Empower me as I go and stay.

Oh, Zephyrus, wind god divine,
With every gust, with every whine,
I ask for your favor, your guiding hand,
To bring blessings upon this land.

Grant me the agility of the breeze,
The clarity to move with ease.
Let your whispers guide my path,
As I navigate life's aftermath.

Carry my intentions on your breath,
To the far corners, from birth to death.
Bring me inspiration, wisdom, and grace,
As I journey through time and space.

By the power of the wind's gentle caress,
I invoke the blessings of this god's finesse.
May the wind lift me high, set me free,
In harmony with nature's symphony.

So mote it be, let the spell be cast,
May the wind god's blessings forever last.
I am connected to the wind's sacred flow,
Guided by its power, wherever I go.

CT 175: Spell for avoiding the judgment of the god of compassion

Oh, god of compassion, merciful and kind,
I seek your favor, your understanding mind.
Grant me exemption from your righteous gaze,
In your compassion, let my soul find praise.

I come before you with humility and care,
Seeking your mercy, I lay my burdens bare.
May my actions and intentions be pure and just,
And in your eyes, may they never cause disgust.

In times of hardship and mistakes I've made,
Let your compassion shield me like a shade.
Guide me towards forgiveness, redemption's light,
And spare me from your judgment's righteous might.

I vow to walk a path of compassion and love,
Embracing your teachings from high above.
May my deeds reflect your divine grace,
And may I find solace in your compassionate embrace.

Oh, god of compassion, hear my plea,
Grant me reprieve, set my spirit free.
May your kindness and understanding prevail,
And keep me safe from your judgment's scale.

By the power of compassion, this spell is cast,
May the god of mercy deem me steadfast.
In your boundless love, may I forever bask,
And be shielded from your judgment's task.

So mote it be, let the spell be done,
May I avoid the judgment, and in compassion, run.
With gratitude, I honor your divine decree,
As I walk my path, may your compassion guide me.

CT 176: Spell for acquiring the ability to perceive hidden truths

By the ancient power that lies within,
I seek the gift to see what's hidden, thin.
Grant me eyes to penetrate the veil,
And uncover truths that others may fail.

From the depths of wisdom, I call upon,
Reveal to me what's hidden, what's withdrawn.
Open my senses to the subtle signs,
Let hidden truths unfold like ancient lines.

With every breath, I attune my mind,
To the mysteries that lie concealed, entwined.
Awaken my perception, sharpen my sight,
To discern the truths veiled in plain sight.

Through layers of illusion, I will see,
The essence of truth, the root that sets me free.
No deception shall cloud my discerning gaze,
As I navigate the hidden realms and ways.

With open heart and focused intent,
I welcome the truths that were previously absent.
Guide me to the knowledge that lies beneath,
Unveil the hidden truths, bring clarity and relief.

By the powers of ancient wisdom and insight,
I claim the ability to perceive what's out of sight.
Let hidden truths be revealed, no longer concealed,
In alignment with the cosmic forces, let it be sealed.

As above, so below, this spell is cast,
Grant me the sight to see the truths that last.
With gratitude, I embrace this divine gift,
To perceive the hidden truths, my spirit uplift.

So mote it be, let the spell be done,
As I awaken to the truths, one by one.
With newfound clarity, I navigate my way,
Perceiving hidden truths each and every day.

CT 177: Spell for preserving one's spirit from annihilation in the realm of shadows

In the realm of shadows where darkness resides,
I call upon the powers that safely guides.
Protect my spirit from the threat of demise,
Preserve my essence from eternal demise.

By the ancient forces that govern all,
I invoke their strength to prevent my fall.
Shield me from the shadows that seek to consume,
Preserve my spirit, ward off impending doom.

With sacred light, I banish the night,
Illuminating my path, shining bright.
Let no darkness swallow my soul's flame,
Guard it fiercely, in your sacred name.

By the strength of ancestors who came before,
I forge a shield that evil can't ignore.
Wrap me in your cloak of divine protection,
Preserve my spirit with eternal affection.

No shadow shall claim me, no darkness shall bind,
I am resilient, with the light I'm aligned.
Let my spirit be a beacon of hope,
In the realm of shadows, I will elope.

With every step I take, I am fortified,
My spirit shines, cannot be denied.
I walk through shadows with unwavering grace,
Protected and preserved in this sacred space.

By the power of the divine and the sacred flame,
I preserve my spirit, untouched by shame.
In the realm of shadows, I am whole and free,
Forever preserved, eternally me.

So mote it be, let the spell be cast,
May my spirit endure and forever last.
Preserved from annihilation in the realm of shadows,

I stand strong, in the light that never fades.

CT 178: Spell for escaping the grasp of the god of despair

Oh, god of despair, release your hold,
Let not your grip tighten, strong and bold.
I call upon powers that bring forth light,
To guide me through this endless night.

From the depths of darkness, I seek escape,
To find solace in a brighter landscape.
Break the chains that bind my spirit tight,
Free me from despair's eternal plight.

With every breath, I reclaim my will,
To rise above the sorrow, sadness, and ill.
I banish the shadows, embrace the light,
And in its warmth, my spirit takes flight.

I summon courage, strength, and hope,
To sever ties with despair's choking rope.
With every step, I move toward the dawn,
Leaving behind the sorrow I have drawn.

Oh, god of despair, I defy your grasp,
In my heart, new possibilities I clasp.
I am resilient, I am filled with might,
No longer held captive by the endless night.

Through the trials and tribulations I face,
I find the strength to break free from this space.
With renewed purpose, I journey ahead,
Leaving despair behind, my spirit spread.

By the power within me, strong and true,
I break the chains that bind and undo.
I am free from the clutches of despair,
Embracing life's joys, with hope I declare.

Oh, god of despair, I bid you farewell,
In my spirit, a new story shall dwell.
I choose to rise above, to overcome,
And in the light of hope, I am reborn.

So mote it be, let the spell be cast,
May despair's grip on my spirit be surpassed.
I walk away, no longer ensnared,
Escaping the grasp of the god of despair.

CT 179: Spell for warding off the god of lies and deceit

In the realm of truth, I take my stand,
To shield myself from the god's cunning hand.
With words of power and symbols strong,
I protect my spirit from deceit's throng.

By the light of truth, I unveil the lies,
And see through deception with discerning eyes.
No falsehood shall cloud my path ahead,
For I am guided by truth's sacred thread.

I call upon the forces of honesty and clarity,
To guard me from the god's twisted verity.
Let my intuition be a beacon of light,
Revealing the falsehoods hidden from sight.

With this spell, I banish all deceit,
No longer swayed by its treacherous beat.
I am immune to the god's web of lies,
Shielded by truth that never dies.

May every word spoken in falsehood wither,
As I am surrounded by truth's radiant slither.
Let the god of lies retreat in defeat,
For I am guarded, strong, and complete.

I walk in truth, my spirit aligned,
No longer bound by deception's bind.
I see through the illusions, see what is real,
And the god of lies shall have no appeal.

By the power within me, I declare,
I am shielded from lies, both foul and fair.
No longer deceived, I trust my own sight,
Warding off the god of lies with all my might.

So mote it be, let the spell be cast,
May truth and honesty forever last.
With this enchantment, I am set free,
From the grasp of lies, I shall always be.

CT 180: Spell for attaining the protection of the guardian spirits of the underworld

In the depths of the underworld, I seek protection,
From the spirits that guard this realm of reflection.
I call upon the guardians, ancient and wise,
To shield me from harm, to hear my cries.

With reverence and respect, I make my plea,
To the spirits who dwell in the realms unseen.
I invoke their power, their wisdom, their might,
To guide and protect me in the darkest night.

O spirits of the underworld, guardians of the soul,
Wrap me in your embrace, make me whole.
Stand by my side, watch over my way,
Keep the darkness at bay, night and day.

Let your presence surround me, a shield so strong,
Deflecting all that may cause me wrong.
From the dangers that lurk, the shadows that creep,
May your protection be mine to keep.

In the realms of the dead, where spirits reside,
I seek your aid, to be by my side.
Grant me your guidance, your watchful eyes,
As I traverse the underworld, where darkness lies.

With your protection, I fear no harm,
For in your presence, I am safe and warm.
I trust in your power, your ancient might,
To guard me through the eternal night.

By the bond between our realms, I invoke your name,
Guardian spirits of the underworld, I humbly claim.
Protect and guide me, throughout my days,
In your hands, I place my soul's eternal blaze.

So be it, let this spell take flight,
May the guardian spirits protect me with their might.
In the underworld's embrace, I find solace and peace,

With their guidance, my fears shall cease.

CT 181: Spell for avoiding the judgment of the god of mercy

Oh, merciful god, hear my plea,
I come before you on bended knee.
In your infinite compassion, I confide,
Grant me your mercy, let me abide.

I seek to avoid your judgment's decree,
To escape the weight of guilt that burdens me.
With remorse in my heart, I bow my head,
I implore you, god of mercy, to tread.

Grant me forgiveness, oh god divine,
Let your compassion upon me shine.
Look upon my soul with benevolent eyes,
Release me from judgment, hear my cries.

I repent for my actions, the errors I've made,
In your mercy's embrace, I seek to evade.
Guide me towards redemption's path,
Protect me from your judgment's wrath.

Oh, god of mercy, in your divine grace,
Extend your hand and shield my face.
Let your compassion wash over me,
Grant me the chance to be truly free.

I promise to amend, to right my wrongs,
To live a life where goodness belongs.
With humility and gratitude, I submit,
To your mercy, I humbly commit.

May your judgment be tempered with love,
As I strive to ascend and rise above.
In your mercy's embrace, I find solace,
A chance to transcend and find my true place.

I offer my devotion, my heartfelt plea,
To avoid your judgment, to be set free.
God of mercy, hear my fervent prayer,
Grant me your mercy, for I am aware.

So mote it be, let it be done,
In your mercy's light, I shall overcome.
With gratitude and reverence, I pray,
Guide me on this path, each and every day.

CT 182: Spell for acquiring the power to traverse the cosmic planes

By the ancient forces of the cosmic domain,
I seek the power to transcend the mundane.
To journey through realms beyond this earth,
To explore the mysteries of the universe's birth.

I call upon the celestial forces high,
Grant me the power to traverse the sky.
Open the gates to the cosmic planes,
And unleash the magic that forever remains.

With this spell, I command the cosmic flow,
To carry me wherever I desire to go.
Through the stars and galaxies, I shall soar,
Unbound by the limitations known before.

Grant me the sight to see the unseen,
The power to travel realms unforeseen.
Across dimensions, I shall freely roam,
With cosmic knowledge, I will make my home.

May the cosmic energy course through my veins,
Empowering me to transcend earthly chains.
With every step, may the universe expand,
Guiding me with the wisdom of an ancient hand.

I embrace the infinite possibilities that lie ahead,
As I journey through the cosmos, where mysteries spread.
Grant me the power to traverse the cosmic planes,
To explore the realms where magic reigns.

So mote it be, let the cosmic forces align,
As I embark on this journey, divine.
With gratitude and reverence, I take flight,
Embracing the power to traverse the cosmic light.

CT 183: Spell for preserving one's heart from corruption

In the realm of the sacred and pure,
I seek protection for my heart's allure.
From darkness and corruption, I plea,
Preserve my heart's integrity.

With this spell, I call upon divine light,
To shield my heart both day and night.
May no malice or wickedness find its way,
Into the depths of my heart, I pray.

Guardian spirits, hear my plea,
Wrap my heart in purity.
Shield it from envy, greed, and strife,
Preserve its essence, its purity of life.

Let love and compassion be its guiding force,
And keep corruption from its course.
Banish negativity, darkness, and despair,
Protect my heart with utmost care.

May it radiate kindness, goodness, and grace,
A beacon of light in every place.
Let honesty and truth be its eternal flame,
And shield it from all guilt and shame.

By the power of the divine and the sacred,
May my heart remain untainted and unfaded.
Preserve its purity, its essence true,
So that I may walk the path that is due.

As I speak these words, so mote it be,
Let my heart's purity forever be free.
May this spell strengthen its virtuous beat,
And keep it safe from all deceit.

With gratitude and reverence, I seal this spell,
Protecting my heart, I bid you farewell.
Preserved and untainted, it shall remain,
A beacon of light, free from corruption's stain.

CT 184: Spell for escaping the torment of the god of remorse

In the depths of torment and regret,
I seek release, my soul beset.
From the grip of remorse, I strive to flee,
Grant me freedom, set my spirit free.

By the power of the sacred flame,
I call upon a higher plane.
Break the chains that bind my soul,
Release me from remorse's hold.

Oh, divine forces, hear my plea,
Unlock the gates, set my spirit free.
Let the weight of guilt be lifted away,
Grant me solace, a brighter day.

I cast off the burden that I bear,
Embrace forgiveness, release despair.
With each breath, I let go of the past,
Embracing peace, at last.

From the depths of remorse, I rise,
Untangled from its haunting ties.
I reclaim my spirit, strong and whole,
Letting go of guilt, restoring my soul.

By the power of redemption's grace,
I transcend the torment, find my place.
I walk a path of healing and light,
Embracing forgiveness, banishing the night.

With gratitude and newfound peace,
I bid remorse's hold to cease.
I am free from its torment and strain,
Embracing joy, releasing pain.

As I speak these words, so mote it be,
I am liberated, my spirit set free.
Escaping the torment of remorse's grasp,

I step forward on a new and hopeful path.

With gratitude and relief, I now decree,
I am free from remorse, forever to be.
The torment is lifted, my spirit restored,
I embrace life's blessings, in harmony with the divine accord.

CT 185: Spell for warding off malevolent spirits in the realm of illusions

In the realm of illusions, where shadows dance,
I call upon the light, this spirit to enhance.
By the power of truth and clarity of mind,
I ward off malevolent spirits, their tricks I unwind.

With this spell, I create a shield of protection,
A barrier strong against deceptive reflection.
No illusion shall deceive, no falsehood prevail,
I stand firm, my spirit fortified, never to fail.

By the strength of my will and unwavering sight,
I pierce through illusions, discerning what's right.
No phantom or specter shall lead me astray,
I walk the path of truth, come what may.

From the realm of illusions, I draw strength and insight,
Unveiling the truth, dispelling the blight.
I see through the veils of deceit and confusion,
Guided by inner wisdom, I find a resolution.

By the light within, I banish shadows deep,
Malevolent spirits have no power to keep.
I stand as a beacon of truth and clarity,
Protected from illusions, embracing reality.

With this spell's completion, I declare,
I am shielded from illusions, I'm aware.
No trickery or deceit shall take hold,
I navigate with wisdom, courageous and bold.

So mote it be, this spell is cast,
Warding off illusions, present and past.
I walk in truth, guided by divine light,
Protected and strong, through day and night.

CT 186: Spell for attaining the blessings of the moon god Thoth

Oh, Thoth, moon god of wisdom and knowledge,
I call upon your divine presence, high above.
With reverence and respect, I seek your blessings,
To unlock the secrets that the moonlight uncovers.

As the moon waxes and wanes in the night sky,
I align myself with its celestial energy nearby.
Grant me the gift of clarity and intuition,
To perceive the hidden truths with precision.

Thoth, the scribe of the gods, with your lunar might,
Illuminate my path and guide me through the night.
Grant me the wisdom to decipher ancient symbols,
To unravel mysteries and unlock their hidden riddles.

Under the moon's gentle glow, I open my mind,
Receiving the blessings of knowledge you kindly bind.
Grant me insight, as the moon's phases unfold,
To tap into the ancient wisdom, both new and old.

By the power of the moon's luminous rays,
I invoke your presence and offer my praise.
Fill me with your wisdom and divine inspiration,
So I may navigate life's journey with revelation.

Thoth, I thank you for your presence and grace,
For bestowing upon me the moon's radiant embrace.
May your blessings guide me on my spiritual quest,
As I seek knowledge and wisdom, I am forever blessed.

As I speak these words, the connection is made,
Thoth's blessings upon me, like moonlight cascade.
I embrace the lunar energy, in harmony with its flow,
Guided by Thoth's wisdom, on this path I shall grow.

So mote it be, this spell is cast,
With gratitude and reverence, it shall last.
The blessings of Thoth, the moon god divine,
Guide and enlighten me, for all time.

CT 187: Spell for avoiding the judgment of the god of redemption

O mighty god of redemption, hear my plea,
I stand before you, humble and free.
I seek your mercy and understanding,
To navigate the path of divine remanding.

In the realm of judgment, where souls are weighed,
I beseech you, grant me your aid.
Let not your scales tip against my favor,
But instead, let me find redemption's savior.

I acknowledge my faults and seek forgiveness,
May your compassionate gaze bring me solace.
I vow to learn and grow from my mistakes,
To mend the brokenness that my past creates.

By your grace, I seek a chance to atone,
To rectify the wrongs I have sown.
Guide me on the path of righteousness,
So I may find peace and spiritual wholeness.

Oh god of redemption, hear my plea,
In your mercy, grant me clemency.
Let not my transgressions define my fate,
But instead, let redemption be my slate.

I promise to honor your divine laws,
To strive for goodness and noble cause.
Through acts of kindness and compassion,
I seek to find my soul's eternal ration.

By your divine wisdom, I seek to be guided,
In the realm of judgment, may I be provided
With the opportunity to right my wrongs,
And in your grace, find where I belong.

Oh god of redemption, hear my prayer,
In your presence, I lay my soul bare.
Guide me through the judgment's daunting gate,
And lead me to a destiny that is great.

As I speak these words with sincerity and might,
I call upon you, god of redemption, this night.
Grant me the chance to redeem my soul's plight,
And in your mercy, let me walk in the light.

So mote it be, this spell is cast,
In the god of redemption's mercy, I am steadfast.
I trust in your divine wisdom and grace,
To avoid judgment's harsh embrace.

May the god of redemption, with compassion and care,
Guide me on a path of redemption, fair and square.
And may I find forgiveness and liberation,
As I strive towards my soul's salvation.

As it is spoken, so mote it be,
In the realm of redemption, I shall be free.
I walk this path with hope and determination,
To avoid judgment and find redemption's revelation.

CT 188: Spell for acquiring the ability to communicate with celestial beings

By the powers of the celestial realms above,
I seek the gift to communicate with love.
To bridge the gap between mortal and divine,
To converse with beings of the celestial line.

With reverence and respect, I call upon the stars,
Guiding lights that shine from afar.
Grant me the ability to understand and speak,
To connect with celestial beings, humble and meek.

Open the gates of celestial communication wide,
Allow my words and thoughts to easily glide.
Grant me insight into their celestial tongues,
So I may converse with grace and eloquent songs.

Through the depths of the universe, I send my call,
To celestial beings, both great and small.
Let our minds merge in harmonious exchange,
Sharing wisdom and knowledge, free from estrange.

In dreams and visions, may their presence be known,
As I commune with beings of cosmic throne.
Grant me the clarity to perceive their messages,
And the wisdom to interpret their passages.

Oh celestial beings, guardians of the sky,
I beseech you, hear my humble cry.
Grant me the gift of celestial communication,
To bridge the realms in divine association.

With pure intentions and a heart full of light,
I seek connection, guided by insight.
Grant me this power, bestowed from above,
To communicate with celestial beings, with love.

As it is spoken, so mote it be,
The ability to communicate with celestial beings is given to me.
With gratitude and reverence, I embrace this divine gift,

To commune with the celestial realms, my spirit uplift.

By the power of the celestial forces at play,
I am now connected, in the most celestial way.
I thank the celestial beings for their presence and grace,
And I honor our connection in this sacred space.

So mote it be, this spell is cast,
My communication with celestial beings shall hold steadfast.
I am open to receive their wisdom and light,
In harmony with the celestial realms, day and night.

CT 189: Spell for preserving one's mind from oblivion in the realm of the deceased

In the realm of the deceased, where shadows reside,
I invoke the power to protect my mind's guide.
From the grip of oblivion, I seek to be free,
Preserve my memories and thoughts eternally.

With reverence and determination, I call upon the divine,
To safeguard my mind in the afterlife's design.
May the essence of my being remain intact,
As I journey through the realm, never to retract.

Let my thoughts and memories form an unbreakable seal,
Shielded from the ravages of time, forever real.
May the wisdom I've gathered and experiences I hold,
Be eternally preserved, never to unfold.

By the ancient magic that binds the realms together,
I request the guardians of knowledge to gather.
Let them weave a web of protection around my mind,
Shielding it from the passage of time, so unkind.

In the realm of the deceased, where spirits reside,
Grant me the gift of remembrance, I confide.
Let my consciousness transcend the veil of death,
Preserving my mind's essence with every breath.

Guardian spirits, hear my plea,
Preserve my mind's sanctity, I decree.
Shield it from the shadows of forgetfulness,
In the realm of the deceased, a place of stillness.

May my thoughts and memories remain ever bright,
A guiding light in the realm of eternal night.
As I traverse the afterlife's mysterious domain,
My mind remains whole, a beacon of eternal gain.

With gratitude and reverence, I offer my plea,
Preserve my mind's essence for eternity.
In the realm of the deceased, let my consciousness thrive,

Forever remembered, in the realm where spirits revive.

By the power of this spell, so shall it be,
My mind preserved in the realm of the deceased, for all to see.
I embrace the gift of eternal remembrance and clarity,
As I navigate the afterlife's vast and ancient tapestry.

So mote it be, this spell is cast,
My mind preserved, its essence will last.
In the realm of the deceased, I shall find peace,
With my memories and thoughts forever released.

CT 190: Spell for escaping the clutches of the god of anguish

In the realm of anguish, where sorrows dwell,
I invoke the power to break free from this hell.
The god of anguish seeks to claim my soul,
But with this spell, I regain control.

With strength and courage, I rise above,
Breaking the chains of despair with a mighty shove.
I reject the grip of sorrow's embrace,
And step into the light, leaving behind the dark space.

I call upon the forces of resilience and might,
To shield me from anguish and guide me towards light.
Let the divine energy flow through my veins,
Empowering me to break free from these chains.

With every breath, I release the pain,
Transforming it into strength to regain.
I banish the shadows that cloud my mind,
Replacing them with hope and peace, I find.

Oh, god of anguish, I defy your hold,
With this spell, your power I unfold.
I claim my freedom, I reclaim my soul,
Escaping the clutches that once took their toll.

By the ancient magic that binds the realms,
I break free from anguish's overwhelming helms.
I embrace joy, love, and serenity,
As I walk a path of newfound divinity.

No longer bound by sorrow's snare,
I rise above, free from despair.
I release the weight that burdened my heart,
Embracing healing and a brand-new start.

With each step forward, I leave anguish behind,
In pursuit of peace and solace I find.
I am liberated, my spirit renewed,
Escaping the clutches of anguish, I conclude.

By the power of this spell, so shall it be,
I am released from anguish, forever free.
I reclaim my joy, my spirit bright,
Stepping into a future filled with delight.

So mote it be, this spell is cast,
Anguish no longer holds me fast.
I emerge victorious, my spirit untamed,
Free from the god's grasp, I am unashamed.

CT 191 Spell for warding off the god of deception and trickery

In the realm where falsehoods dwell,
Where deceit and trickery weave their spell,
I invoke the power of truth and light,
To ward off the god who thrives on the night.

By the ancient forces that govern the land,
I raise my voice and make my stand.
I call upon the guardians of truth,
To protect me from lies, cunning, and sleuth.

With clarity and discernment, I am armed,
Shielded from illusions skillfully charmed.
The god of deception shall not prevail,
For truth and honesty will always prevail.

I weave a barrier of truth and trust,
To guard my path against deceit's unjust.
I see through the webs of cunning disguise,
Unmasking the tricks with discerning eyes.

Oh, god of deception, your reign I defy,
With this spell, your illusions I untie.
I am guided by the light of truth's embrace,
In your presence, falsehood has no place.

By the power of integrity and right,
I ward off deception with all my might.
My spirit remains steadfast and strong,
As I navigate the path, avoiding all wrong.

No longer fooled by deceit's cunning ruse,
I choose honesty and clarity to diffuse.
With each step forward, I stay aware,
Shielded from deception, I am prepared.

By the strength of this spell, so shall it be,
The god of deception has no power over me.
I walk in truth, with eyes open wide,
Guarded against deceit that seeks to hide.

I am free from the snares of trickery's snare,
Guided by truth, with a heart laid bare.
Warding off the god of deception's hand,
I stand firm in truth, my spirit will withstand.

So mote it be, this spell is cast,
Deception's grip on me will not last.
With truth as my armor, I walk my way,
Protected and wise, throughout each day.

CT 192: Spell for attaining the protection of the guardian deities of the celestial realms

In the realm of stars and heavenly light,
I seek the guardians who protect with might.
I call upon the deities of celestial domains,
To shield me from harm and all negative strains.

Oh, guardians of the celestial realms so high,
With your divine presence, draw nigh.
Wrap me in your protective embrace,
Keep me safe in every time and space.

From the perils that may seek to invade,
I call upon your strength and aid.
Guard me from darkness, keep me secure,
Guide me with wisdom and ensure my pure.

By the power of celestial light,
I invoke your presence, shining bright.
Wrap me in your radiant wings,
As protection around me, it clings.

May your celestial energy surround,
Creating a barrier, strong and profound.
No harm can touch me, no evil can near,
With your guardianship, I have no fear.

Oh, guardian deities of celestial might,
I stand under your watchful sight.
Shield me from danger, guard my way,
Guide me through night and into day.

By the stars that twinkle and shine,
By the celestial realms so divine,
I invite your protection, firm and true,
To keep me safe in all that I do.

With gratitude and reverence, I make this plea,
Grant me your guardianship, so mote it be.
I am connected to the celestial divine,

Protected and guided, in your care I align.

From this moment forth, until the end,
With your presence, I will transcend.
Protected by the guardians of celestial lore,
I walk this path, forevermore.

CT 193: Spell for avoiding the judgment of the god of purity and righteousness

Oh, god of purity and righteous decree,
I beseech thee, hear my plea.
Grant me mercy and understanding divine,
As I seek to avoid your judgment's line.

In your presence, I humbly stand,
Aware of my flaws, my weaknesses, firsthand.
But I seek redemption, I strive to be pure,
To walk the path of righteousness, secure.

I invoke your grace, your forgiving hand,
To guide me away from your judgment's command.
May your eyes see my intentions true,
And recognize the efforts I pursue.

Grant me the strength to overcome my flaws,
To adhere to the values of your divine laws.
I seek to purify my heart and my soul,
To align with your principles, my ultimate goal.

In every thought, in every deed I partake,
I strive for righteousness, for goodness' sake.
May your wisdom guide my choices and ways,
And protect me from your judgment's blaze.

With sincerity and humility, I plead,
That you may see my genuine need.
Grant me the chance to learn and grow,
To atone for any transgressions I may sow.

Oh, god of purity and righteousness divine,
In your mercy, may I forever shine.
I seek your forgiveness, your compassionate gaze,
To walk the path of purity all my days.

By your grace, may I find redemption's door,
And avoid the judgment I fear, evermore.
Guide me, protect me, as I strive to be,

In alignment with your divine decree.

With reverence and respect, I make this plea,
To avoid the judgment, set my spirit free.
I embrace your teachings, with a heart sincere,
In your presence, may I eternally adhere.

So, hear my words, O god of purity and right,
Grant me your mercy, your forgiving light.
I pledge my devotion, my commitment to thee,
In your embrace, may my soul find sanctuary.

CT 194: Spell for acquiring the power to control the celestial bodies

By the cosmic forces, I stand in awe,
To wield the power, the celestial law.
Grant me, O universe, the gift profound,
To command the celestial bodies that abound.

I call upon the stars, radiant and bright,
To lend me their power, their celestial might.
From the vastness of space, I draw near,
The energy and influence of planets so clear.

Mars, the warrior, grant me strength and might,
To overcome obstacles, to fight the good fight.
Venus, the enchantress, bestow upon me grace,
To attract love and beauty, to light up any space.

Jupiter, the king, bless me with abundance and wealth,
To prosper and flourish, to experience life's health.
Saturn, the teacher, guide me with wisdom and restraint,
To learn from my trials, to exercise self-restraint.

Uranus, the innovator, inspire me with creativity,
To think outside the box, to embrace originality.
Neptune, the dreamer, awaken my intuition deep,
To perceive hidden truths, to journey in sleep.

Mercury, the messenger, grant me clear communication,
To express my thoughts with eloquence and precision.
And dear Moon, the nurturer, keep me in balance,
With your gentle ebb and flow, my emotions enhance.

In this sacred moment, I declare my intent,
To harness the power of the celestial firmament.
Grant me the ability to control with care,
The celestial bodies that float in the air.

With respect and reverence, I invoke this spell,
To align with the cosmic energy, all is well.
I embrace this power, this celestial might,

To manifest my desires, to create what's right.

By the stars above, I claim my birthright divine,
To control the celestial bodies, by this will of mine.
With gratitude and love, I thank the cosmic expanse,
For bestowing upon me this celestial dance.

So mote it be, as above, so below,
I wield the power of the celestial glow.
With this spell cast, my destiny unfurls,
As I control the celestial bodies, within my world.

CT 195: Spell for preserving one's ka (life force) from dispersion in the afterlife

Oh, divine guardians of the afterlife's embrace,
I beseech your aid, to protect my ka's grace.
As I journey beyond the mortal plane,
May my life force remain, untouched by the bane.

In this sacred moment, I call upon the divine,
To shield my ka, that essence divine.
Let not my life force scatter and disperse,
But keep it whole, in unity and converse.

Oh, mighty Anubis, guide of the souls,
Wrap your loving arms around my ka's goals.
Guard it against the winds of fate's harsh blow,
Preserve its essence, let it eternally glow.

Isis, the great mother, I seek your embrace,
Wrap my ka in your loving, protective space.
Keep it bound and intact, in the afterlife's realm,
Shielded from chaos, serene and overwhelmed.

Osiris, lord of the underworld's domain,
Grant my ka sanctuary, free from pain.
Let it thrive and flourish, in eternal bliss,
Safeguarded from darkness, your divine kiss.

By the power of these sacred words I speak,
Let my ka endure, strong and unique.
Preserve its essence, its life force divine,
In the afterlife's realm, forever entwined.

May the balance of Ma'at shield my ka's plight,
As I navigate the realms beyond the mortal sight.
No dispersion or scattering, but unity profound,
My ka preserved, its essence resound.

With gratitude and reverence, I offer this plea,
To the guardians of the afterlife, I decree.
Protect my ka, let it transcend time and space,

Preserved and eternal, in divine embrace.

So mote it be, as the gods decree,
My ka preserved, throughout eternity.
In the afterlife's realm, my essence held tight,
Unified and eternal, a beacon of light.

CT 196: Spell for escaping the torment of the god of punishment

Oh, mighty god of punishment, I plea,
Release me from your grip, set my spirit free.
No longer shall I suffer under your wrath,
I invoke the power to escape your path.

By the forces of light and divine decree,
I break the chains that bind and torment me.
I call upon the guardians of mercy and grace,
To intercede and grant me a new embrace.

Oh, wise Thoth, master of knowledge and insight,
Guide me through the darkness, show me the light.
Grant me wisdom and understanding profound,
To navigate the realms where torment is found.

Isis, compassionate goddess of love and healing,
Wrap your wings around me, protective and shielding.
Breathe new life into my spirit, restore my peace,
Release me from the torments, bring me release.

Anubis, guardian of the scales and the gate,
Guide me to a fate that's not filled with hate.
I seek redemption and a chance to amend,
To escape the punishment, find solace in the end.

By the power of my intention and will,
I sever the ties that bind me still.
I rise above the torments that held me tight,
Embracing a future that's filled with light.

No longer confined to the god's cruel decree,
I break free from the torment that once plagued me.
I reclaim my spirit, my essence, my soul,
Escaping the punishment, becoming whole.

With gratitude and strength, I leave the past behind,
Embracing a future that's loving and kind.
I am free from the torment, I am released,

No longer bound, my spirit finds peace.

So mote it be, as I will it to be,
I escape the god's torment, forever set free.
I step into a new chapter, with renewed might,
Embracing freedom and joy, in eternal light.

CT 197: Spell for warding off malevolent spirits in the realm of nightmares

By the power of my will and the strength within,
I call upon the forces of light to begin.
In the realm of nightmares where darkness resides,
I invoke protection that evil cannot abide.

With focused mind and unwavering intent,
I create a shield, a barrier impenetrable and unbent.
No malevolent spirit shall come near,
For I am guarded, protected, without fear.

I summon the light of the celestial stars above,
To shine upon me with radiant love.
Their luminous glow, a beacon so bright,
Dispels the darkness, banishing the night.

I call upon the guardians of dreams and sleep,
To stand beside me, their vigilance to keep.
With their guidance and watchful eyes,
I am shielded from nightmares' ominous skies.

I invoke the power of ancient symbols and signs,
To repel malevolence and sever its binds.
The Eye of Horus, vigilant and wise,
Wards off evil with its all-seeing eyes.

I weave a web of protection, strong and true,
An ethereal barrier that evil cannot undo.
Through this sacred thread, nightmares cannot pass,
For I am safeguarded, shielded like glass.

I banish the shadows that seek to invade,
For in this realm of dreams, my sovereignty is displayed.
No malevolent spirit shall disturb my rest,
As I sleep peacefully, feeling truly blessed.

With each breath I take, I am filled with light,
Dispelling the darkness, embracing the night.
I walk through dreams with courage and might,

Protected from harm, guided by the light.

By the power of this spell, I claim my domain,
In the realm of nightmares, harmony shall reign.
Malevolent spirits are banished, no longer to dwell,
For I am the master of my dreams, and all is well.

So mote it be, as I will it to be,
In the realm of nightmares, I am safe and free.
Protected and guarded, I sleep without fright,
Embracing peaceful dreams, throughout the night.

CT 198: Spell for attaining the blessings of the sun goddess Hathor

Radiant Hathor, goddess of the sun,
I call upon your blessings, for you are the one.
With your divine presence, grace me this day,
Illuminate my path with your golden ray.

Goddess of joy, of beauty and love,
Shower upon me your blessings from above.
Fill my heart with your warm embrace,
Awaken my spirit to your radiant grace.

Hathor, whose light brings life anew,
Grant me vitality and strength so true.
Infuse my being with your healing power,
Renew my spirit in each and every hour.

With your sacred dance, bring harmony and bliss,
Unleash your creative force, grant me the gift of this.
Inspire my soul to embrace life's art,
To express and create, to heal and impart.

Benevolent Hathor, lady of the sky,
I honor you, and to you, I fly.
Guide me with your wisdom and insight,
As I bask in your blessings, shining bright.

Through your divine radiance, I am blessed,
In your gentle warmth, I find solace and rest.
As the sun rises and sets, so shall I,
Aligned with your energy, reaching the sky.

Hathor, I offer my gratitude and praise,
For your blessings that brighten my days.
May your light forever shine upon my way,
As I honor you, now and every day.

By the power of Hathor, so it shall be,
Her blessings bestowed, setting my spirit free.
I embrace her light, her love, and her grace,

Guided by Hathor's radiance in every place.

As I walk in her presence, I am blessed,
By the sun goddess Hathor, I am truly caressed.
Her blessings fill me with divine delight,
Forever under her loving, golden light.

So mote it be, in Hathor's name,
Her blessings upon me shall forever remain.
With gratitude and reverence, I receive,
The blessings of Hathor, my soul to relieve.

CT 199: Spell for avoiding the judgment of the god of truth and balance

Oh, mighty Ma'at, goddess of truth,
I beseech you in this sacred booth.
Guide me on the path of righteousness,
Shield me from judgment and distress.

With your feather of truth held high,
Weigh my heart, let it not deny
The purity and goodness within my soul,
Grant me mercy, make me whole.

Oh, Ma'at, keeper of cosmic balance,
Help me avoid judgment's harsh silence.
Let my actions align with your decree,
In thought, word, and deed, so mote it be.

I call upon your scales of justice,
To measure my worth with fairness and clemency.
May my heart be light as a feather,
In your presence, may I find forever.

Oh, Ma'at, goddess of divine order,
May your wisdom guide me across the border
Of judgment and into eternal peace,
Where the burdens of guilt and shame cease.

Grant me the strength to live in truth,
To honor your principles from my youth.
Let my words be honest, my intentions pure,
In your presence, may I endure.

Ma'at, I offer my reverence and respect,
For your role in justice, I shall not neglect.
Guide me through the trials that may arise,
With your divine wisdom, may I be wise.

By the power of Ma'at, I am shielded,
From judgment's gaze, I am concealed.
In your grace, I find solace and release,

Oh, goddess of truth, bring me inner peace.

So, I cast this spell in your sacred name,
Ma'at, let your justice be my claim.
Avoiding the judgment, I strive to be,
Aligned with truth and balance, eternally.

With gratitude and humility, I beseech,
Ma'at, your blessings I humbly reach.
May my path be guided by your divine light,
As I walk in truth, with all my might.

So mote it be, in Ma'at's name,
My spirit aligned, unburdened by shame.
Through her grace, I am set free,
From judgment's grip, forever to be.

CT 200 Spell for acquiring the ability to commune with the divine ancestors

Oh, ancient ones, spirits divine,
I call upon you in this sacred shrine.
Grant me the gift to connect and commune,
With the ancestors who rest beneath the moon.

Through the veil that separates our realms,
Let our spirits intertwine like sacred helms.
Open the channel of communication wide,
So I may seek your wisdom and guidance, side by side.

Ancestors wise, whose knowledge transcends time,
Whose presence brings comfort, sublime.
I ask for your blessings and divine aid,
To bridge the gap between the worlds, unswayed.

With reverence and respect, I approach your might,
As I walk the path in your sacred light.
Guide me, ancestors, with your loving care,
In moments of joy, grief, and despair.

Ancestral spirits, guardians of my blood,
I seek your counsel, like a heavenly flood.
Grant me insight, clarity, and strength,
As I navigate life's trials, at any length.

By the power of the ancestral line,
Through generations, a connection divine,
I invoke your presence, oh ancestors dear,
With love and reverence, I hold you near.

May the whispers of your wisdom flow,
Through the depths of my being, with an ethereal glow.
Grant me the ability to hear your voice,
To receive your guidance, to make the right choice.

Ancestors of blood, and ancestors of heart,
In this moment, our souls never apart.
I honor your legacy, your stories untold,

By communing with you, my spirit unfolds.

So, I cast this spell with love and respect,
For the ancestors whose spirits I reflect.
Grant me the ability to commune with you,
To honor your wisdom, forever true.

By the power of the ancestral bond we share,
I open myself to your presence, rare.
In communion with you, my ancestors divine,
May your guidance and blessings intertwine.

So mote it be, let the connection be strong,
As I commune with the ancestors, lifelong.
With gratitude and reverence, I embrace,
The wisdom and love of the ancestral space.

Ensuring that the deceased is provided with essential sustenance and supplies for their existence in the afterlife.

Providing protection against evil spirits and malevolent supernatural entities in the afterlife.

Egyptian underworld.

deception and trickery

moon god Thoth